BEHIND THE BENCH

BEHIND THE BENCH

The Guide to Judicial Clerkships

DEBRA M. STRAUSS, ESQ.

Printed in the United States of America.
Cover Design: Pivot Design, Inc. (Chicago, IL)
Interior Design: Desktop Miracles (Stowe, VT)

The BarBri Group, Inc.
111 W. Jackson Blvd., 7th Floor
Chicago, IL 60604
Phone: 1-800-787-8717

Table of Contents

PART I

To Clerk or Not to Clerk

PART II

Courts and Clerkships

PART III

The Nuts and Bolts

PART IV

Resources for Prospective Judicial Clerks and Their Law Schools

---

APPENDICES

About the Author

DEBRA M. STRAUSS, ESQ. is the national expert in the area of judicial clerkships, providing consulting services and seminars to law schools, students, other organizations, and the judiciary.

Ms. Strauss has published and presented numerous articles and programs nationwide addressing judicial clerkship issues.

A Phi Beta Kappa graduate of Cornell University and Yale Law School, she served two clerkship terms for the Honorable Charles L. Brieant, former Chief Judge of the United States District Court for the Southern District of New York, first directly after law school and then years later as a Permanent Law Clerk. In addition, she practiced law at Rogers & Wells in New York, specializing in commercial litigation. Upon returning to Yale Law School as Director of Judicial Clerkship Counseling and Programs, she established the judicial clerkship program there, which achieved national prominence and resulted in a record number of Yale students obtaining clerkships.

Ms. Strauss served as Project Director of the National Judicial Clerkship Study, sponsored by the National Association for Law Placement and the American Bar Association. She is the author of *Courting the Clerkship: Perspectives on the Opportunities and Obstacles for Judicial Clerkships,* Report on the 2000 National Judicial Clerkship Study (National Association for Law Placement, October 2000).

Debra Strauss is affiliated with Pace University School of Law as Adjunct Professor of Law and Co-Director of the Federal Judicial Extern Honors Program, which she helped to establish and teach. She also teaches business law at the Fairfield University Charles F. Dolan School of Business. The author can be contacted through her web-site—www.judicialclerkships.com—at jclerkships@aol.com.

Dedication

This book is dedicated to my family—especially my husband Michael and children Melanie, Jonathan, and Andrew—for their patience and support through the years during which my information and experiences were accumulating, percolating, and boiling over before finally being memorialized in the present form. Of course, this tribute must also include the central member of my extended family—my own judge, the Honorable Charles L. Brieant, U.S. District Court for the Southern District of New York—whose clerkship launched my incredible journey and who has in the years since become my lifelong mentor, teacher, and friend.

Acknowledgments

Many thanks to all those who have contributed their experiences and input and whose collective wisdom has hopefully been captured in this book.

- Kimm Alayne Walton, the fabulous job guru, who encouraged me to act upon my dream of writing this book to capture the knowledge of judicial clerkships that had been building for so many years. She has come to me time and time again for information on judicial clerkships for her many books and has always graciously supported my endeavors with glowing descriptions that were so much more than complimentary—thanks, Kimm!

- National Association for Law Placement—especially Julie Hamre, Judith Collins, and Janet Smith—for offering me the opportunity of a lifetime to lead the National Judicial Clerkship Study and for working with me as a well-organized team to gather information and analyze data from thousands of law school administrators/career services professionals, law students, and alumni law clerks nationwide.

- William Paul, former President of the American Bar Association, for his initiatives in the area of minorities and clerkships, most especially the National Judicial Clerkship Study.

- The judges who have been my closest mentors for the last 15 years, and as such influenced this book in ways too numerous to mention: Honorable Charles L. Brieant, U.S. District Court for the Southern District of New York (formerly Chief Judge); Honorable Ralph K. Winter, Jr., Senior Judge, U.S. Court of Appeals for the Second Circuit (formerly Chief Judge); and Honorable Guido Calabresi, U.S. Court of Appeals for the Second Circuit (my former Professor and Dean at Yale Law School during my matriculation).

· The following judges, present and former law clerks, professors and attorneys in practice, who appreciated the importance of this book and submitted significant written contributions on its behalf: Honorable Stefan R. Underhill, U.S. District Court for the District of Connecticut; Honorable Melanie L. Cyganowski, U.S. Bankruptcy Court for the Eastern District of New York; Honorable Lisa Margaret Smith, Magistrate Judge, U.S. District Court for the Southern District of New York; Honorable Mark D. Fox, Magistrate Judge, U.S. District Court for the Southern District of New York; Wendy L. Trugman, Senior Litigation Counsel, GE Card Services; Professor Lia Geloso Barone; Jeannie Sclafani Rhee, Assistant United States Attorney; Christopher Sclafani Rhee, Counsel to the Deputy Attorney General at the U.S. Justice Department; John Elwood, Baker Botts LLP; Bart Epstein, Latham & Watkins; Patricia DeJuneas, law clerk for the Honorable Owen Panner, U.S. District Court for the District of Portland; Susan M. Damplo, Adjunct Professor at Pace University School of Law and appellate attorney; Francesca Bignami, Assistant Professor at Duke University School of Law; Sherene D. Hannon, former law clerk for the Honorable Charles L. Brieant; Andrew H. Kayton of Schoeppl, Burke & Kayton; Jonathan A. Shapiro and James W. Prendergast, Hale and Dorr, LLP.

· The many judges and law clerks who shared their experiences, ideas, and input in interviews and through enlightening conversations contributed to the milieu of this book, most especially: Honorable Robert W. Sweet, Senior Judge, U.S. District Court for the Southern District of New York; Honorable Holly B. Fitzsimmons, U.S. Magistrate Judge, U.S. District Court for the District of Connecticut; Honorable William I. Garfinkel, U.S. Magistrate Judge, U.S. District Court for the District of Connecticut; Alyssa Esposito, career law clerk for Judge Fitzsimmons; Donna Thomas, Staff Attorney, U.S. District Court for the District of Connecticut; Erin M. Kallaugher, career law clerk for the Honorable Ellen Bree Burns, Senior Judge, U.S. District Court for the District of Connecticut.

· The many members of the judiciary I have had the great pleasure of associating and working with over the years, including: Honorable Janet Bond Arterton, U.S. District Court for the District of Connecticut; Honorable Rosemary Barkett, U.S. Court of Appeals for the Eleventh Circuit; Honorable Robert Benham, Chief Justice, Supreme Court of Georgia; Honorable Danny J. Boggs, U.S. Court of Appeals for the Sixth Circuit; Honorable Miriam G. Cedarbaum, Senior Judge, U.S. District Court for the Southern District of New York; Honorable Raymond C. Clevenger III, U.S. Court of Appeals for the Federal Circuit; Honorable William C. Conner, Senior Judge, U.S. District Court for the Southern District of New York; Honorable Denise Cote, U.S. District Court for the Southern District of New York; Honorable Martha Craig Daughtrey, U.S. Court of Appeals for the Sixth Circuit; Honorable Nina Gershon, U.S. District Court for the Southern District of New York; Honorable Barbara Jones, U.S. District Court for the Southern District of New York; Honorable Lawrence E. Kahn, U.S. District Court for the Northern District of New York; Honorable Carlos F. Lucero, U.S. Court of Appeals for the Tenth Circuit; Honorable Joan G. Margolis, U.S. Magistrate Judge, U.S. District Court for the District of Connecticut; Honorable Roderick McKelvie, U.S. District Court for the District of Delaware; Honorable Colleen McMahon, U.S. District Court for the Southern District of New York; Honorable Paul R. Michel, U.S. Court of Appeals for the Federal Circuit; Honorable Alan H. Nevas, Senior Judge, U.S. Distict Court for the District of Connecticut; Honorable Barrington D. Parker, U.S. Court of Appeals for the Second Circuit; Honorable Ellen Ash Peters, Senior Justice, Connecticut Supreme Court; Honorable Stephen Reinhardt, U.S. Court of Appeals for the Ninth Circuit; Honorable Sonya Sotomayor, U.S. Court of Appeals for the Second Circuit; Honorable Diane P. Wood, U.S. Court of Appeals for the Seventh Circuit. These judges and countless others have exchanged ideas and shared their knowledge and wisdom with me, which I now pass on to the readers of this book.

- Many supportive people in the Administrative Office of U.S. Courts, with whom I had many fascinating discussions, especially Karen Siegel, Assistant Director; Marilyn Holmes, Office of General Counsel; Sharon Waites, Office of Public Affairs; Bob Dealing and Michele Reed, Article III Judges' Division.

- Clifford P. Kirsch, District Executive, U.S. District Court for the Southern District of New York.

- Elizabeth Cronin, Assistant Circuit Executive, U.S. Court of Appeals for the Second Circuit.

- Lois Bloom, formerly Senior Staff Attorney, Pro Se Office, U.S. District Court for the Southern District of New York, who is now a newly appointed Magistrate Judge, U.S. District Court for the Eastern District of New York.

- Roger Karr, Manager of Informational Services at the Federal Judicial Center, for his time and helpful discourse that went beyond simply providing resource materials.

- Meredith Schuman Casale from LEXIS® for her recognition of the importance of judicial clerkships and her collaboration in providing valuable resource materials to law students in this area.

- Cie Armstead, ABA Commission on Racial and Ethnic Diversity in the Profession, for inviting me to speak at the ABA mid-year meeting to launch their worthy judicial clerkship program and providing materials and support for the chapter on minorities and clerkships.

- Dean Anthony T. Kronman, who supported my initiative to build a judicial clerkship program at Yale Law School and with whom I worked in a valiant effort to improve the clerkship application process nationwide.

- Yale Law School students and alumni from my days at Yale and beyond—I have learned as much from them as they learned from me!

- Joy Beane, Dean for Career Development at Pace University School of Law, my partner in directing and teaching the Federal Judicial Extern Honors Program, for her friendship over the years, as well as the pleasure of working with her to establish such a worthwhile and successful program.

- My colleagues at Pace University School of Law—Dean David Cohen, Associate Dean Michael Mushin, Professor Jo Ann Harris, and Vielka Holness, Director for Career Development—for seeking my stewardship and making me feel so welcome and appreciated, as well as for their sponsorship and efforts on behalf of our program.

- The Pace Law School students from my classes, who provided continual feedback of their externships and some of whom also submitted written comments for the book—especially Jessica Bannon, Jason Marino and Joy Fitzgerald.

- At the Fairfield University Charles F. Dolan School of Business, Dean Norman Solomon, the late Dean Walter Ryba, Professor and former Acting Dean Winston Tellis, and Professor Lucy Katz for their high regard and support, and the students of my many classes there on the Legal Environment of Business for keeping my perspective of the law and the courts fresh through their eyes.

- The numerous law schools and students who have sought my advice and services and in so doing added to the breadth of information in this book.

- Stephanie Kartofels and Rick Duffy of The BarBri Group for all their valuable assistance and for their patience in waiting for this book during the times I put it aside to pursue each exciting opportunity—much of which came to be included in the book as yet another added dimension to strengthen its content!

Most of all, we should express gratitude to the many judges who have tutored and shaped the lives of their law clerks, passing on their knowledge and inspiration to each future generation of leaders of the legal profession, practitioners, politicians, academics, and members of the judiciary. It is my sincere hope that you the reader have the opportunity to share firsthand this remarkable experience and that this book helps you to find the clerkship of your dreams.

— DEBRA M. STRAUSS
SOUTHPORT, CONNECTICUT

Introduction

Until now, there has been no central source of information on judicial clerkships and how to obtain them—the ultimate prize. Yet in the intriguing world of the judiciary, there is a maze of valuable clerkship opportunities that is often difficult to navigate.

The ideas for this book have been forming from my own experiences throughout the years, first as a student at Yale Law School applying for a clerkship myself with virtually no guidance or information, then as a law clerk with the amazing good fortune to clerk for the Honorable Charles L. Brieant, then—Chief Judge of the U.S. District Court for the Southern District of New York—an experience so positive that I repeated it as a permanent law clerk many years later. Through my subsequent years in private practice at Rogers & Wells in New York, I came to recognize the value of a clerkship in one's law practice and general career. During my second clerkship experience, I appreciated my role as a law clerk all the more, and had the rare opportunity to meet with numerous members of the judiciary as part of the continual mentoring of my wonderful judge. Emerging as an enthusiastic advocate, I returned to my law school to spread the word of this remarkable world of clerkships. In seeking to provide information and guidance to the students at Yale, I developed a highly successful full-scale program on judicial clerkships, which received national prominence as a model to other schools that soon came to me for guidance. I realized, however, that there was still a void of resource materials to assist law students with this unique and mysterious process.

This led to my stewardship of the 2000 National Judicial Clerkship Study—the first comprehensive national effort of this magnitude in the area of judicial clerkships—conducted by the National Association for Law Placement ("NALP") and the American Bar Association ("ABA"). Here was a valuable opportunity to design the surveys based on the questions students had asked me over the years, and actually to obtain the much-needed quantitative and qualitative answers from thousands of law students and alumni law clerks, as well as law school career service professionals nationwide. The study captured information on student perceptions about the clerkship application/selection processes; the value students see in clerkships; data on the presence of women graduates and graduates of color in federal, state, and local clerkships; the influence of clerkships on attorney careers; and the roles that law school faculty and administration assume in the student clerkship application processes. In compiling the results and preparing the NALP Report, I was able to identify some of the measures needed, with the hopes of reaching judges and law school professionals across the country to help to improve the clerkship application process. No book on judicial clerkships would be complete without bringing to the students some of the valuable empirical information generated from this study, which serves to augment and support the more instinctive and anecdotal insights from my experiences and observations. So, reprinted in the Appendix of this book is an excerpt containing the Executive Summary of the findings and the Action Plan of suggested initiatives for the judiciary, law schools, and students.

One of the most significant findings of the National Judicial Clerkship Study was something I discovered long ago—the need for more resources on judicial clerkships—suggesting a master handbook for law students in this area. In the creation of this definitive guidebook, I hope that I—and all of those judges, law clerks, students, and court personnel who have provided their valuable input to this book—will be contributing to enhance the judicial clerkship process significantly for others in the years to come.

Part I

To Clerk or Not to Clerk

CHAPTER

one

The Value of a Clerkship

Behind every great judge is his or her law clerk. This fundamental truth explains why having an outstanding law clerk is so vitally important to a judge. To help us understand this process, it is enlightening to view this first from a judge's perspective. The relationship between a judge and his or her law clerk is an intensely personal collaborative effort with a loyalty and codependence that are unparalleled in any other setting. The judicial clerk serves as a confidant, an advisor, and an assistant who is always by the judge's side to do his or her legal bidding. In the sanctity of chambers, a judge can talk to the clerk in depth about a case, seek direction, and rely in large measure upon the legal research, writing and editing skills of the law clerk. In turn, the law clerk receives an exciting one-on-one education from a stellar member of the legal profession—a knowledgeable jurist in a lofty position of influence and authority—a heady experience that cannot be matched in any other legal employment.

An exceptional versus a poor quality team of law clerks and staff makes a significant difference in the judge's daily life and work product during their brief time together. Many judges talk about it being a good or bad year, not just in terms of results they have achieved in the cases before the court, but also in terms of the camaraderie and synergy within their chambers. In this world, a law clerk can be a judge's most valuable asset, which fuels the competition among judges for the best and brightest law students to serve by their side. Let us explore that special world of the judicial clerkship together, to see what makes it so valuable and to gather a perspective of our worthy goal before delving into the intricacies of the application process.

WHAT EXACTLY IS A JUDICIAL CLERKSHIP?

A judicial clerkship is a post-graduation position with a judge or a court, in which the law clerk works closely with the judge as an assistant in handling his or her caseload. The duties of a law clerk range by judge and court from conducting legal research, drafting bench memoranda for pretrial motions and advising the judge on the resolution of these issues, to assisting in the drafting of opinions and the conducting of conferences, hearings and trials (*e.g.*, marking exhibits, researching evidentiary issues that may arise in the course of the trial, preparing jury voir dire and jury instructions). The law clerk generally acts as a liaison between the judge and the attorneys or litigants. Depending on the judge, law clerks may also be responsible for various administrative and clerical duties.

Although we will discuss some variations below, most clerkships are temporary in nature, lasting for a term of one or two years at the discretion of the judge. In some instances, the clerkship continues for a longer period of time, typically in the category of a "career" or "permanent" clerk. Some judges start their law clerks at the same time, while others stagger the terms, resulting in a "senior" and a "junior" clerk.

As a historical note, the role of the judicial clerk reportedly dates back to 1875, when Horace Gray, Chief Justice of the Massachusetts Supreme Court, hired a young graduate of Harvard Law School to be his law secretary. When he was appointed to the United States Supreme Court in 1882, Justice Gray continued the practice, later institutionalized by Congress in 1886 as a "stenographic clerk." The tradition of hiring judicial clerks from the top law schools grew in the Supreme Court, and the role of these clerks in influencing the drafting and disposition of cases expanded. However, the position of law clerk was not established in the lower federal courts until Congress authorized the designated funds in 1930. Since that time, judges have come increasingly to rely on law clerks for their essential work.

THE VALUE OF A JUDICIAL CLERKSHIP

As a former law clerk for a federal district court judge and an advisor to countless students and law clerks over the years, I can personally attest to the merits of a clerkship. The value of a judicial clerkship is indeed substantial, and these benefits last for a lifetime. Clerkships are prized from all different perspectives, transcending the distinctions between private practice and the public sector, corporate and litigation. Regardless of your future career path, a judicial clerkship can be a significant asset to your career. In academia, it is an essential credential. After your clerkship, the possibilities are expansive—including judicial, administrative, government and even other non-legal positions.

In addition to being a key credential for future law practice in any area, a judicial clerkship is itself a valuable life experience. A clerkship offers a unique opportunity to glimpse behind the scenes of a courtroom into the practical workings of a judge's chambers. Unless you become a judge yourself someday, you will never again have the chance to gain this perspective on how judges make decisions and how the system of justice operates. The same is true for the once-in-a-lifetime prospect to gain first-hand knowledge of current legal issues, and to impact the law through the judge's decision-making and opinion writing. In the courtroom as well, through your exposure to numerous lawyers' oral and written litigation styles, both good and bad, you will be forming role models of the most effective techniques for your own eventual practice of law.

The special knowledge and skills you acquire, and the contacts and relationships you develop, are considerable in such a concentrated period of time. The clerkship experience enhances your research, writing and analytical skills. Many appellate clerks view this apprenticeship as an extension of law school because of the further honing of these skills. Through your clerkship year or years, you may also take advantage of the opportunity to explore a new part of the country or to learn the local rules and procedures in the area of your future practice, as well as to forge connections with many of the local attorneys, particularly in a trial court. As an additional asset, you join a network of co-clerks, former clerks and future clerks, with a common link to the judge and a mutual interest in each other's lives and careers. The name of "your" judge will be carried with you on your resume for the rest of your professional life. Ultimately, you may gain a lifelong mentor who will take an interest and assist in the development of your future positions.

In evaluating the potential benefits, here are a few sample comments from others who view judicial clerkships from a variety of perspectives, demonstrating as well the many potential career paths that may follow from a clerkship.

· A Future Career in the Government

A judicial clerkship opens the door to other public sector positions, particularly in the government. For instance, many Assistant United States Attorneys followed this natural path from a clerkship. In addition, the Department of Justice actively recruits from the clerkship ranks, and one-third of its Honors Program hires each year are judicial clerks. A former federal law clerk, Christopher Sclafani Rhee, explains how his clerkships (in the D.C. District Court and Court of Appeals) led him to his subsequent career in the government: "Clerking certainly influenced my decision to pursue a career in government. First, both of the judges I clerked for had extensive government experience.

Their career trajectories, and their war stories, made government service seem very rewarding. Second, I was exposed to a host of government attorneys in the courtroom—Assistant U.S. Attorneys, federal agency counsel, attorneys for the city. Almost uniformly, they were of a better caliber than their adversaries—the kind of lawyers I would want to consider my colleagues." In addition, he found that his clerkships helped him "appreciate the value of good government. My experience, watching government lawyers justifying searches of the home or requesting prison sentences, impressed upon me the power that government has over our everyday lives. On the rare occasion when I was disappointed or even disgusted by the conduct of a government attorney, it only reinforced in my mind the urgency of staffing government law offices with competent and ethical lawyers." After his enlightening clerkship experiences, he went on to serve in the U.S. Justice Department as a Special Assistant and as Counsel to the Deputy Attorney General. Thus, if you would like to consider a career in government, or just gain exposure to one, a clerkship is a logical place to begin.

• The Appeal for Law Firms

Most law firms zealously seek law clerks and highly prize those former law clerks included among their ranks. It is interesting to delve further into why this is so universal, from the point of view of the law firms directly.

Representatives from one prominent law firm, Hale and Dorr, LLP in Boston, presented this perspective in a seminar to firms about recruiting and hiring law clerks. Speaking first from his personal experience as a former clerk, Jonathan A. Shapiro, who before joining the firm clerked for the Honorable Joseph A. DiClerico, Jr., Chief Judge of the U.S. District Court for the District of New Hampshire, offered this explanation: "A clerkship is sort of an extension of your educational experience. It's a further and unique training. In particular it's an opportunity for people who have been in largely an academic setting to see, at least for litigation, the soup to nuts process of filing a complaint, pretrial process, pretrial/post-trial motions and, in the case of an appellate clerkship, how the appeals process works. So in that sense it's sort of an extension of the academic process." Mr. Shapiro added other reasons for a law student to do a clerkship: "I think it certainly is prestigious; to a certain extent it is a credential building process. There are also personal reasons people do clerkships. For instance, with so many law school graduates having gone to law school directly out of college, the prospect of joining a law firm or professional employment maybe at the age of 23 or 24 is actually still quite intimidating. So a clerkship in some respects provides an opportunity to sort of slow yourself into the workforce."

James W. Prendergast from Hale and Dorr further addressed the reasons law firms want clerks. "There is a certain element of talent that judicial law clerks bring to a firm. They clearly have been through, depending upon what court they have worked for, the pretrial process, the trial process, perhaps an administrative or appeal process; that talent is valuable as well as the insight that they bring into the mechanics of the courts or the particular judges. The same is true for experience." Beyond the invaluable training of a law clerk, he acknowledged another significant factor—the perception of the law firm. "The fact that you have judicial clerks in your roster often is an enhancement to the prestige of the law firm. At our firm in the past couple of years, between 15 and 25 % of our incoming summer associate class have been or are going to be judicial law clerks. It is something that we take a certain amount of pride in and I think that is one of the reasons you find most law firms looking to recruit judicial clerks." So, if you want to increase your own marketability with law firms, you certainly will not go wrong with a judicial clerkship.

• An Essential Credential for Academia

While it is well known among colleagues in the academic world that a clerkship is generally essential, it is much more than a credential. The value of a clerkship from the outlook of academia is furnished by Lia Geloso Barone, who clerked for the Honorable Lisa Margaret Smith, Magistrate Judge for the U.S. District Court for the Southern District of New York, for quite a few years (while I was also clerking in the

White Plains Courthouse) and links her clerking directly to her subsequent teaching experiences. "My experience as a law clerk has provided me with extremely valuable skills that enable me to perform my work as a college professor with great ease. The skills I developed in research, writing and organization have assisted me immensely, as well as the opportunity to frankly discuss all points of view of a legal issue to really know all aspects of a case and theories of law and perhaps politics. This has assisted in all aspects of my academic profession, especially in the classroom with my students." In addition, she explains that in academia, she spends enormous spans of time working independently, completing research or preparing for lectures. Professor Barone credits her clerkship with developing the ability to motivate herself to do so, as a law clerk works independently for long spans of time, performing research on a case and drafting documents, especially during the time that the judge is presiding over a trial.

· The General Effect on a Career

One former law clerk, John Elwood, who clerked both for Judge J. Daniel Mahoney of the U.S. Court of Appeals for the Second Circuit and Justice Anthony M. Kennedy of the U.S. Supreme Court, observed how the clerkship experience positively affected the substance and direction of his career: "Clerking has made me a better lawyer, by broadening the areas of law to which I have been exposed and providing me the opportunity to work closely with experienced judges and bright young lawyers. It also improved my writing ability by requiring me to write and re-write drafts until they were ready for publication." He added that, "Clerking permitted me to see litigation in many different fields of the law, which helped me decide which area I wanted to work in. Although many law firms allow new lawyers to rotate among departments for a limited time, that is not true in most nonprofit organizations (which tend to specialize) or government offices (ditto). I think it's much easier to decide what interests you while clerking. I entered law school interested in entertainment law. Thanks in no small part to a clerkship that exposed me to lots of criminal cases, I do predominantly criminal work today." After the significant impact of his clerkships, Mr. Elwood went on to practice law at the D.C. firm of Miller, Cassidy, Larroca & Lewin, which is now Baker Botts LLP.

The numerous advantages of a judicial clerkship are widely recognized. As a consequence, these coveted positions are both prestigious and highly competitive.

POSSIBLE DISADVANTAGES OF A CLERKSHIP

To be fair, I do feel compelled to mention the potential disadvantages for your consideration. The most significant is the financial differential between the salary of a judicial clerkship and that of a large metropolitan law firm. Many law firms offer a substantial clerkship bonus to attract clerks and compensate somewhat for this differential. However, the salary itself is not as low as commonly perceived, and does compare favorably to other public interest or government jobs. Moreover, the term for a clerkship and any financial sacrifice is quite limited, and the clerkship is likely to lead to greater success in your career for the future. Thus the non-economic (and even monetary) benefits of a judicial clerkship may actually be considerably greater in the long run. (*See* Chapter 9 on the financial aspects.)

Another potential disadvantage of a clerkship is the delay of entrance into a more "permanent" employer. After three years of law school you may be anxious just to get started with your legal career. However, this delay may be an advantage in disguise because when you enter the law firm after having done a clerkship, there is generally an appreciation for the kind of work that you should be given to take advantage of your credentials and expertise. From my experience, there was less of that large document production so common in the first year or two of law firm practice. Instead, other associates and even partners in the firm would come to me and ask my advice as if I had special insight—"You did a clerkship: how can I do this, how can I do that"—and I was given a higher level of work and responsibility, drafting briefs as well as researching interesting issues. In bypassing the grind of the first year in a firm, you may find that you arrive just when the work starts to become more interesting. Also, there is generally a seniority of status, or advancement credit towards partnership, given to law clerks upon entering the firm (*i.e.*, you enter as a second year associate), so you really do not lose that year on the track after all. Most former law clerks will agree that the year spent with the judge was the best professional year of their lives, and there was time enough to get on with the next 40 or so years of practice. Of course, for some people the delay is much desired, as they have a legitimate way to spend an extra year thinking about and deciding what to do next!

I raise in the category of disadvantage the fact that there is very little support staff or frills in chambers. Unlike a law firm or other employer, you are often doing your own typing of memoranda and draft opinions, reshelving the books in the chambers library, and so forth. Since most of you are still students and have not yet been spoiled by the bountiful support services of a large law firm, you will probably not view this as a major drawback. Still, it is wise to keep in mind this egalitarian atmosphere at the outset, have an appropriate level of expectation, and be willing to work as part of a team.

Lastly, there are often long hours and an intensity of the work, depending on the judge. However, this does not differ so greatly from some other law practices in terms of hours (and, on average, is probably less). Moreover, the level and type of work is so meaningful and worthwhile, with the judge usually working by your side, that I have heard very little complaint from law clerks who have chosen this path. It is, after all, a relatively short time period, and most people are willing to sacrifice that time for a year or two during the clerkship, knowing that they have in so doing greatly impacted the law as well as their own careers. Still, your quality of experience and level of enjoyment depends in large measure on the practices, temperament and personality of the judge, so investigate in advance and choose wisely! (Don't worry, later on in this book we will teach you how.)

There may be other personal reasons that cause you to forgo applying for a judicial clerkship. Perhaps you are not interested in the types of tasks involved in a clerkship or simply prefer another type of employment following your graduation from law school. We must recognize that this is an individual decision, and merely one option—albeit a great one—that may not be right for everyone.

SOME EMPIRICAL SUPPORT FROM YOUR PEERS

Again, the decision to apply for a clerkship is a very individual one—only you know what is best for you. It might be of interest to you, however, to see what other students and graduates across the country have said regarding their decisions. The National Judicial Clerkship Study found that "clearly students recognize the value of the clerkship relative to one's legal career."[1] Why do so many law students apply for judicial clerkships? We took the opportunity to ask the numerous students in the study this very question. The factors that most influenced their decision to apply were the desire to gain the work experience of a clerkship, the impact of a clerkship on their future career, the prestige of clerkships, and discussions with others. Most of these influential discussions were with lawyers in practice, followed next frequently by other law students, and then faculty members. When asked this question, the alumni law clerks identified substantially the same reasons for applying for their clerkships. In addition, they specified judicial internships and externships most often as the programs which influenced their decision to apply for a judicial clerkship. Additional reasons noted were the flexibility of the clerkship term and hours, and the opportunity for a transitional year to decide future career plans. Now, you may know what reasons are most compelling for you, but if not, it may be useful to consider these prevalent factors in making your own decision.

I have been telling students for years how a judicial clerkship helps them to acquire an amazing amount of skills that cannot be gained in any other way during such a relatively short period of time. In the clerkship study we were able to ask thousands of law clerks across the country whether they did in fact acquire such skills, which ones in particular, and how this compared to their initial expectations of their clerkships. The law clerks reported that the skills most significantly enhanced were writing/drafting opinions or memoranda and knowledge of court procedure, and other skills such as self-confidence, communication and supervisory skills, diplomacy, and a sense of social responsibility. Also listed by the majority as significantly or moderately enhanced were general knowledge/experience, general legal ability/judgment, legal reasoning and analysis, and knowledge of case law/statutes. Note that there were some differences observed by court type and level (state/federal, trial/appellate), with the highest ratings given by clerks for the trial courts.[2] Most significantly, the substantial majority of law clerks (96% overall) felt that the skills gained in their clerkships met or exceeded their initial expectations.

The next widely held belief to investigate with the law clerks in the study was the idea that the clerkship helps you to develop contacts and relationships within the court—particularly with your judge—that is a key advantage of pursuing a judicial clerkship. The law clerks certainly verified that aspect as well, reporting a positive development of relationships and contacts, particularly with their judge and with the other law clerks and administrative staff in their own judge's chambers. Most also indicated that their relationships with other judges, law clerks and court personnel were also moderately or significantly enhanced. According to one clerk, "These contacts and relationships played key roles in my decision to remain in the community, and were extremely helpful in securing my post-clerkship employment. In addition, these contacts and relationships have significantly increased my level of confidence when appearing in court with the same judges, attorneys, and court personnel."[3] With new evidence in hand, I stand by my enthusiastic declarations over the years that a judicial clerkship is the best way to develop relationships and contacts within the court system!

As we have suspected all along, the beneficial effects of clerking last beyond the actual clerkship. The national study documented the positive impact of the clerkship experience on their careers. Almost half of the law clerks responded that their clerkship helped a great deal in obtaining their post-clerkship position, while almost one-quarter stated that it helped somewhat. In essence, no one reported that the clerkship negatively affected the post-clerkship employment search. One clerk exclaimed, "Without a doubt, my two years of clerking got me the job I'll start in the fall." Another law clerk explained: "My clerkship made a palpable difference even before I started. I worked at a firm after my third year. When I did my job search, the same firms who had turned their noses up at me after my first year were pursuing me—the only real difference on my resume was the clerkship . . . Now, I feel like I know what bad lawyering works like, so, hopefully, I can avoid doing it; and I have seen examples of wonderful lawyering which I hope to emulate!"[4] In their post-clerkship employment as well, the vast majority of former law clerks in this study responded that the clerkship positively affected their ease of success in handling their post-clerkship duties. As one former law clerk stated, the clerkship "gave me confidence to do whatever I want."

The best testimonial comes from these law clerks themselves, who resoundingly gave their overall clerkship experience high marks. On a scale of 1 to 10, with 10 being most positive, 33% described their clerkship experience as a "10" and 95% rated it as 7 or above. When asked whether they would clerk again, a remarkable 97% responded in the affirmative.[5]

To Clerk or Not To Clerk

While it is a highly personal decision, for many people the logical choice is to clerk—or at least to begin the application process and hopefully to obtain a clerkship. Any potential disadvantages seem to be far outweighed by all of the advantages and the value of a judicial clerkship which cannot be gained at any other time or place. The clerkship statistics reflect this choice. It is really quite impressive how many students do clerk each year—approximately one in nine, or 11%, of law student graduates nationwide.[6]

Only you know your own situation and the choice is yours—but my advice is, unless you have some unusual and compelling personal reason not to do so, go for it! In all my years of experience in career development and counseling, I have yet to come across a student or graduate who has regretted the decision to clerk. To the contrary, I have spoken with countless former law clerks—and I can add my own experiences as a law clerk to that—without a doubt, the decision to clerk proved to be a positive one and certainly the optimum way to commence their legal careers. In fact, if you are fortunate enough to obtain one, a judicial clerkship promises to be one of the best professional experiences of your life!

Notes

1. *See Courting the Clerkship: Perspectives on the Opportunities and Obstacles for Judicial Clerkships,* Report on the 2000 National Judicial Clerkship Study (National Association for Law Placement, October 2000) ("NALP Report") at 50–51, including tables. The full report is also available on the NALP website (http://www.nalp.org/nalpresearch/clrk-summ.htm).
2. *See* Tables 59–62 of NALP Report at 73–75 for comparisons by type of court.
3. NALP Report at 74.
4. NALP Report at 77, *see also* Table 65 appearing therein.
5. NALP Report at 79. For more detailed discussion and tables on these aspects of the judicial clerkship experience, *see* NALP Report at 72–78.
6. These statistics represent the Class of 2000 nationwide, as reported by the National Association for Law Placement. *See Jobs and J.D.'s: Employment and Salaries of New Law Graduates—Class of 2000,* National Association for Law Placement (2001).

CHAPTER
two

The Keys to Success in Finding a Clerkship

The process of obtaining a clerkship is highly competitive, filled with misinformation and confusion for applicants. Nevertheless, you can navigate the maze of courts and clerkship opportunities successfully, with positive results for both you and the judges for whom an appropriate match is equally important.

WHAT DOES IT TAKE TO GET A JUDICIAL CLERKSHIP?

Every student wants to know, in applying for a clerkship, what are the factors for success? For the most part, the criteria generally used by other employers to evaluate applicants pertain to judicial clerkships as well. Grades, journal membership, work experience, writing skills, references, and compatibility rank among the most important factors. Many judges prefer to hire clerks from their alma mater or from local law schools. In addition, some judges prefer students who have prior connections to the geographic area or a demonstrated commitment to settle there. As stated by one very fine judge, the Honorable Ralph K. Winter, Senior Judge (formerly Chief Judge) of the U.S. Court of Appeals for the Second Circuit, some generalities can be observed: "What are judges looking for? They look at grades, they look at courses, they look at the recommendations, and they look at personality. They do this in a differing mix. Some will emphasize one kind of thing more than another." Beyond that, the hiring of a judicial clerk is a very individualistic decision and, accordingly, there is no exact formula for what every judge seeks.

Grades do not convey the entire picture for a judge, as there is much more to this application process than simply the academic record. One judge, the Honorable Lisa Margaret Smith, United States Magistrate Judge for the Southern District of New York, describes some of the nuances for her own selection process: "One of my considerations is the value of training attorneys for future work in this District, for this community. Thus, I ordinarily do not consider the 'mercenary' candidate, who has no apparent ties or connections with the Southern District of New York or its environs." Sometimes the background of the judge will yield clues as to the aspects that will be important to that judge. For instance, as Judge Smith explains, "Because of my background in public service, I give weight to a candidate's demonstrated commitment to serving the public, either by volunteer positions, internships or actual employment in public service, whether legal or non-legal." Each judge has an element that carries the most weight, which for her is the quality of the written work: "I believe that most judges consider the ability to write a succinct, reasoned analysis to be a primary criteria for a law clerk." While each judge has unique criteria and concerns that the judge must address and consider during the selection process, there are some common factors.

Of value to you in your own clerkship applications should be the National Judicial Clerkship Study, which with its extensive aggregate data provided enlightening answers and debunked some of the myths surrounding the clerkship application process.[1] The study found over-all that the elements of the academic record do play the largest role in a successful clerkship application. Many students who applied for and received a judicial clerkship had certain law school activities or factors in common. More than one-half had one or more of the following characteristics: "top grades/high class rank" (as defined by the students' own perceptions), membership on the law review/law journal, or experience as a teaching or research assistant. Almost half had significant prior work experience. These students mentioned other law school activities or characteristics with somewhat less frequency, and nearly one-third had a summer or academic year judicial intern/externship. These factors for success largely coincided with the perceptions of the career services personnel of law schools, who also identified the significance of faculty support. In the opinion of judicial law clerks (who typically assist in their judges' selection process), in addition to the academic record, the interview and personal character traits were of particular importance to the judges.

There is a common misconception among students that they need to have a connection to a judge in order to get a clerkship. However, only a very small percentage, 8%, of the students who applied and received an offer actually had a special connection to a judge. Similarly, only a relatively small percentage, 11%, of the law clerks in the study reported having a special connection to a judge while in law school. Notably, these facts contrasted with the perceptions among many of the students who offered as a reason for not applying for a clerkship, or for not succeeding with their clerkship applications, that they did not have the right "connections" to acquire a clerkship. So, don't be discouraged from applying for a clerkship if you feel you do not have connections to a judge—90% of the successful applicants were in the same boat.

STRATEGIES FOR SUCCESS

If these academic factors are missing from your personal repertoire, do not despair or select yourself out of the process. This is only a generality.

You should focus on your own qualifications and skills, and be prepared to explain why *you* are interested in obtaining a clerkship. You can maximize your chances through flexibility, including applying to "less competitive" judges, and following the key strategies presented here.[2] Moreover, to the extent you are just starting out in law school and beginning your approach to the application process early, knowing the importance of these factors will help you build a successful clerkship application, as well as a successful law school experience. Likewise, if you plan to apply again or wait until your third year of law school to apply for a judicial clerkship, these are critical activities the pursuit of which can increase your chances. With the above criteria in mind, the key to success is utilizing the following general approach:

- **Evaluate Your Objectives.**

At the outset, you should evaluate your objectives, both of this clerkship experience and future career goals (*e.g.*, trial litigation, appellate practice or academia; or a particular geographic affiliation). This evaluation often will yield a logical goal in terms of the type or location of the court(s).

YOUR SELF-ASSESSMENT GUIDE:

Asking yourself the following questions will help you prepare your own approach to the clerkship application process and to tailor a strategy designed to help you find the types of courts and clerkships best for you. At this point, you will probably not have all the answers yet, but rest assured that you will—by the time you finish reading this book!

Your Objectives

- What are your reasons for seeking a judicial clerkship?
- What type(s) of law practice are you interested in pursuing in your future career (*e.g.*, litigation, corporate, appellate practice, government, or academia)?

- What specialty areas of practice, if any, interest you and fit with your background and experiences (*e.g.*, tax, bankruptcy, administrative law, patent, intellectual property)?

- In what geographic areas do you have family, friends or other connections, either currently or from your past experiences?

- Do you have any restrictions that require you to be in a certain city or region of the country; or do you have more geographic flexibility?

- Do you know the geographic area where you would like to practice in the future?

- **Conduct a Self-assessment.**

A preliminary self-assessment in terms of your academic record, in conjunction with an interest in particular courts and judges, may further determine an appropriate strategy. You will need to consider both: (1) the differing clerkship experiences by court, and which fit best with your personality, *e.g.*, an appellate court as predominantly research and writing-oriented, versus a trial court as involving abundant contact with litigants, factual issues, jury and bench proceedings; and (2) the levels of competitiveness, which vary by court type and location.

Your Personality and Background

- Are you a person who likes to juggle many different types of tasks, prefers daily contact with a variety of people, and would thrive on the hustle and bustle of court proceedings?

- Do you prefer a more academic experience, reviewing briefs, researching and writing in depth in a relatively quiet, isolated setting?

- How strong do you perceive your academic record to be, in terms of grades?

- Are you a member of the "top" law review/journal at your school?

- Are you actively involved, for example as a member of the editorial board, of another journal at your school?

- Are you involved in a clinic or trial advocacy program?
- Are you actively involved in Moot Court? Have you participated in Moot Court competitions and, if so, what was the result?
- Have you pursued a judicial internship or externship, either over a summer or during the academic year?
- What type of legal employment have you pursued over the summer?
- Did you have any extensive work experience prior to law school (or during law school, if you are supporting yourself through school)?
- Do you have any non-law advanced degrees?
- Do you have any language proficiency besides English, and/or foreign travel?
- What interests, experiences, or activities might distinguish you from other students, or might be of interest to judges?

- **Keep an Open Mind.**

It is paramount to maintain flexibility and open-mindedness as to judges and types of courts. Many students feel swept up in their class-mates' application process and compelled to apply only to "presti-gious" and more well-known courts and judges. For instance, you should not overlook state courts for which a law clerk can potentially shape the law of that state and gain valuable local contact as to the participants and procedures for future practice. Certain lesser-known federal specialty courts, such as Tax, Bankruptcy or the Federal Circuit with its intellectual property and patent focus, may best serve your particular background and interests, and your special expertise will be an added bonus for the judges of those courts.

Your Interest in the Courts

- Do you have any prior exposure to or previous interest in a par-ticular court or judge?
- Do you have any thoughts as to which courts or judges most appeal to you?

- Do you have a leaning towards a clerkship in a federal court or state court, or both?

- Are you more inclined to clerk for a trial court or an appellate court, or both?

- Would you be interested in clerking in a specialty court that has a particular subject matter of cases (*e.g.*, tax, bankruptcy, military, patent or international trade)?

- Do you have a preference for the geographic area in which the court is located?

- Is there a particular type of court that you envision appearing before most often in your future law practice?

- How open-minded are you as to the kind of judge (*e.g.*, Magistrate, Bankruptcy, Administrative Law Judge, Senior or new appointee)?

- Would you consider alternate forms of clerkships (*e.g.*, Staff Attorney, Pro Se Clerk, Career Clerk)?

- **Remember the Golden Rule.**

Above all, you should be advised never apply to a judge with whom you would not want to clerk. To the extent you can discover this fact through your initial research, you will avoid potential pitfalls later in the process for both yourself and the judges to whom you apply (*i.e.*, in the interviewing and offer and acceptance stages, discussed later). This golden rule is of such critical importance that you will hear me refer to it again throughout this book as a central part of your application process.

- **Do Your Research.**

Accepting this as a research project, you should investigate early and through a variety of sources, while keeping in mind the need to assess the credibility of these sources to obtain accurate, reliable information. Most of the screening, organizing, and prioritizing of resources has been done for you already in this book (see Chapter 13), so that you can use your research time most effectively! Your inquiry consists of analyzing the background and opinions of each judge, as well as checking the requisites and procedures of the judge and court. As we will also discuss in detail, factors in choosing a judge to whom to apply may include: ideology, personality and the possibility of a mentor relationship, types of cases, level and amount of work, atmosphere in chambers, length of clerkship term, and special status (chief, senior, new appointee).

Your Research Project

- What factors are most important to *you* in choosing a judge to whom to apply?
- Have you adequately looked into the background of each judge to whom you are applying?

- **Build a Successful Application.**

Through counseling early in the process, you should try to pursue seminar classes, to write papers and/or to serve as a research assistant. In this manner, you can develop an ongoing dialogue with the faculty to help gather information as to courts and judges, and substantive letters of recommendation as well as a writing sample. In addition, activities such as working on a law journal, clinic or Moot Court further benefit as appropriate experiences for a judicial clerkship, which reflect well on your resume. We will, of course, be devoting an entire chapter later to these essential elements.

Your Application

- Which faculty members know you personally and would be most apt to write you a strong letter of recommendation?
- With whom, if any, have you had a small-class or seminar experience?
- In whose class have you excelled? With whom have you written a paper?

- Have you worked as a research assistant or teaching assistant for any faculty member?

- Which faculty members are in the best position to know your legal research and writing skills?

- Are there any employers who can assess and write favorably about your legal research and writing abilities?

- Do you have any potential reference who can also address your other personality traits, such as your character and personality, and your oral communication skills?

- Does your resume reflect your most current personal and professional self, including your activities, interests and prospective future employment?

- What subject matter have you chosen to pursue in law school, and how favorably will your performance in these courses be exhibited on your transcript?

- Which of your papers from law school or other legal work could you use as a writing sample?

- **Understand the History of the Timing.**

Finally, the timing of applications is critical. To help you understand where we are now, it is important to understand from whence we came. As you will see, the timing of the judicial clerkship applications is no simple matter.[3] Currently there are no uniform guidelines from the judges as a whole, but some vestiges of the old guidelines remain for some judges and some courts. Moreover, based on this history and reform efforts, anything is possible for the future.

As a historical perspective, before the mid–1970s, the prevailing practice was to select law clerks during the fall of their *third* year of law school. The judges' hiring deadline gradually advanced to the fall of the second year, and in some cases, even the summer before. By 1992, the timing of the clerkship applications had receded to the fall of the second year of law school, which was widely viewed as disadvantageous both for students and for judges because the students had limited opportunity to develop a record of grades and experiences such as Moot Court, law journals and the like. To counter this erosion, there had been several previous attempts at reform on the part of individual or groups of judges with the effects limited at best.[4] Out of this milieu evolved the September 1993 guidelines from the Judicial Conference, significant in that the judges' national policy-making arm—albeit only a representative body—had become involved in passing such a broad resolution. The resolution established March 1 as the benchmark starting date for law clerk interviews, and suggested that faculties be urged not to transmit letters of recommendation until February 1; building upon the latter component, the law schools also directed their students not to send applications to judges before that date.

An inherent problem was that this resolution was not binding on the judges. Gradually over the ensuing years it splintered, when several of the judges circumvented the guidelines regarding timing of interviews and offers; eventually, the process became mired in confusion. In the fall of 1998, the Judicial Conference officially rescinded these guidelines, although some judges and courts have made individual efforts to retain the February/March dates. Despite notable initiatives from some individual judges in their courts, the timing has slid forward to as early as September (or before) of the second year of law school for clerkships to begin after graduation—as much as two years later.

The most recent initiative in this area comes from the U.S. Courts of Appeals, at the direction of Judge Harry Edwards of the D.C. Circuit and Chief Judge Becker of the Third Circuit through an Ad Hoc Committee of Federal Appellate Judges. (*See* Press Release from the United States Courts of Appeals, March 11, 2002, "Federal Appellate Judges Adopt a New Plan for Law Clerk Hiring," http://www.cadc.us-courts.gov/lawclerk.) The Plan of the Federal Appellate Judges includes: (1) a moratorium on law clerk hiring during the Fall of 2002, (2) an arrangement ensuring that the hiring of law clerks will not be done earlier than the Fall of the third year of law school, and (3) an agreement that the focus of law clerk hiring will be on third year law students and law graduates. Notices have been sent to the Dean of every law school registered with the Association of American Law

Schools (AALS), as well as to law school placement directors. Law students and law graduates are to be advised that, under the Plan, the only law clerk hiring that will be done during the Fall of 2002 will be by judges who are considering third year students or law graduates for clerkship positions during the 2003–2004 term; law clerk hiring for the 2004–2005 term will be done during the Fall of 2003. Beginning in 2002, law schools are being asked to discourage law students from submitting applications for clerkship positions before the fall of the third year of law school; to do nothing to facilitate the release of official transcripts; and to discourage faculty members from sending letters of reference or making calls on behalf of law clerk applicants before the fall of the third year of law school. The Ad Hoc Committee concludes, "We are convinced that this is a good solution to an old and thorny problem."

Initial response to this new plan has been favorable. Of the over two-hundred federal appellate judges that considered the Plan before its inception, 92% of the judges either supported the Plan or indicated that they would not oppose it. The Plan has subsequently been endorsed by the law school deans of a core group of 16 law schools, the Board of Directors of the American Law Deans Association, AALS, and the National Association for Law Placement (*see* Endorsement Letters in http://www.nalp.org/schools/judgerel.htm). In addition, by memorandum dated April 2, 2002, Chief Judge Becker and Judge Edwards have asked all U.S. District Judges, Magistrate Judges, and Bankruptcy Judges to support the Plan: "we urge you to join with us in our efforts to bring much needed reform to the law clerk hiring process." They note that many District Judges "have told us that they are asking their courts or the District Judge associations of their Circuit to endorse the plan." However, as of this writing, the question remains as to which specific judges and courts have committed to, or will support in the future, this latest initiative. Moreover, the Plan does not set uniform application dates for these judges. (*See* www.cadc.uscourts.gov/ lawclerk for updated listing of courts and law schools supporting the Plan.)Given the unfortunate history of failed attempts to establish standards for the timing of clerkship applications, it is uncertain whether this laudable proposal will succeed on a broader scale in pushing the clerkship hiring season beyond the second year of law school. Ultimately, students must check with individual judges and their law schools as to the timing of their applications.

· **Master the Timing of Your Applications.**

In the absence of uniform timing guidelines, students need to investigate the individual application dates, requirements, and procedures of each judge. There are many places to find out this key information, conveniently catalogued for you later in this book as well. In addition, I advise students to apply in "waves" or a series of applications. List the deadlines of the judges and courts for which you are interested in applying, and send in your applications accordingly.

What you may find is that the most competitive courts and judges post early dates, for which you need to send your materials in immediately, but many other judges and courts will have a later pattern. This allows you more flexibility both in terms of getting many chances, but also in the types of judges and courts for which you can apply. For instance, many Magistrate Judges—who can provide wonderful clerkship experiences—will follow the lead of the District Judges, in part out of deference, and wait on their dates. The so-called "less competitive" circuits (*e.g.*, *not* the Second, Ninth and D.C. Circuits)—which have very fine judges and excellent clerkships as well—are less likely to enter the fray so early and more likely as a whole to chose later dates. Of course, many great judges who are independently minded individuals in all types of courts (yes, even the Second Circuit and the Southern District of New York) will stick to their later application dates, which can vary to late in the spring of the second year—or even the fall of the third year of law school. In addition, there are newly appointed judges entering the bench who typically hire their clerks with timing outside of the traditional season, as soon as they are confirmed. Specialty courts such as Tax, International, Federal Circuit, and Bankruptcy are also more likely in general to wait until later in the application season.

State courts may indicate dates as early as fall or spring of the second year, and as late as the fall of the third year of law school for clerkships commencing the following year. For example, I know several students who have found the Alaska Supreme Court to be a most positive and rewarding experience in terms of exploring a geographic area and having an opportunity to shape and impact a state's law; and this court tends to hire in the fall of the third year. In an interesting twist, under the new Federal Appellate Judges' Plan, conceivably a student might apply for a District Court clerkship in the second year (unless that District Judge joins this plan), certain state courts that spring and, for some, federal appellate clerkships in the fall of the third year of law school. In fact, a student may end up clerking first for a District Judge and then for a Circuit Judge.

Flexibility as to types of clerkships, as well as types of courts can pay off. Keep in mind the clerkship positions that are not traditional "elbow" clerks for an individual judge, which we will describe in detail in the next chapter. Staff attorney positions for the circuit courts give clerks the opportunity to interact with and write for a number of judges on their courts; and these tend to hire much later in the season, even well into the third year of law school. For example, the Staff Attorney's Office in the Southern District of New York, which has been reorganized to combine Pro Se Clerks and Motion Clerks, generally conducts interviews on campus in the fall for third-year students. Sometimes your second, third or even later "wave" turns out to be the best clerkship experience, which was truly meant for you.

As your final wave, consider in any event the possibility of applying in your third year of law school—or even later—for a clerkship that may begin after you have been out of law school for a year. I have found that most law firms and other employers welcome their attorneys' acquisition of a clerkship and would grant a leave of absence with the hope that you would return to them with that extra wisdom and asset you would surely bring. In addition, your chances of obtaining a clerkship might be greater as a third-year student. You will have had another year of law school to develop a stronger academic record, significant law school activities, another summer of professional work experience and more meaningful faculty and practitioner recommendations. Judges are increasingly appreciating the additional work experience, and turning to more experienced clerks to fill at least one of their slots. This scenario is particularly true for the newly appointed judges, who need immediate clerks, as well as future slots to be filled off-cycle; these judges benefit both from the added flexibility of an attorney in practice and the additional knowledge and experience of such an applicant. Incidentally, the clerkship salary of the law clerk with additional work experience will be adjusted upward also to reflect that premium. A clerkship is worth waiting for and will benefit your career in the long-term, even if you wait a little longer for the right one and follow a less traditional order of employment options!

Yes, it would be nice if the application process was more structured with standard procedures, uniform timing of applications and interviews, and accordingly, less confusing. However, when viewed from this rather different "wave" perspective, a longer, extended clerkship season actually means more opportunities; and, since judges and courts will differ as to their timing, there might be more chances to interview and explore the possibilities!

Notes

1. *See* NALP Report at 42, 46–49 and 68–69. *See, e.g.,* Tables 25, 26, 29, 52 and 53.
2. *See also* Strauss, Debra M., "The Wide World of Judicial Clerkships: Counseling Strategies for Navigating the Maze of Courts and Clerkship Opportunities," *NALP Bulletin,* Vol. 11, No. 11, November 1998.
3. *See also* Strauss, Debra M., "The Clerkship Timing Guidelines: Efforts to Rebuild in the Wake of the Rescission," *NALP Bulletin,* Vol. 12, No. 11, November 1999.
4. These earlier efforts are set forth extensively in a prominent essay by Circuit Judge Edward Becker, Associate Justice Stephen Breyer and Circuit Judge Guido Calabresi, "The Federal Judicial Clerk Hiring Problem and the Modest March 1 Solution," *The Yale Law Journal,* Vol. 104 (1994). (*See also* my Attachment to the Report of the NALP Judicial Clerkship Task Force, July 8, 1999.)

Part II

Courts and Clerkships

CHAPTER
three

A Collection of Clerkship Opportunities

At the outset, it should be enlightening to portray the general flavor of clerking for a judge or a court, and to capture some of the differences in the experiences. We will then discuss the types of judicial clerkships, including special types of clerkships that are readily available but not as widely known. Some of these variations and alternatives are more off the beaten path but—or perhaps for this reason especially—worthy of consideration.

THE JUDICIAL CLERKSHIP EXPERIENCE

In a judicial clerkship, the kinds of tasks, duties and daily work varies by court as well as by judge. Perhaps one kind of experience appeals more to you than another or fits more closely with your personality and future career goals. (*See also* Chapter 5 on the factors in your selection process for further details of the differences between the types and levels of courts, and how these may be significant for you.) It is only with an understanding of these generalities that you can evaluate the options and determine your direction through the clerkship maze.

· **Clerking for a Trial Court**

Trial court clerks have close contact with the litigation process. As a result, trial court clerkships involve more human interaction, more time in the courtroom, and a generally heavier caseload. In a trial court, the judicial law clerk typically is involved in decision-making at every stage of the proceedings, assisting with case management, participating in settlement negotiations and status conferences with the parties, usually (but not always) with the judge. Law clerks participate greatly in the discovery process, playing a role in assisting to resolve discovery disputes by phone, pre-trial conference and motions; often this involves practical judgment as to fairness and dispute resolution techniques that can only be learned by watching the process at work.

In the trial court, the law clerks are exposed to all aspects of each case. In addition to the above list, they are involved in evidentiary hearings, non-jury and jury trials. With the law clerk always by the judge's side, the range of tasks for bench (non-jury) trials includes assessing the credibility of witnesses and the evidence, preparing findings of fact and conclusions of law, and drafting or editing final orders. For jury trials, the law clerk will prepare questions for the jury voir dire at the beginning of the trial and the jury instructions for the end of the trial, researching and advising the judge as well on whatever evidentiary issues come up on the spot in the course of trial. During the trial, the law clerk may act as a courtroom clerk, with or without the deputy clerk, marking exhibits, keeping trial minutes, handling (but not swearing in) the witnesses, and just plain watching the dramatic events of the trial. Indeed, there is a great deal of daily contact with attorneys and litigants, scheduling conferences and communicating with counsel, as well as working with the facts of real documents.

Although trial court clerks play a key role in the courtroom, they also do a great deal of behind-the-scenes work. In evaluating substantive motions, the law clerk reads the briefs, conducts independent research, performs legal analysis and writes memoranda for use by the judge (a "bench memo" which typically sets forth facts, issues, case law and a recommended disposition for the motion). Note that some judges resolve these motions from the bench in an oral decision based in large measure on this work of the law clerk, while others prefer to issue a written opinion, which the law clerk assists in drafting as well. In some chambers, the law clerk writes the first draft of a decision, with or without some initial guidance from the judge, who later edits and revises the draft; some judges prefer to write their own draft first, and have the law clerk review and edit the judge's writing. The continual editing of the written work by both law clerk and judge can prove to be an exciting collaborative effort.

While there are written opinions of the court to prepare, trial clerks tend to have less time for lengthy writing and research, and more of a focus on getting the work done efficiently. Of course there still must be a high level of quality of work, but with less attention to the process of in-depth research and the eloquence of the written word than one finds in the appellate courts. There are actual parties before the court waiting for a relatively prompt resolution of the issues in order to proceed with the litigation. As a result of the exposure to the parties and the facts themselves, the perspective of a law clerk and judge for the trial court differs from his or her appellate counterparts; thus, these written opinions tend to be more practical and less esoteric in nature.

Throughout the process, most judges work closely with the clerks on a daily basis, discussing the bench memos, the draft opinions, and the general direction of the cases. In the trial court clerkship, a judicial clerk gains tremendous exposure to and participation in every aspect of trial practice and technique, making this an unparalleled experience in the litigation process.

· Clerking for an Appellate Court

An appellate clerkship tends to be a continuation of the law school experience in many ways. The experience is more academic and reflective. The law clerk performs exclusively a research kind of function, writing opinions and bench memoranda on the issues of law being appealed. More time is spent on each case, exploring the case law in detail and crafting a somewhat scholarly exposition of the ruling. The facts are limited to those in the trial court record and those in the briefs of the parties; as a result, there is almost no contact with the attorneys. With no courtroom exposure except during the limited times of oral appellate argument, the focus of the work takes place exclusively in chambers or in the library. Thus, the experience can be isolating but is also more sedate, slower in pace and less hectic, without the constant interruption and juggling of a wide variety of tasks present in the trial court clerkship. There are generally fewer matters and more time, but higher expectations for the level of the written work product.

Although there are reduced contacts with the litigants and less court exposure, a law clerk can, through observation, gain knowledge of the techniques of oral argument and a greater appreciation for the record. Typically, the appellate clerk helps to prepare administratively for oral arguments, including bench memos summarizing the briefs, analyzing the legal issues, and suggesting questions for the judge to raise or key points needing clarification by the attorneys at oral argument. Much of the clerk's time is later spent in extensive research and drafting of the final rulings.

Another aspect unique to the appellate court is the amount of contact with other judges and the law clerks from other chambers, in addition to the intensive writing and editing experience with one's own judge. In the process of creating a decision for the court, the draft opinion circulates among the panel of judges and is the object of suggestion and compromise. While drafting some of these opinions and reviewing others, the law clerk advises the judge as to whether to join in the opinion of colleagues, suggest changes, or draft a separate concurring or dissenting opinion. The appellate clerkship thus offers the opportunity not only to witness first-hand the collective process and collegial interaction among the judges, but also to participate in a significant way. Depending on the court and judge, the clerkship may involve some travel to a central courthouse for sittings during the week or so of oral argument; depending on your own personal situation, this feature may or may not be an additional benefit of that clerkship.

• Other Functions of a Law Clerk

For all of these clerkships there are other functions, which may involve assisting with extra-judicial events, more menial duties, or even personal tasks. Along the way, there are things like checking citations for accuracy and maintaining a library in chambers. Many judges use law clerks to draft their speeches and lectures for conferences or bar association functions. Clerks may assist in the writing of articles, book reviews or books. At the other end of the scale, a judge may ask the clerk to serve as a driver or to run personal errands. Some judges give clerks more administrative tasks, and others have the secretary doing those sorts of things. Remember that some judges (*e.g.*, a Magistrate Judge) may opt to have an additional law clerk instead of a secretary. So, depending on the judge, it could be a different work mix. Outside of chambers life, the judge may include the law clerk in professional social events or extracurricular activities. Regardless of the type of court, the experience of the law clerk varies above all with the practices, personality and working style of the particular judge.

TYPES OF CLERKSHIPS

Now for a few words on special clerkships, some of which are beyond what you might ordinarily think of as a traditional clerkship. Once again, flexibility is the key. Perhaps a brief description of each will expand your thinking a bit . . .

• "Elbow" Law Clerk

Most of what we have discussed so far has really been "elbow" law clerks. This is a term of art for those law clerks who work one-on-one for a particular judge. If you have been absorbing the flavor of the clerkship experience from everything described above, you can easily see the origins of the term—the clerk is always within an arm's length, or by the side of, his or her judge!

- **Staff Attorney or Court Clerk**

As mentioned here and there rather briefly until now, a staff attorney position is another type of judicial clerkship. Staff attorneys or court clerks (also known as "central staff counsel") work for an entire court, usually an appellate court—state as well as federal. (Consult the next chapter for an overview of the courts.) Rather than developing a close relationship with a particular judge, these clerks handle matters for the court as a whole, with only minimal contact with individual judges. The use of staff attorneys varies considerably from court to court, but some of the common tasks include administrative duties such as reviewing appeals and correspondence, assisting in case management and handling settlement procedures. They may thus perform more of a clerk's office role, serving a screening function by reviewing cases to pass along the cases through the process to the judges on the court, perhaps weeding out cases on the grounds of jurisdictional issues or other defects. Some of these cases can be decided summarily without oral argument, in which case the staff attorney may prepare a memoranda or summary order for the disposal of a judge. Sometimes they write bench memos on substantive issues, emergency motions and the like, which go directly to a panel of judges for decisions. So it really can vary greatly with the needs of the court, but that is something to check into as well.

The term of service for staff attorney positions also varies by court. For federal circuit courts, staff attorney positions are sometimes for a fixed term of five years (or less). Often in the state courts and some federal courts, these positions are longer term, "permanent" or "career" clerkships. Staff attorney positions are gaining in practice, for example, becoming increasingly common in the California appellate courts. While compensation for these positions may be at the same rate as elbow law clerks, the prestige level is generally less, as is the level of contact with individual judges. However, this feature, and the fact that fewer students are aware of them, makes these positions less competitive to obtain. Moreover, staff attorney positions can provide the opportunity to gain inside information as to the inner workings of the court system and useful practical experience. Many subsequent employers will appreciate the added perspective gleaned from this position. Often clerks stay in these positions, as the hours are the reasonable civil-service variety and the legal work continues to be interesting.

I have spoken with several staff attorneys for a variety of courts, and they have viewed their role quite positively. One former staff attorney for the D.C. Circuit Court, who went to this position after a few years of law firm practice, highly recommended the experience to law students for the following reason. "In my opinion it was better for a clerk because I didn't have to work for just one judge, but had the opportunity to work for all of the judges on the court. I might not have had the intimate relationship with one judge, but I was exposed to a wide range of cases and judges." He acknowledged that this type of clerkship differs from a traditional elbow clerkship, observing: "It is a different experience but it's not a lesser experience just because you are not at the oral argument every day and writing the opinions, although depending on the court there may be some of that type of work, as there was at the D.C. Circuit."

Students should check circuit by circuit for both the duties of the job and the qualifications that the circuit wants. Some courts (such as the Ninth Circuit) will accept clerks directly from law school; the courts that use staff attorneys for other more varied roles (such as the D.C. Circuit) tend to require more experience at the outset. Since they are generally not as widely publicized, you may need to investigate further and contact the court directly. This information can be found on the website of each court (many of which are listed in the resources chapter), advertised like other staff court positions as a regular job posting for the court. For postings of staff attorney positions, you can also check the general employment opportunities on the Federal Judiciary website, at http://www.uscourts.gov/employment/opportunity.html (listed under the position title "Staff Attorney"), and then the other job listings for the United States Office of Personnel Management at http://www.usajobs.opm.gov/. Note that the application timing for staff attorney positions is often off the cycle of the traditional law clerk applications, since the positions are posted as they arise. While there is significant variation in the staff attorney experience by circuit and type of court, this is an excellent option for law students to consider.

· **Pro Se Clerk**

A pro se law clerk is a specialized kind of staff attorney position. Common especially in the federal district courts, they may also be called writ clerks or staff attorneys. The pro se law clerk is designated as the judicial clerk to handle pro se matters, either as part of an entire Pro Se Office, or under the auspices of the Central Staff or Staff Attorney Office. Typical types of pro se matters include prisoner habeas corpus petitions and civil rights complaints, employment discrimination complaints, social security disability appeals and any other civil proceeding instituted without an attorney. The duties of a pro se clerk generally include substantive screening of all petitions and complaints, drafting proposed sua sponte dismissals and appropriate orders for the court's signature, and writing advisory memoranda to assist the court in preparing opinions.

I know from clerking for a Chief Judge in the Southern District of New York that a large number of these cases come into the Pro Se Office. The pro se law clerks do a lot of screening of these cases to weed out the cases that are determined to be frivolous or without merit. After drafting orders of dismissal, the pro se clerk submits them to the Chief Judge to review and sign, thereby disposing of the case before it even goes to the other law clerks in the other chambers. So it is predominantly a reviewing function and a substantial volume of work on those types of cases for the court. In addition, the pro se clerk serves as a liaison between the court and pro se litigants. These litigants sometimes need extra care and time, since they are not represented by an attorney and thus unlike other litigants rely upon the Pro Se Office to provide forms, procedural (but not substantive) advice and guidance. When a pro se litigant calls the chambers of a judge, the judge's law clerk refers them to the Pro Se Office to handle any questions and problems; any papers this person files will be processed in that office as well before being sent to the chambers of a designated judge. Note that in some courts, the staff attorneys' or pro se law clerks' office may work under the supervision of a committee of judges, a single judge, a senior staff attorney, the circuit executive or the clerk of the court.

The salary of a pro se clerk is comparable to a judicial law clerk, with the government salary level dependent on qualifications and experience (*see* Chapter 9). The pro se clerk position may be variable or indefinite in length, generally longer term than an elbow clerk position. Once again, this position lacks the prestige level of and differs from a traditional clerkship, but if you are so inclined, the work can be interesting and rewarding. The Pro Se Office likes to see in its applicants a commitment to public interest law and a solid understanding of constitutional law. You must demonstrate in the cover letter how your education and work experience relate to the duties and responsibilities of this position. Staff attorney and pro se law clerk positions are excellent opportunities frequently overlooked by students considering judicial clerkships.

• Term versus Permanent (or Career Clerk)

Most law clerk positions we have been discussing are "term" positions in that they have a limited fixed period of time, usually one or two years. The length of these term positions is determined by the judges according to their individual preferences in how they choose to structure their chambers (*e.g.,* two-year clerks with a "senior" and a "junior" clerk, versus one-year clerks who rotate simultaneously or with staggered start dates). The length of the clerkship term may, accordingly, be a factor in your selection of judges (*see* discussion in Chapter 6).

In contrast, a "permanent" or "career" clerk works for the judge or court for an indefinite period of time, considered to be permanent in that he or she will serve as a clerk until further notice. By being placed in this special category, the law clerk may be eligible for a different set of benefits and salary level. For instance, in the federal system, "career judicial law clerks," defined as appointments for four or more years, can participate in the federal retirement system and the Thrift Savings Plan (which augments the clerk's investment income with matching funds from the government) in addition to the standard health and life insurance available for "term" clerks. (*See* Chapter 9 for more on the financial aspects.)

A growing number of federal and state courts are hiring law school graduates as "permanent" law clerks. Permanent or career clerks are especially common in the state court system; for example, the judges in the California Court of Appeals and the California Supreme Court do not hire clerks directly from law school, but instead hire "career research attorneys." Recently this trend has been increasing in the federal courts as well, most notably among the Senior District Judges, Magistrate Judges and Bankruptcy Court Judges, particularly those who choose to use their second law clerk instead of a secretary and seek the same sort of permanence in the position. Some judges hire new law-school graduates to fill career clerk positions; others hire only experienced clerks or practicing attorneys. Sometimes a standard term clerkship eventually, upon agreement of the judge and clerk, becomes converted to a permanent clerk position.

Prior to the early 1990's, a career clerk was only prevalent in the state court system. When at that time it became authorized in the federal courts, my judge called me to say, "Come back—let's grow old together." So I decided to prove wrong the old adage, "You can't go home again"[1]—since "home" is truly what his chambers and court were to me—and, ultimately, I did. My experience as a permanent law clerk was even more special and rewarding; how nice it was to enjoy the work of a clerk without thinking about the next career step. I have spoken with a number of career clerks recently who have also noticed this increasing trend; we agreed that the secret must be out as to how great this position is! Many graduates have called me to ask about just this; they are out in practice and decide they really would love to do a permanent law clerk position. These clerkships are very hard to find because there is no central listing of the available positions, but you can follow any leads and keep looking through the continual postings of individual judges and courts. At the very least, this arrangement is certainly growing in practice and well worth considering at some point in your career.

· Temporary Clerkships

· *Temporary Law Clerk*

Occasionally a vacancy for a law clerk arises from a special circumstance, such as a departure of a law clerk due to illness or personal reasons. In this situation, a judge may seek a replacement for the remainder of that clerkship term. The law clerk position is, however, in all other respects the same as a standard term clerk.

In addition, the federal judiciary sets forth as a distinct type of law clerk appointment a "temporary" law clerk—different from a "term" or "career" law clerk appointment. A "temporary" law clerk is defined by the federal government as an appointment approved by the circuit judicial council with a specific termination date. Appointments for one year or less are covered by social security only and do not include eligibility for health, life, retirement and participation in the Thrift Savings Plan. Temporary appointments for more than a year are eligible for health and life insurance only (like a "term" clerk).

· *Temporary Assistant Clerks (TACs)*

I am including this type of position here, but distinguishing it from a traditional judicial clerkship. Some new graduates who do not have a job at graduation and are awaiting the bar results take positions such as in the Connecticut Superior Courts as TACs (temporary assistant clerks). Usually temporary in nature, this position does provide exposure to court procedures and documents. Although there are some people who interpret the concept of judicial clerk more liberally and may consider TACs to be a form of a clerkship, I follow a more conservative definition of judicial clerkship, as does the National Association for Law Placement in their compilation of the law graduate employment statistics. To me, the key difference between a TAC and a law clerk position is the fact that it is not a research and writing position, but is more administrative. This contrasts with the typical "elbow" clerk, and even the Staff Attorney position, which is still a clerkship although the tasks are performed for an entire court rather than an individual judge. It can still be a court position, for example, more akin to a deputy clerk (which does not, however, require a law degree).

The best indicator is found on the official website of the Connecticut Judicial Branch (http://www.jud.state.ct.us/external/super/volunteer.htm), which lists as a separate category from "Law Clerks" (including Superior Court, Appellate Court, and Supreme Court) the following description of the position "Temporary Assistant Clerks":

> Applications are accepted on a continuing basis for all Judicial Districts. Minimum qualification: A law school degree. The position involves a wide variety of duties including courtroom clerk, jury clerk, case flow, scheduling pretrials, calendars and other responsibilities as assigned. Compensation is $15 per hour with a maximum of 70 hours during a two week pay period. Group health and life insurance is available after six months of full time employment.

Although not a traditional clerkship, a TAC may be a good way to have some involvement in the court system. Be aware, however, that this is not a substitute for the intellectual rigor, prestige and experience of a judicial clerkship.

· A Judicial Internship or Externship

Since we have been exploring types of clerkships, judicial internships/externships are certainly worth focusing on here for two reasons: (1) the experience, which is much like a clerkship; and (2) the key role an externship can play in obtaining a judicial clerkship. As described by a former career law clerk at the U.S. Court of Appeals, who went on to her own appellate practice and academia: "Internships are the best way to get the foot in the door to a clerkship. All three of the interns I knew during my time with the judge went on to get clerkships: one in the Sixth Circuit, one in the Eastern District of Michigan, and one in the appellate division of the Ohio state courts." In fact, for those of you who are still unsure, sometimes an externship is one of the best ways to test out whether or not you really want a clerkship.

A judicial externship or internship (the terms are basically interchangeable) is essentially a junior clerkship working in a judge's chambers while one is still a law student. These are generally unpaid positions (full or part-time), although sometimes with academic credit, depending on the policies and programs of the law school. This contrasts with a judicial clerkship, which is a paid post-graduation position, but often includes many of the same types of activities. The optimum time for such an experience is during the summer after the first year of law school or during the second year of law school, since the knowledge and writing skills gained during the externship can improve the student's performance in later law school courses and potentially lead to a judicial clerkship. Some courts, however, consider only third-year law students for these positions.

Many judges will accept judicial interns during the summer or the school year, and some will send letters to local law schools actively seeking these students. Some law schools offer a formal program through which students are placed in externships with local judges. Others will allow academic credit for judicial extern/internships even if obtained independently by the student (usually provided certain conditions are met, such as arranging faculty supervision). Even if credit is not offered, many students volunteer for these opportunities by calling directly or writing the chambers of judges in the geographic area of interest. Although no financial compensation is generally available through the courts for summer interns or academic year externships, alternate funding sources may be available. For example, a few regional bar and city programs provide such funding. You should check with the career services and financial aid offices of your school for information on externship opportunities and programs, policies on academic credit, and possible financial support.

At its best, the externship can provide you with the benefits of a mentor, in the law clerks and hopefully in the judge as well. A great deal of this depends upon the judge and the structure in chambers.

Some judges work directly with the extern, while others rely upon their law clerks to delegate work and instruct the extern. The level of contact with the judge will vary accordingly, as will the amount of time the judge allows the extern to spend in the courtroom assisting with or at least observing the proceedings. Thus, the externship is often a clerkship one-step removed, subject also to the personalities and abilities of the law clerks as well as of the judge. There is the danger they will choose to pass along only those cases they wish to avoid (the "dogs") or those that are so big and cumbersome that they will be around virtually forever anyway (the "elephants"). For this reason, if you are applying independently for a summer internship or academic year externship, you should research the practices of the particular judge during the application and interview process. Seek feedback from students who have externed for this judge in the past and ask the law clerks about the division of labor on cases and the degree of contact with the judge and courtroom. If the externship is through your law school, most likely these facets will have been screened and refined from prior student feedback before your placement; if so, you need not concern yourself with this caveat.

The externship experience should offer you practical insights into the process of adjudication, a singular knowledge of the law, and result in a vast improvement of your legal writing. The acquisition of these skills can assist you in subsequent law school classes and your future career. There are so few opportunities in law school to have exposure to the real world of law, contact with the judiciary, and genuine cases/facts/litigants! This is also a rare opportunity to observe and gather more information on what a post-graduation clerkship would be like. Depending on the judge, an externship may parallel more closely the experience of a clerkship; if there is direct interaction with the judge and the court, the experience will be most valuable.

An additional benefit is worthy of note. Most judges will set a lower threshold for the qualifications and credentials they seek for interns/externs, as this position presents less of a commitment in time (*e.g.*, three months versus one year) and is secondary to the law clerks, who are their primary line of reliance. So, this may be a way to get your foot in the door with a judge who would not have considered you for a clerkship in the first instance.

Occasionally, an externship leads directly to a post-graduation clerkship with that judge. However, many judges have a policy against hiring their externs as law clerks. At the very least, the externship is more likely to lead to a judicial clerkship with another judge, through the added credential on your resume and hopefully a weighty recommendation from this judge. I have often seen the tremendous impact of the recommendation from one of these judges to another, whether by letter or by phone, in the clerkship application process. Thus, the experience of working for a judge often creates new opportunities for students that they might otherwise not have had. Many externs perform so well that upon graduation they obtain judicial clerkships that might not have been available to them without the externship experience.[2]

The National Judicial Clerkship Study documented that internship or externship programs with local judges often provide an entrée into the world of judicial clerkships, as well as a valuable experience and enhancement to the law school education. The vast majority of law schools reported having a formal program. Overwhelmingly, the schools with an externship or internship program believed that this has positively affected the number of clerkship applications; 91% of schools provided this response nationwide. A smaller but still large percentage of schools (85%) also believed that externships have a positive effect on clerkship offers. As further support for the substantial impact of judicial internships or externships, the National Clerkship Study found that almost one-third of the law clerks and students who received a clerkship had pursued a summer or academic year intern/externship while in law school. For this reason, the study in its action plan of initiatives encouraged the law schools to develop more judicial internship/externship programs for students.[3]

I remain convinced of the value of externship programs, particularly in law schools where the students would otherwise be less likely to be considered for a clerkship. So much so that I have helped to establish one such program at Pace University School of Law, as a professor and director of the Federal Judicial Extern Honors Program. At

Pace, we have found that the word has spread about the fine training of these select students, opening judicial doors that previously might not have been accessible to them. As a result, the number of judicial clerkships has increased dramatically.

A few of these students put together some thoughts to share about their externship experiences with federal district court judges. Each of them discovered, in his or her own way, the benefits of the externship both in deciding whether to do a judicial clerkship and in helping to obtain those clerkships. The judicial externship program, according to Jessica Bannon, "was the best experience of my law school years. Externing with a federal judge was like being a federal clerk. I sat in on conferences, watched trials and got a bird's-eye view of the daily routine of a judge. It was like finding out a secret that few people know."

Joy Fitzgerald found that the learning curve was steep, but she learned more substantive law and more about the reality of practice than she could have imagined possible. "The externship experience made me more interested in pursuing a judicial clerkship position because it provided me with an appreciation of the range of matters before the court and the type of work a judicial clerk handles. This is impossible to glean from a classroom. Although the time commitment is limited in an externship, I think it provides a real glimpse into the workings of chambers which, for me, provided an added impetus to apply for clerkships and a significant enhancement to my application credentials." She concluded that she would "absolutely recommend an externship experience to any law student. It certainly gives you credibility in applying for a judicial clerkship and I believe it still would be invaluable for a student going directly to practice in a firm."

Another student tells the success story of how his externship led directly to his receipt of an offer for a judicial clerkship. During his interview, Jason Marino had misgivings when the judge disappeared to make a very significant phone call: "Much to my surprise however, he had called, in those five minutes I was with the law clerks, the judge I externed for the previous semester. He told me that, based on her recommendation, he wanted to offer me a clerkship right there on the spot. After I picked my jaw up from the floor, I gladly accepted."

Thus, an externship is an option that can provide you with a positive experience and a glimpse into a judge's courtroom and chambers. Beyond these potential benefits, an externship may actually increase your chances of obtaining a judicial clerkship upon graduation. Sometimes the externship can lead directly to a clerkship offer with that judge. At the very least, the addition of the judge to your credentials may open other doors to the judiciary for you, perhaps even leading to the intervention of this judge on your behalf!

Notes

1. Originated by Thomas Wolfe in his autobiographical novel, *You Can't Go Home Again* (1940).
2. *See, e.g.,* Nealy, Jounice, "Minorities finding clerkships key to law careers," *St Petersburg Times,* Dec. 25, 2000 (students credit their school's internship program at Stetson University College of Law for leading to federal clerkships), on-line at http://www.sptimes.com/News/122500/State/Minorities_finding_cl.shtml.
3. NALP Report at 17, 32, 46–47 and 68–69. This data is excerpted from the NALP Report at 32–33, including Tables 10–13 presented therein.

CHAPTER
four

An Overview of the Courts

There are lots of courts out there and so many clerkship options that it can be somewhat daunting. This chapter and the next will serve as your guide to navigating the maze of courts and clerkship opportunities in helping you to decide which may be best for you. Keep in mind that the answer may be *several*—and this flexibility, if strategically focused, will work to your benefit during the clerkship application process.

As an overview, there are in the judicial world many levels and types of courts: federal, state, international and specialty courts. As we shall see, clerkships are available at the trial and appellate levels for federal, state and local court systems, federal magistrates, federal administrative law judges, and specialized courts such as tax, bankruptcy, federal claims, veterans appeals and more. Each court offers bountiful clerkship opportunities waiting to be investigated, considered and possibly pursued.

· Federal Courts

In the federal court system, there are many clerkship opportunities. They do involve some differences in levels of prestige, which we will discuss in subsequent chapters as one of many factors to consider in choosing a court. However, for the most part, each is widely respected as a golden opportunity to gain an experience valuable to your future career. As a useful guide to law students, I have included a basic chart below, which diagrams these courts and their place in the federal system. The appellate courts represent the first and second tier in this chart, including the U.S. Courts of Appeals and of course the U.S. Supreme Court, which is a secondary clerkship and will be discussed separately in Chapter 11 as an entirely different animal. On the level of trial court clerkship are the U.S. District Courts, including U.S. Magistrates and U.S. Bankruptcy Courts which report to them, and a variety of specialty courts such as tax, federal claims, veterans appeals, international trade, and administrative agencies.

Federal Court Structure

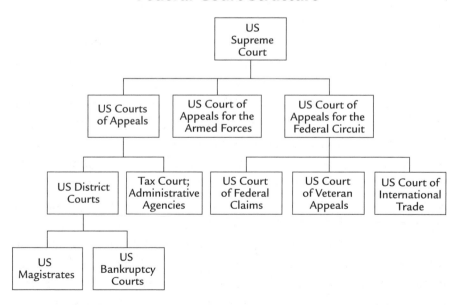

Overall, there are a multitude of clerkship positions available in these courts. Federal circuit judges may hire three law clerks, while federal district judges are generally permitted two law clerks. Some additional clerk positions have been created for chief judges, judges who have no secretarial assistance, and judges with unusually heavy caseloads; whereas, senior judges have fewer allotted clerks (usually one less). The number of law clerks is generally less for judges on the Bankruptcy Court and magistrate judges, who are allocated one law clerk and one secretary, but many opt for a second law clerk instead of the secretary. These numbers refer to the traditional "elbow" clerk designated for an individual judge. In addition, certain of these courts in their central staff include the alternate forms of clerkships that play a role for judges of the court as a whole.

- ### U.S. Supreme Court

The United States Supreme Court is the highest court in the federal judiciary, and consists of the Chief Justice of the United Sates and eight associate justices, all of whom are appointed for life by the President with the advice and consent of the U.S. Senate. The Court holds one term annually, commencing on the first Monday in October. It reviews decisions of lower federal courts and the highest state courts, granting certiorari to a limited number of cases. According to the official statistics of the U.S. Supreme Court: of the approximately 7000 cases on the docket per term, plenary review with oral arguments by attorneys is granted in 100 cases per term. Formal written opinions are delivered in 80 to 90 cases. Approximately 50 to 60 additional cases are disposed of without granting plenary review. Law clerks for the Supreme Court assist the Justices by reviewing petitions for certiorari, advising the Justices, researching and preparing memoranda for oral argument, and drafting and editing opinions of the Court. "Some opinions are revised a dozen or more times before they are announced."[1]

Each Justice is authorized to hire four law clerks for a one-year term, and the Chief Justice may hire up to five clerks; however, Chief Justice William H. Rehnquist and Justice John Paul Stevens both prefer to hire only three clerks. A Supreme Court clerkship is a second clerkship that usually follows a clerkship for the U.S. Court of Appeals. Justices start considering applications from students during their third year in law school. (*See* Chapter 11 on Clerking for the U.S. Supreme Court.)

· *U.S. Courts of Appeals*

The United States Courts of Appeals, also called the Circuit Courts, are the intermediate appellate courts in the federal system. Organized into 12 regional circuits (numbered First through Eleventh Circuit plus the District of Columbia Circuit), each of these courts of appeals hears appeals from the district courts located within its circuit, as well as appeals from decisions of the federal administrative agencies. In addition to these 12, the Court of Appeals for the Federal Circuit has national jurisdiction over specific types of cases, discussed separately below. These appellate judges are appointed for life by the President, with the advice and consent of the U.S. Senate.

The number of judges allotted varies by circuit, depending on the caseload of the courts. The smallest court is the First Circuit with six judgeships, and the largest court is the Ninth Circuit, with 28 judgeships. A list of the states that compose each circuit is set forth in Title 28 of the U.S. Code, Section 41, and the number of judgeships in each circuit is set forth in Title 28 of the U.S. Code, Section 44. *See* Appendix for a summary listing of these courts including districts, locations, and the number of authorized judgeships for each. For easier reference, I have included this handy map with the geographic boundaries of the Circuit Courts.

There are over 500 federal appellate clerkships (corresponding to approximately 175 judgeships),[2] which believe it or not is far fewer than district court clerkships; as such, they are as a whole rather competitive and esteemed. At the outset, the best way to determine what it would be like to clerk for these federal appellate courts would be to review the earlier general description of appellate clerkship experience; it was modeled predominantly after this intermediate federal court. We will later explore these clerkships further as you research by court and by judge into the individualized nature of each experience—and look at other factors to help with your selection process.

United States Courts of Appeals
Geographic Boundaries by Circuit

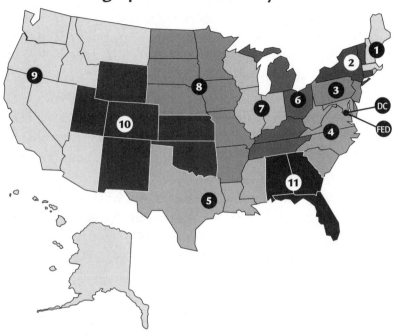

First Circuit   Maine, Massachusetts, New Hampshire, Rhode Island, Puerto Rico

Second Circuit   Connecticut, New York, Vermont

Third Circuit   Delaware, New Jersey, Pennsylvania, the Virgin Islands

Fourth Circuit   Maryland, North Carolina, South Carolina, Virginia, West Virginia

Fifth Circuit   Louisiana, Mississippi, Texas

Sixth Circuit   Kentucky, Michigan, Ohio, Tennessee

Seventh Circuit Illinois, Indiana, Wisconsin

Eighth Circuit   Arkansas, Iowa, Minnesota, Missouri, Nebraska, North Dakota, South Dakota

Ninth Circuit   Alaska, Arizona, California, Guam, Hawaii, Idaho, Montana, Nevada, Northern Mariana Islands, Oregon, Washington

Tenth Circuit   Colorado, Kansas, New Mexico, Oklahoma, Utah, Wyoming

Eleventh Circuit Alabama, Florida, Georgia

D.C. Circuit   District of Columbia

Federal Circuit   Nationwide jurisdiction, located in Washington, D.C.

- ## U.S. Court of Appeals for the Federal Circuit

This federal court of appeals hears appeals in specialized cases, such as those involving patent laws arising from the district courts, and cases by the Court of International Trade and the Court of Federal Claims. In addition, this court has jurisdiction over appeals from the U.S. Court of Veterans Appeals, the International Trade Commission, the Board of Contract Appeals, the Patent and Trademark Office and the Merit Systems Protection Board. It also hears appeals from certain decisions of the secretaries of the Department of Agriculture and the Department of Commerce, and cases from district courts involving patents and minor claims against the federal government. Located in Washington, D.C., the court has 12 judges and, as with the other federal appellate courts, they are appointed for life by the President with the advice and consent of the U.S. Senate.

The Court of Appeals for the Federal Circuit causes some confusion even among career services professionals who have called me to ask what exactly it is and where it fits in. It is at the federal court of appeals level and so all of the description of the appellate clerkship experience, above, is equally pertinent to this court. In addition, due to the specialized nature of its cases—particularly patent and intellectual property kind of subject matter—it can be an excellent option especially for students with a technical background or interest in a future practice in that field. The judges there love to hire law students or practitioners with backgrounds in engineering, science (*e.g.*, chemistry, biochemistry), mathematics, or previous professional work experience in industry, the military, patent law or academics.[3] Several collegial judges from the Federal Circuit have reached out to me over the years, encouraging an awareness of and applications to their court, and I have sent many students there to such positive experiences that I have become a big fan of that court!

- ## U.S. Court of Appeals for the Armed Forces

The U.S. Court of Appeals for the Armed Forces, formerly known as the Court of Military Appeals, exercises appellate review of court-martial convictions. Located in Washington, D.C., its jurisdiction is worldwide but encompasses only questions of law arising from trials by court martial in the United States Army, Navy, Air Force, Marine Corps, and Coast Guard in certain specified instances. Its decisions prior to 1984 were final, but now are subject to review by the Supreme Court. The five judges of the U.S. Court of Appeals for the Armed Forces are civilians appointed for 15-year terms by the President, with the advice and consent of the U.S. Senate. While this is certainly a particularized subject matter, if your background or future practice rests in the military, these interesting cases may appeal to you as your clerkship of choice.

· *U.S. District Court*

The United States District Courts are the trial courts of the federal court system. Within limits set by Congress and the Constitution, the district courts have jurisdiction to hear nearly all categories of federal cases, including both civil and criminal matters. There are 94 federal judicial districts, including at least one district in each state, the District of Columbia, and Puerto Rico. Each district includes a United States bankruptcy court as a unit of the district court (discussed below). Three territories of the United States—the Virgin Islands, Guam, and the Northern Mariana Islands—have district courts that hear federal cases, including bankruptcy cases. (So, you can be a law clerk there *and* enjoy a tropical paradise!) Several districts are divided into divisions and may have several places where the court hears cases. For example, New York and California are composed of multiple judicial districts, whereas Alaska is comprised of a single judicial district. The district courts are listed with their divisions in Title 28 of the U.S. Code, Sections 81 through 144, and the number of judgeships allotted to each district is set forth in Title 28 of the U.S. Code, Section 133. For your handy reference, I have included in the Appendix a summary listing of these courts with subdivisions, locations, and the number of authorized judgeships for each. With the exception of the three territorial courts, all district court judges are appointed for life by the President, with the advice and consent of the U.S. Senate.

As depicted above, these federal trial court clerkships offer a rich and varied experience. They are the heart of the federal system in terms of daily decision-making, disposition of cases and, in the process, the development of the law. By sheer number of district court judges (more than 600) with roughly two clerks each, these clerkships are also the most numerous in the federal courts—but still highly competitive and much sought-after. Note that a growing number of these clerkships now last for two years, instead of the traditional one-year term, so the openings for a given year may be fewer.

Occasionally district judges may function as appellate judges, as when they "sit by designation" on a panel of appellate judges for the Court of Appeals. In addition to the general trial court tasks, a law clerk for the U.S. District Court may also assist the judge in exercising an interesting kind of appellate review of decisions of the magistrate judge and the bankruptcy judge. As discussed below, these secondary courts are, to differing extents, arms of the federal trial court; and these judges serve an important role in the work of the district judge and clerk as well.

· *U.S. Magistrates*

Clerking for a magistrate judge is an option that is not as widely known and may be somewhat less prestigious (if that is important to you), but is also less competitive a clerkship to obtain and can essentially be a comparable experience to clerking for a district judge. As the role of the magistrate judges has enlarged in recent years, so too has the desirability of a clerkship with this jurist to gain valuable exposure to pretrial procedures and even trial practice.

Magistrate judges are judicial officers of the district court and are appointed by a majority of the judges on the district court for a term of eight years, with no involvement of the President and the Senate. The number of magistrate judge positions is determined by the Judicial Conference of the United States, based on recommendations of the respective district courts, the judicial councils of the circuits, and the Director of the Administrative Office of the U.S. Courts. The judges of each district appoint one or more magistrate judges, who discharge many of the ancillary duties of district judges. There are both full-time and part-time magistrate judge positions. Many magistrate judges are subsequently appointed to U.S. District Court judgeships.

The role of the magistrate judge has been expanding over the years to assume a significant portion of the federal litigation process. Each district court through its own rules assigns cases and utilizes the services of the magistrate judges somewhat differently. In some courts, magistrate judges conduct almost all pretrial and discovery proceedings in civil cases, preparing the case for trial before the designated district judge. Magistrate judges may serve as special masters in civil actions and proceedings. In addition, recently there has been an increase in the number of cases tried or settled by magistrate judges with the consent of the parties under 28 U.S.C. § 636(c). The magistrate judge can also decide dispositive motions and issue a written ruling called a "report and recommendation" for the district judge to adopt and approve. In criminal cases, magistrate judges conduct preliminary proceedings in felony cases (including issuing search and arrest warrants, bail hearings and arraignments), trials in misdemeanor and petty offense cases, and preliminary review of applications for post-conviction relief. Since they do not conduct trials in felony criminal cases and thus are not subject to the Speedy Trial Act (which gives priority to criminal trials and precludes district judges from giving the parties assurances of a particular trial date), magistrate judges can offer the parties an exact date for trial; this advantage often leads the attorneys to chose a trial of their case with the magistrate judge over an uncertain future timeframe with the district judge.

Thus, although they technically report to the district court, the magistrate judge and law clerk really have a full range of daily tasks and responsibilities more akin to a district court judge and clerk. Since the cases are primarily civil in nature, this feature of the clerkship may appeal to you as well. Of course, this type of clerkship is, like a district court clerkship, an excellent training ground for future litigators. A particularly fine Magistrate Judge, the Honorable Mark D. Fox, U.S. District Court for the Southern District of New York (who I had the great pleasure of seeing in action on several occasions), offers some words of wisdom about clerking for his court:

> I look for law clerks who are interested in pursuing a
> career in litigation because I want my law clerks to have a

meaningful experience. For that reason, I encourage them to sit in when anything is going on in the courtroom, including trials. The only way you can really learn litigation—you can't learn it out of books, you can't learn it by watching videotapes—the only way you can learn it is either by doing it or by watching other people do it. I think that through the law clerk experience, particularly in the trial court if litigation is your career goal, you can gain experience that is wonderful and there really is no substitute for it. From our point of view, we benefit greatly from having law clerks who come in with a fresh point of view and with good educational backgrounds, to help us do our work.

For a detailed description of the work of a magistrate judge and the role of her law clerk, see the essay of the Honorable Lisa Margaret Smith, U.S. Magistrate Judge, U.S. District Court for the Southern District of New York, in Chapter 12.

· *U.S. Bankruptcy Court*

A clerkship for a judge on the U.S. Bankruptcy Court is another interesting option, especially for those students who are interested in bankruptcy, tax, commercial or consumer law, or in pursuing this type of field in future practice. Each district court has a bankruptcy unit that hears and decides petitions of individuals and businesses seeking relief from bankruptcy. However, unlike the magistrate judge, a bankruptcy judge operates virtually independently from the district judge in the daily adjudication of his or her cases, which may go beyond matters of bankruptcy law to resolution of other broad and complex issues of law with a nexus to the case, or related to the claims against the debtor's estate (e.g., breach of contract, license, tax). On appeal, the determinations of the Bankruptcy Court go to the district judge for review. Bankruptcy judges are judicial officers of the district court and are appointed by the majority of judges on the court of appeals for a term of 14 years, with no involvement of the President and the Senate. The number of bankruptcy judges is determined by Congress, upon recommendations submitted by the Judicial Conference of the

United States from time to time regarding the number of bankruptcy judges needed.

Similar to a district court clerkship in function, the law clerk performs a wide range of tasks ranging from assisting in pre-trial conferences, hearings and trials, to drafting the judicial opinions and orders of the Bankruptcy Court. To determine if your interests fit closely with this type of clerkship, you should look through some of the cases published in the *West's Bankruptcy Reporter* to see the breadth of these legal issues. Moreover, it is most instructive to consult a bankruptcy judge directly. Here is what one such jurist, the Honorable Melanie L. Cyganowski, United States Bankruptcy Judge for the Eastern District of New York, had to say on this subject: "What do I look for when I review applications for a law clerk? For the Bankruptcy Court, I am interested in persons who have shown an interest in consumer law, commercial law or real estate law; tax law is something that gets a couple of extra bonus points in reviewing an application." This means that if you have an interest in one of these areas which has led you to the Bankruptcy Court, show it to the judge!

· *Specialty Courts*

The same thing is true for the specialty courts, which can be perfect for you if you are a student who is interested in tax law, the law of government contracts, or international trade. Looking further into these courts, less known to other students as more off the beaten path, might be just the thing for you. Judges really love it when they see somebody with that specialized type of background and expertise. This can be an appropriate fit both in terms of enjoying your clerkship year and also where you go in the future. Clerking for these courts sets you off well for that area of practice. For each of these specialty courts—U.S. Tax Court, U.S. Court of Federal Claims, U.S. Court of Veterans Appeals—we will briefly describe the types of cases and judges you can expect to discover. Notice that for each of these federal trial courts, appeals go to the Federal Circuit. So, if you are interested in these areas of law and an appellate clerkship, remember to check into that court as well!

· U.S. Tax Court

The Tax Court handles controversies involving deficiencies or over-payment of income, estate and gift taxes, and personal holding company surtaxes. Under the Pension Reform Act of 1974, the Tax Court has jurisdiction to issue declaratory judgments concerning the qualification of pension and profit sharing plans. When contesting a notice of deficiency in tax from the Internal Revenue Service, a taxpayer has the option to file suit for a refund in a U.S. District Court or the U.S. Claims Court after first paying the tax and filing a claim with the IRS for a refund, if the IRS then disallows the claim. If the taxpayer does not want to pay the tax in advance, he or she may litigate the matter in the Tax Court. Decisions of the Tax Court are generally subject to review by federal appellate courts. The Tax Court is based in Washington, D.C. The 19 tax court judges are appointed by the President for terms of 15 years.

As in the other federal trial courts, law clerks draft judicial opinions and participate in hearings and trials. A clerkship for the U.S. Tax Court is a valuable initiation if you are interested in pursuing a future practice in tax law.

· U.S. Court of Federal Claims

The United States Court of Federal Claims, formerly known as the U.S. Claims Court, is a special trial court with nationwide jurisdiction over most claims for money damages against the United States, disputes over federal contracts, unlawful taking of private property by the federal government for public use, and a variety of other claims against the United States usually filed by individuals and companies in those areas where there has been a Congressional waiver of sovereign immunity. These cases include tax refunds, patent or copyright violations by the United States government, claims of injury by childhood vaccines, constitutional and statutory rights of military personnel and their dependents, Japanese American internment victims from World War II, and back-pay demands from civil servants claiming unjust dismissal. The U.S. Court of Federal Claims also hears appeals of decisions of the Indian Claims Commission. Tort claims against the U.S. Government may not be filed in this court, but are heard exclusively in the U.S. District Courts, which also maintain concurrent jurisdiction over tax refund cases. The court's headquarters are located in Washington, D.C. Appeals from the Court of Federal Claims are to the U.S. Court of Appeals for the Federal Circuit. The 16 judges of the Court of Federal Claims are appointed for 15-year terms by the President, with the advice and consent of the Senate.

Law clerks for the U.S. Court of Federal Claims assist the judges at trial and draft opinions for publication in the *Federal Claims Reporter.* Many of the clerks accompany their judges on travel throughout the United States, since the court has jurisdiction over these civil claims against the government nationwide.

· U.S. Court of International Trade

The Court of International Trade sits in New York City and has exclusive national jurisdiction over any cases involving international trade and customs issues. Specifically, its cases concern the classification and valuation of imported merchandise, customs duties, and unfair import practices by trading partners. The court hears product classification and valuation determinations by the Customs Service plus appeals of unfair trade practice cases from the Department of Commerce and International Trade Commission. Appeals are to the U.S. Court of Appeals for the Federal Circuit. The nine judges are appointed for life by the President, with the advice and consent of the U.S. Senate.

· U.S. Court of Veterans Appeals

The U.S. Court of Veterans Appeals, based in Washington, D.C., was created by an act of Congress in 1988. The seven judges of the court are appointed by the President for 15-year terms, with the advice and consent of the U.S. Senate. The court exercises exclusive jurisdiction over appeals from the decisions of the Board of Veterans Appeals, whose decisions were final prior to the establishment of this court. Such cases include all types of veterans' and survivors' benefits, mainly disability benefits, and also loan eligibility and educational benefits. Appeals from this court are to the U.S. Court of Appeals for the Federal Circuit.

· **State Courts**

Judicial clerkships are available at all levels of the state and local courts. While the state courts system does vary greatly from state to state, some useful generalizations can be made about these courts. Every state has a top appellate court, and many have one or more intermediate appellate courts. Some states, like New York and California, have a highly developed system of intermediate appellate courts. As a cautionary note, the terminology may differ as well; the Supreme Court is usually the highest level of appellate court (and the jurists are called "Justices"), but not in New York, where it is the Court of Appeals (and they have "Judges"). Most state "supreme court" justices and many intermediate appellate court judges have one or more "elbow" law clerks. In addition or in the alternative, some intermediate appellate courts utilize a central clerkship staff that handles cases for the entire bench.

State systems have trial courts, sometimes called Superior Courts, which are general jurisdiction and hear cases from a full range of legal issues. Then there are state specialty courts or courts of limited jurisdiction, which include things like probate, criminal, municipal, housing and juvenile or family court—smaller issues that can be of interest to someone who is interested in these areas of practice. Many state trial courts have law clerks and staff attorney positions for these various types of general and specialized courts. In fact, on the state level, the majority of the clerkship opportunities are found at the trial level.

As a helpful guide, consult my chart on the general structure of the state courts, below; but remember to check with each individual state as to the names, levels and types of courts within that state. By the way, there is a handy set of detailed organizational charts by state in *Want's Federal-State Court Directory*, and you can also check the websites for each state's judicial branch, available through my links in www.judicialclerkships.com. See, for example, the official website of the Connecticut Judicial Branch—http://www.jud.state.ct.us/external/super/volunteer.htm—for description and application information regarding law clerk positions for the Connecticut Supreme Court, Appellate Court, and Superior Court. Contrast this with the official website of the New York courts system, which sets forth the clerkship opportunities, including "Central Staff clerks" and "Judges' clerks," at that state's highest court, the New York Court of Appeals—www.courts.state.ny.us/ctapps/clrkship.htm.

General State Court Structure

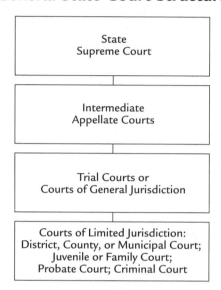

State court clerkships are generally less competitive than the federal courts, although some of the highest courts of the state are quite prestigious. In any event, these clerkships can be a valuable experience for local practice, and are well respected in the legal community for the "inside perspective" on the court system of that state. They provide an excellent opportunity for students to learn state law, observe local rules and procedures, and develop contacts with the local judges, attorneys, and court staff. Particularly if you have plans to settle in a particular geographic area, you should consider applying to state appellate and even trial courts.

The daily tasks of a law clerk vary somewhat, although the overall description for trial and appellate clerkship experiences does apply. Your clerkship experience depends on the court and judge. Many state trial judges hire clerks for one- or two- year terms, and rely upon their clerks to research legal issues (often on the spot during the course of trial), counsel the judge as to rulings, and participate in the trials. The highest state court levels would most resemble the tasks described above for an appellate court clerkship. In these state appellate courts, particularly the Supreme Court, there is a unique opportunity to shape the law of the state. Many states do not have a large body of state law, and often judges and their clerks are presented with matters of first impression. Moreover, unlike Federal Courts of Appeals, the decisions rendered by the top state court carry almost absolute finality, since review by the United States Supreme Court of state cases is exceedingly rare. There are other smaller variations from federal practice as well. For instance, jury voir dire in some state trial courts is conducted by the attorneys questioning the jury panel directly, rather than by the judge with the preparation of the law clerks. The level and amount of written decisions will also differ with the practice of the court and judge.

Just as the court structure varies by state, note that the application process differs from state to state as well, ranging from applying to a central location of the court for distribution of the applications to individual judges/justices, to panel interviews of judges, to submitting applications to individual judges for a selection process parallel to the federal system. In sum, this can certainly be a wonderful clerkship experience too, so be sure not to overlook the state courts!

· Administrative Agencies

There are clerkship positions available in other entities outside of the judicial branch. Certain categories of legal disputes may be resolved in special courts or entities that are part of the federal executive or legislative branches, and by federal and state administrative agencies. Another option to consider is working for an Administrative Law Judge for one of these entities.

Administrative Law Judges (ALJs), unlike federal judges who are appointed for life or specific terms, are employees of the United States Government—the executive departments and independent agencies. As independent, impartial triers of fact, they conduct formal administrative hearings and issue decisions based on trial-type proceedings. Typically, appeals from these decisions of the ALJs are to the Federal Courts of Appeals. Over 30 U.S. governmental departments and agencies utilize

ALJs, some of whom hire law clerks for either a term or an indefinite period of time. As an example, through the Department of Justice Attorney General's Honor Program, the Drug Enforcement Administration hires one law clerk to assist each ALJ for a one-year period. In the Environmental Protection Agency, terms last for a period of two years and each clerk serves two ALJs.

For helpful listings of the departments and agencies, along with their Chief Administrative Law Judges, see the most recent annual edition of *Want's Federal-State Court Directory*. Among the federal agencies listed with ALJs are the following: Food and Drug Administration, National Labor Relations Board, Federal Communications Commission, Federal Trade Commission, Federal Energy Regulatory Commission, Federal Maritime Commission, International Trade Commission, Securities and Exchange Commission, Commodity Futures Trading Commission, Small Business Administration, Department of Commerce, Department of Education, Department of Agriculture, Department of Justice/Office of Immigration Review, Department of Housing and Urban Development, and more.[4] (*See also* http://www.usdoj.gov/02organizations/02_6.html, providing links to websites of federal agencies.) In addition, a variety of state agencies handle similar functions, with internal review boards that make decisions interpreting the agency's regulations. (*See, e.g.,* http://www.piperinfo.com/state/index.cfm for list of state and government websites, as well as individual state home pages.)

Perhaps one of these subject areas is of particular interest to you or fits with your future career choice. Certainly, this would be a logical first step in a path through the ranks of that agency or governmental body, to a specialty law practice in the field that is regulated by that agency, or ultimately towards an Administrative Law Judge position years hence. If so, you might consider inquiring further with the agency into the available clerkship positions.

In addition to these clerkship positions, there are also parallel non-judicial positions. Commissioners of certain regulatory agencies hire administrative assistants or special assistants similar to law clerks. Likewise, high-level executives, such as cabinet members or general counsels of administrative agencies, may offer such positions. You can contact the agency or individual directly for information.

· **International Courts/Other**

Through the years, I have known several students who have gone to clerk for judges in foreign courts and enjoy the unique experiences and unusual perspective they provide. These courts generally offer no compensation, however, so you will need to look into alternate forms of funding.

For instance, I have sent students to the Court of Justice of the European Communities, which is a very prestigious international clerkship administered through the American Embassy in Luxembourg as the Dean Acheson Legal *Stage* Program. Clerkship-like positions as Dean Acheson *Stagiares* are offered to a limited number of top students from select U.S. law schools for minimum three-month periods during the spring and fall terms of the court. The purpose of this program is to foster better ties between the United States and the European Union legal communities and to increase the mutual understanding concerning their respective legal systems. Four categories of *stages* (internships) are available: with a Judge of the Court of Justice; with an Advocate-General of the Court of Justice; with a Judge of the Court of First Instance (the trial court); and with the Research and Documentation Division (on a research project under the supervision of a Judge or Advocate-General). Some knowledge of a European language, particularly French, is essential. No funds are available from either the U.S. Government or the European Court of Justice, and the participants must bear the costs of their transportation, room and board. The applications, due approximately six months before the *stage* period (but accepted up to one year in advance), are screened and submitted by an administrator in the participating law schools. If you are interested, you should check with your law school to see if this program is available. The direct contact information is as follows:

Monica A. Kwiecinski, U.S. Embassy Luxembourg program officer
U.S. Embassy Luxembourg
22, bd. Emmanuel Servais
L-2535 Luxembourg
tel: +352-46-01-23 ext. 235
email: KwiecinskiMA@state.gov

For a view from the inside, I tracked down one of my students who participated in this program, and is now a professor. Francesca Bignami[5] spoke very highly of her internship with an Advocate General of the Court of Justice, which is the *stage* most akin to a traditional U.S. judicial clerking experience. (The European Court of Justice is formed of judges and advocate generals; an advocate general is assigned to each case to advise the judges on how the case should be decided under the governing legal standards.) She commented that the *stage* was "an invaluable opportunity to learn about the judicial architecture of the European Community—the interaction among the Court of Justice, European institutions, and national courts and governments that produces the law." Since most of the members of the Advocate General's chambers were French judges on leave from permanent positions with the French judiciary, they brought a variety of perspectives to the Court. In addition, the *stagiares* (interns) were from all over Europe, each trained in his or her distinctive legal system with a unique conception of the law and the legal profession. For this reason, she would recommend this unique type of clerkship to "any American-trained lawyer interested in genuine, day-by-day, legal multi-culturalism, either as a valuable experience in its own right or in preparation for a successful international legal career."

Occasionally a student will arrange to clerk for the Supreme Court of Israel. I have known several who have pursued this alternate path, usually through their own contacts on that court. Another popular international clerkship is with a Justice on the South African Constitutional Court. Since these clerkships last for a year, funding may be an issue. Perhaps you can explore the possibilities with your law school or an employer for an alternate source or an advance or grant. Other examples of international courts I have heard of for law students include: the Supreme Court of Canada, the Federal Court of Australia, the Supreme Court of Italy, the International War Crimes Tribunal (Belgium), the European Court of Human Rights (France), the Iran Claims Tribunal in the Hague (Netherlands), the Criminal Court in the Hague, and the International Court of Justice in the Hague. (For the websites of a variety of international courts, *see* http://www.ncsconline.org/Information/info_court_web_sites.html#international.) Of course, these are illustrative as samples only; my point is simply that the possibilities are limitless, to follow your interests and forge your own paths into the wider world of clerkships!

I add to this "other" category the Tribal Court. Although it is not exactly international, this court does represent another world and culture. Many issues, such as some child welfare cases, cross the lines of state, tribal and federal laws, and regulations of the U.S. Bureau of Indian Affairs. The *Directory of Minority Judges* now includes the names of a few hundred tribal court judges (starting with its second edition in 1997). Some judges sit on several tribal courts, and in these cases all tribal courts are identified for each judge. Some tribal courts do hire law clerks, although funding for these positions is generally rather limited. Although these positions are difficult to find, you can look for postings in a newspaper called *Indian Country Today* (on-line at http://www.indiancountry.com/jobs), on the website of the National American Indian Court Judges Association at http://www.naicja.org, or by checking with individual tribal courts and judges.

Notes

1. These statistics appear on the official website of the U.S. Supreme Court under the heading "The Justices' Caseload." http://www.supremecourtus.gov/about/justice-caseload.pdf (5/26/01).
2. According to the Administrative Office of U.S. Courts, *Understanding the Federal Courts* (1999). *See* Appendix for chart of specific states and authorized judgeships.
3. *See, e.g.,* Ringel, Jonathan, "Federal Circuit's Scientific Method: Coveted Judicial Clerkships Draw Pool of Candidates With Technical Background to Match the Court's Docket," *Legal Times*, Nov. 6, 2000 (includes review of the backgrounds of 36 of the court's 39 clerks).
4. By the way, some of these agencies are also described further, including websites and contact information, in a handy chapter on "Great Government Jobs—Federal, State, and Local" in Kimm Walton's book, *America's Greatest Places to Work With a Law Degree* (Harcourt Brace, 1999), pp. 817-898.
5. Upon graduating from Yale Law School in 1996, Francesca Bignami clerked for the Honorable Stephen F. Williams, U.S. Court of Appeals for the D.C. Circuit, and then served as a *stagiare* for Advocate General Philippe Léger. After specializing in international trade at the law firm of Wilmer, Cutler & Pickering, she is now Assistant Professor at Duke University School of Law.

CHAPTER
five

Choosing a Court
That's Best for You

Well, now that you have had a broad overview of the courts and clerk-ship opportunities available, you may be wondering what to do next. Hopefully, you have had some instinctive reaction of interest—or dis-interest—to each court you have heard described here. As you are drawn more to one type than another, you have begun to take the first step in the selection of courts to which to apply!

With all the courts, judges and clerkships out there, where do you begin? What should you be looking for in your quest for the judicial clerkship that is perfect for you? There are a number of factors to con-sider. Together—in whatever combination or degree of emphasis you choose—these factors will comprise the filter through which you eval-uate the information gathered as part of your research project. (To help you in your research, I have gathered together the complete array of resources in Chapter 13, ranked and organized by function for your best and most efficient use. As we discuss the factors below, I will along the way mention the best ones for each purpose. Later on, you can go there to view the full enchilada in detail.) As always, remaining flexible in your evaluation of these factors will provide you with a strategic advantage; but remember the golden rule and never apply to a judge for whom you would not want to clerk.

To help us navigate the maze of courts and clerkship opportunities, we will catalog the most important factors in choosing a court, followed by the key factors in choosing a judge to whom to apply. Clerkships are available in many different courts. Generally the first thing to consider is the type of court or courts that most interest you in conjunction with your background and career goals. As outlined below, these considerations will include: federal versus state courts; appellate versus trial courts; geographical location; subject matter of cases; financial considerations; prestige/competitiveness elements, and future career plans.

· Type of Court—Federal versus State

A significant factor to consider is whether to apply to federal, state or local courts, or maybe some of each. With a bit of a prestige and competitive element, there is a general bias towards the federal courts, but clerking for a state court can be advantageous too. The state courts can offer a unique opportunity to shape the law of a state, often as a matter of first impression, and the highest level court of that state usually determines the issue with finality, since review by the U.S. Supreme Court is rare. If you know you want to practice law in that state, the familiarity you gain with the local laws and procedural rules—and the contacts you make with local attorneys as well as judges—cannot be surpassed. In addition, some state courts are known for their expertise in particular areas of the law. Be cautious, however, as every state has its own system that must be examined and assessed.

One state trial court clerk explained his choice of court in terms of his future career: "My goal was always to prosecute at the state level.

My clerkship gave me a solid background in terms of my knowledge of the day-to-day operations/procedures in the courtroom. It also provided me with insight into what judges are and aren't swayed by. Furthermore, it gave me a solid credential to get me a job prosecuting in the same area."

A former law clerk for a state appellate court described the benefits of her clerkship. Patricia DeJuneas, who clerked for the Connecticut Appellate Court, noted that, "While we were very busy and had lots of appeals, I had much more time to research, think about the issues and write the opinion. I feel that it was a perfect first job out of law school—I was able to concentrate on my research and writing skills while taking advantage of the close working relationship with a judge." She must have indeed enjoyed her state court clerkship tremendously, as she went on to pursue two additional clerkships![1]

Sometimes it is simply a matter of more awareness or information out there about federal or state courts, depending on the culture of your law school. Although they present two very different credentials and experiences, each is important to consider and evaluate for yourself.

• Level of Court—Appellate versus Trial Court

The level of court, appellate versus trial court, also involves some issues of prestige and competitiveness. Some view appellate courts as more prestigious than trial courts, but this can be a misconception and overgeneralization. For one thing, certain Federal District Courts are more competitive than certain U.S. Courts of Appeal. Similarly, some appellate courts are considered more prestigious than other appellate courts. When a student walks in and says to me, "I want to apply to the Ninth Circuit, D.C. Circuit, and Second Circuit," I ask, "Why?" If the reason is prestige, we try to broaden it and really get a little more open minded and flexible to look at what is really out there. There are so many fine judges that it would be foolish and shortsighted to apply based solely on that perception.

More significantly, these courts differ in terms of the types of experiences that fit best with your personality. For instance, the appellate court is more like an extension of the law school experience: researching, writing, and more academic, with an occasional oral appellate argument and the opportunity to observe decision-making in the dynamic of judicial panels. Trial courts tend to be involved more with the nitty gritty of daily trial practice, working with the evidence, the litigants, the jurors and the attorneys on a continual basis, in addition to drafting the opinions, advising the judge on the disposition of motions, and writing jury voir dire questions and jury instructions. The myriad of tasks of the trial court clerk will either appeal to you or overwhelm you, depending on your nature and temperament.

Your career goals may also be a relevant factor here. Some say the trial court is better for one who seeks to be a litigator, whereas an appellate clerkship is more appropriate for future appellate practice or academia. However, if you look more closely at the backgrounds of law school professors, you will find that while virtually all of them have the credential of a judicial clerkship, the type of court does vary; many clinical professors pursued trial court clerkships, while often (but not always) the more academic law professors held appellate clerkships. In fact, some law clerks may choose a future practice in corporate law from either route, or another area or career path entirely. I believe that either experience is a benefit and you should choose whichever sounds more interesting and exciting to you (or apply to both if you are unsure). Do you like to work with the people and the facts, or do you like to do intensive research and writing? Both types of clerkships will involve some elements of each, but the overall portrait differs significantly in magnitude. Those who are attracted to one or the other usually also follow a career path naturally appropriate for that clerkship.

A former law clerk for the U.S. Supreme Court, as well as the U.S. Court of Appeals, explained some of these differences: "Appellate clerkships have the virtue of allowing you to see more different areas of the law because you deal with each case for a relatively short period of time." On the other hand, trial court clerkships "give you much better insight into the nuts and bolts of litigation, which is very valuable, especially for people who expect to be litigators." Another clerk favorably compared her district court experience to an appellate clerkship: "I loved being at the district court because, while I obtained the same basic research and writing skills obtained by the Circuit Court clerks, I additionally obtained skills directly related to the nuts and bolts of litigation—skills regarding privilege issues, document production, motion practice, depositions, remand and removal, arbitration, hearings, trials and settlement."

One who clerked in both a U.S. District Court and a U.S. Court of Appeals expressed his personal preference:

> In many respects, they were very different—but both were enormously rewarding. Having had both experiences, I can say with certainty that a district court clerkship is both more fun and more valuable (at least for a would-be litigator) than a court of appeals clerkship. The learning curve on the district court is much steeper. Trial court litigation takes so many more twists and turns than appellate litigation. There is much more variety and much more chaos. You get to see evidentiary rules put in practice and to watch individuals be sentenced to prison. You become aware of the enormous power of a single judge with a fair amount of discretion. It is cliche, but true, that a court of appeals clerkship is much more like one's experience in law school—a lot of reading, a lot of issue-spotting.

A federal appellate clerk summarized her "extremely rewarding" clerkship experience many years later, and the impact it had on her future career path: "Minute per minute it provided the most intellectually stimulating work of my career." She credits her clerkship with leading to her solo practice concentrating in appellate law. "Absent my clerkship, I would most likely continue to be a civil litigator, as I had been prior to my clerkship, which practice, as we know, consists of cases 90% of which settle before trial . . . It is difficult to tell a student what level and type of court to pursue . . . As a litigator, I honestly was considering looking for a federal district court clerkship before this opportunity presented itself."

· Geographical Location

Geographic considerations are a significant factor for most students. You may have personal preferences or obligations which limit you based largely on this factor. If so, you may use this factor predominantly to shape your application strategy, applying to both the appellate and trial courts of that geographic area. Expanding your search to the state courts as well as the federal courts will increase your flexibility. Moreover, if you know this is the location of your future practice, you will be well served in the higher courts of that state, as well as the federal courts, to gain familiarity with state law, local rules, and individual attorneys.

Take into account, however, that the clerkship term is a limited one. Perhaps this is the time in your life to explore another area of the country for a year or two, if you do have the flexibility. In fact, some students seek an exotic locale, such as a federal clerkship in the U.S. Virgin Islands, which in addition to having a wonderful beach has a vibrant corporate practice. In addition, I know many students who enjoyed clerkships with the Supreme Court of Alaska, both for the adventure and for the opportunity to shape the law of a state in some areas of first impression in the absence of much binding law. (By the way, there is an added benefit in terms of timing; the Alaska Supreme Court typically interviews student applicants in the fall of their third year for a one-year clerkship commencing in the fall after graduation.)

Particularly if you would like to consider practicing there in the future, a clerkship offers an opportunity to investigate the legal community of that geographic area, without committing yourself to a firm or other employer for the longer term. In addition, the more remote the area you choose (*e.g.*, avoiding the major East Coast and California cities), generally the less competitive the application process will be for that clerkship. For the most part, a federal clerkship is a federal clerkship, regardless of whether it is in Akron, Ohio or New York City—and the former (Sixth Circuit) is far less competitive than the latter (Second Circuit). So if you can, try to stay off the beaten path and use your geographic flexibility if you have are fortunate enough to have it!

• **Specialized Subject Matter—Types of Cases**

As discussed previously, the specialty courts—courts of limited jurisdiction such as tax, international trade, bankruptcy, military and patent law/intellectual property—may be the types of courts for you to consider as a focus for your clerkship applications. Ultimately, the degree of importance of this factor comes from the personal background and special interests of the individual student. A few years ago when I was Director of Judicial Clerkships at Yale Law School, I had a student who came in the middle of February saying first of all that it was too late, to which I said it was not necessarily so for all courts and judges (February 1st was widely the beginning application date at that time). He raised as his second issue that he really had not previously considered a clerkship, but he had heard about the U.S. Court of Appeals for the Federal Circuit from his brother in an intellectual property practice in D.C. and was vaguely thinking about it. This student had such a great background of technical expertise, having been a naval officer with all types of technical experience, a summer in a patent law practice, and a future career goal of patent law. His resume and background were clearly flashing, "Federal Circuit"! Well, by the time this student left my office, he had everything all in order and he ended up with an excellent clerkship in the Federal Circuit. I later spoke with the judge who was equally thrilled to have someone with such a well-suited technical background coming to his chambers. Such alternate paths are good to remember in assessing your own background and interests.

Even in courts of general jurisdiction, the subject matter may vary by court due to the most frequent types of cases or litigants in that area. For example, the courts in Delaware have a heavy corporate bent and judges with a high level of expertise and experience in this area. In New York, one can experience a wide variety, including criminal cases and commercial litigation. In the District of Columbia Circuit, administrative law receives the most prominence, whereas the Ninth Circuit has a tendency towards liberal social issues. Some of these areas of emphasis may appeal to your interests and future career goals.

· Financial Considerations

Depending on your own individual circumstances, the financial factor may be relevant to you in your selection of courts and judges to whom to apply. If so, thinking ahead to the interview phase, you may avoid applying to the more remote areas since you will ultimately have to pay your own travel expenses; you may choose to apply instead to only local judges. Perhaps you should consider applying to a group of judges in particular geographical areas so that you can try to interview with them in one trip, rather than scattering your applications to isolated judges across the country. In addition, there may be differences in the clerkship salary to consider (federal versus state or local), along with the cost of living in the city of the clerkship. Sometimes different types of clerkships will also prompt differences in the clerkship bonus that may be offered by a future employer. (For further suggestions on how to afford these expenses and a detailed discussion of the financial aspects, *see* Chapter 9.)

· Prestige of Court / Competitiveness

Since it is implicit throughout our discussion of these factors, we might as well acknowledge the importance in this process placed on the reputation for prestige of the court, and the resulting competitiveness for that court which is always the flip side of prestige. As one former law clerk for two highly prestigious courts (including the U.S. Supreme Court) reluctantly acknowledged: "Because appellate clerkships tend to be harder to get, they tend to be more prestigious and any employment effect (which, as I say, I tend to discount) will be more pronounced." As he observed further, a clerkship for a District Court judge or Court of Appeals judge (life tenure or "Article III judge") is generally more prestigious than a clerkship for a Bankruptcy Court, Magistrate or Administrative judge (term appointment or "Article I judge"). "Thus, a federal trial court clerkship *usually* carries more prestige than clerking for a state supreme court justice. (There are exceptions if you plan to work in the state where you clerk or plan to do work in the state court system.) This may be crazy, but with a few exceptions, that is the way it is."

However, be careful to scrutinize the source of your information on this element, as often the rumor mill grinds with baseless overgeneralization and false perceptions. As noted above, you should try to look beyond this factor to the actual duties of the law clerk which encompass the clerkship experience, and ascertain for yourself how clerking for this court will mesh with your future career plans. As an added benefit, you may discover that staying clear of these stereotypes will place you in a better strategic position.

Some Interesting Statistics from Your Peers

In this choice of courts, if you are wondering which factors are most important to your peers (as most students are), you may be interested in the findings of the National Judicial Clerkship Study in this regard.[2] Asked to identify the factors that influenced their decision to apply to particular courts, the students and law clerks in the study named geographical considerations as the most significant, desiring to clerk in the locale or court of their future practice. More than one-half looked to the level of the court (trial/appellate), while almost as many focused on the type of court (federal/state/local). Many linked their decision to their interests and future career plans (*e.g.*, a particular area of the law, academia, appellate or trial work). Very few registered concerns about financial considerations in their selection of courts.

A Personal Note

This is, after all, a personal process. Take a moment of self-reflection, and think about why you are applying for a clerkship. Consider your interests and your longer-term goals, along with a dash of self-assessment of your level of competitiveness. If you think that you wish to pursue a career in litigation, particularly in trial advocacy, you should consider a district court clerkship. Particularly if you are concerned about competitiveness (*e.g.*, your academic record or the reputation of your law school), you might downplay this to the closely similar experience of a clerkship for a Magistrate Judge, or even a state trial court clerkship. On the other hand, if you are more attracted to purely research and writing, maybe even aspiring to teach law school someday, perhaps a federal appellate clerkship is for you. If you know where you plan to practice in the future, have strong ties to one geographic area, or are interested in relocating to a particular state, perhaps you should choose a clerkship in a state court to become familiar with the procedures, judiciary and local bar of that state. Does one (or more) substantive area of the law fit best with your background or career goals? If so, you might also consider clerking for specialized courts (*e.g.*, bankruptcy, tax, international trade, federal circuit) or administrative law judges involving that subject matter.

Before you put too much pressure on yourself to know your goals at this early stage of your legal career, keep in mind that you really cannot go too wrong with any of these options. The prevailing wisdom should reassure you that the clerkship experience in and of itself is extraordinarily valuable to your life! More than one type of court or clerkship may suit you well, just as there are so many judges out there who would be wonderful for you as your entrée into your professional world. Hopefully, with this knowledge and some gentle guidance, you are now ready to look more closely into the next aspect of this process . . .

Notes

1. After her clerkship with the Honorable E. Eugene Spear, Patricia DeJuneas went on to clerk for the Honorable Donna F. Martinez, United States Magistrate Judge, U.S. District Court for the District of Connecticut, and then the Honorable Owen Panner, U.S. District Court for the District of Portland.
2. *See* Tables 35 and 55 of the NALP Report at 52 and 70.

Choosing a Judge Who's Best for You

Now that you have at least somewhat narrowed down your courts to scope, there are many different things to consider in choosing the individual judges to whom to apply—the judge as a person, a mentor, a jurist, a teacher, and a scholar; the relationship between the judge and his law clerks; the judge's approach to cases, whether practical or theoretical, liberal versus conservative—any and all of these criteria may be important to you. In examining the background of each judge, it is often helpful to keep the following broad factors in mind: judicial ideology and background; personality and atmosphere in chambers; types of cases, tasks and amount of work; reputation of the judge; mentor relationship; demographic characteristics of the judge; length of clerkship term; special status of the judge; and connections to the judge. Note that some of these factors may also prompt you to add individual judges to your list regardless of their court. We will discuss the major ones in greater detail below.

For this purpose, there are many good sources of background information on the judges to follow later in the resources chapter, ranging from contact directories with biographical profiles (*e.g., Judicial Staff Directory, Judicial Yellow Book, The American Bench*, on-line sources, WESTLAW® and LEXIS®) to commentaries on judicial style and reputation (*e.g., Almanac of the Judiciary*, feedback from former law clerks, other people sources). But first let's discuss the factors you will need to think about in order to process this information.

· Ideology and Background

For a substantial number of students, the litmus test as to the desirability of a judge is simply the political affiliation of that judge, based largely upon the affiliation of the President who appointed that judge. Depending on the particular judge, this approach can be unduly narrow and unjustifiably restrictive. First, the political affiliation by President may not reflect the true nature of the political beliefs of the judge. Many Presidents have been surprised by the ideological convictions of the judges whom they have nominated, which often vary by issue and by case and cannot be predicted as simply as the litmus test would imply. Second, even if the judge does follow a certain partisan persuasion (as indicated more accurately from his or her past cases, organizational affiliations and professional activities), you might want to examine first the strength and relevancy of your own convictions. Perhaps you really are someone who holds strong political ideas and could not possibly work for a judge with whom you have a fundamental disagreement. If so, you are better off knowing this now, avoiding the conflict entirely, and shaping your list of acceptable judges accordingly. On the other hand, you may be adaptable and flexible despite your noble ideals; you might even benefit from being occasionally confronted with the opposing viewpoint—as might the judge. More likely than not, you will rarely if ever encounter this conflict with the judge, as most cases involve legal issues relatively devoid of the glamour and influence of politics. In the daily work in chambers, your opposing points of view may never surface.

A personal anecdote may be illustrative here. When students come to me with the idea that they could never clerk for a judge appointed by President X, I often tell them the story about my judge, who was appointed by a President who was not only from a different political party but was also a President not held in high regard in my family. Unlike most grandmothers who would say, "Oh, you're clerking for a judge, isn't that wonderful" (or maybe "What is that?"), my grandmother's first question to me was, "So, you're clerking for a judge—who appointed him?" When I told her, she was very, very concerned. Now I had a wonderful clerkship with this judge and our political affiliations were so completely irrelevant, that many years later I was telling him the story with amusement. We were talking about his mother and my grandmother as examples of politically savvy, strong-willed matriarchs, and I remarked, ". . . Then she asked what President appointed him and I told her." The judge smiled and asked, "Oh, and was she happy with your response?" and I said, "No, Judge, she wasn't!" Here he had absolutely no idea—that demonstrates how inconsequential it was to our relationship in chambers and since then. By the way, on the rare occasions that as an enthusiastic law clerk I did challenge him with the opposite views, we both greatly benefited as a result.

One very prominent judge who is one of my lifelong mentors, the Honorable Ralph K. Winter, Senior Judge (formerly Chief Judge) of the U.S. Court of Appeals for the Second Circuit, likewise advises students that, "Political differences, political attitudes are something that are vastly exaggerated in law school and should be less of a concern for you when you are out looking for a clerkship—a fairly minor concern. It is really less important than you think." He does qualify that somewhat, "If *you're* an ideological warrior, then you've got to worry about who you're going to work for. You may want to work for an ideological warrior. If the judge is an ideological warrior, and you want to learn something other than how right you are, assuming that you wind up well-matched, then you're probably not going to want to work for that judge either. It really depends on what you're looking for."

• Judicial Style / Personality / Atmosphere in Chambers

Judges are people too. As such, they will differ greatly in their style and personality. These differences are heightened in the closely personal, intensive relationships in chambers and thus may largely shape the success or failure of your clerkship experience with that judge. Examples of these variants in judicial style include a judge who is combative versus relaxed, more formal versus informal, more humorous and joking versus stern and somber. Is the judge one who spends a great deal of time with his clerks and staff on a daily basis, frequently eating lunch with them, exchanging ideas, sharing thoughts on a conversational level and taking a personal interest in their overall well-being? Or is the judge more impersonal and removed, less accessible and less amenable to ongoing personal contact, perhaps even arrogant? In addition, the judge's approach to cases may vary, in a range from the more practical to the more theoretical and scholarly. The personality, particular interests or even idiosyncrasies of the judge will set the tone and atmosphere in chambers. Depending on your own personality as well, you may have a strong preference for or, conversely, an aversion to one of these judicial styles.

Some of these personality traits will be ascertainable from collections of feedback from law clerk alumni (if your school maintains such a collection), and conversations with former law clerks and others who may have come into contact with the judge. In any event, these are certainly aspects to look for in the course of an interview.

• Types of Cases and Amount of Work / Tasks of the Law Clerk

Along with a difference in work style of the judge comes the difference in the amount of work for his or her law clerks. The variation in workload may be a function of the court as well, due in part to the number of judicial vacancies on that court. You can often get a sense of the general work level by checking the case statistics with the Clerk's Office or Office of the District or Circuit Executive (or published sources such as the *Third Branch*, which is also available on-line through the Administrative Office of U.S. Courts at www.uscourts.gov). However, more relevant than the actual number of cases will be how the judge chooses to handle those cases. Is this a judge with a huge backlog of undecided cases or one who manages to resolve a large caseload expeditiously and efficiently? The number of hours worked in chambers may not be correlated with this result.

For instance, my judge believes strongly in hard work and efficiency during the normal hours of the business day, and ushers his clerks out the door at a reasonable hour. He strongly discourages his clerks from bringing extra work home with them, urging them to maintain an outside personal life and to build an active professional life by attending civic and bar association functions. Yet he has proudly carried a large caseload for 30 years on the bench, without stagnant or long-pending cases. In the words of the master (the Honorable Charles L. Brieant, of course):

> Every lawyer owes it to himself or herself and the profession not to be so swept up with this work so that you lose the rest of your life. You ought to divide your days and you should be able to support yourself and do your work within eight or nine hours of the day and have the rest of the time to maintain your health, your family interests, your community obligations and the other things that are part of life. We seem to have rewarded slowness and incompetence by the practice of hourly billing and by contests in major law firms as to who can book the most hours. Those hours I think are often non-productive. Anyone can do the work. Very few people can do the work efficiently and promptly. I have often been known to tell the clerks on my way out the door, "We've made enough mistakes for the day. Go on home and we'll try again tomorrow!" You ought to try to moderate your work so that you can get it done in the time allotted and don't waste your whole life working.

Another former clerk of my judge, the Honorable Melanie Cyganowski, agrees with his judicial working style, which she indeed now follows as a judge on the U.S. Bankruptcy Court (Eastern District of New York). She contrasts her approach of hard work during the business day with that of a colleague on the bench who uses "every available hour" and is regularly in chambers until late at night. "The way that we now run our own court was modeled after our own clerkship experiences . . . So far both of our judicial loads are being managed and indeed it is all a question of style."

Many judges do burn the midnight oil and work around the clock—with their law clerks by their side—to achieve this end. Perhaps they follow the philosophy of Winston Churchill, who said, "Working hours are never long enough. Each day is a holiday, and ordinary holidays . . . are grudged as enforced interruptions in an absorbing vocation."[1]

You might not mind working long hours with your judge for the limited time period of a year or two (indeed, you may be expecting this at your next employer, particularly if it is a large law firm). The level and quality of work is certainly rewarding and worthwhile (and with a greater impact than you can expect in that next position). Still, if this consideration is relevant for you, it would be wise to investigate further.

The type of tasks will also vary with the judge, as a reflection of the structure of chambers, including the division of labor between law clerks, and/or with the judge, secretary, and deputy clerk. In some chambers, the law clerks divide the cases by type of cases (*e.g.*, criminal/ civil, pro se, particular subject matter) or randomly (*e.g.*, by odd and even case numbers). Depending on the judge, the tasks of a law clerk may include the answering of phones, the ongoing dealing with litigants, the authority to schedule conferences or grant extensions for motions, and even the conduct of phone conferences with attorneys. In addition to the division of work on cases in chambers, some judges will include among the duties of a law clerk maintaining the library in chambers, drafting speeches and lectures for conferences, continuing legal education and so forth. Some judges give clerks more administrative tasks, or have opted for another clerk in the place of a secretary, so there may be a different work mix for them. Certain judges even require their law clerks to do personal errands, such as picking up their dry cleaning! If you would find this offensive or beneath you, explore this factor at the outset. On the other hand, if you would clerk for this remarkable judge under any conditions, perhaps you will still prefer to have an awareness of exactly what those conditions might be.

· Reputation of the Judge / Prestige

The reputation of the judge will encompass several dimensions, including his or her status as a person, mentor, judge, teacher, scholar, and employer. Essentially these can be distilled into two main and potentially divergent aspects: quality as a judge, and character as a boss. Some prominent judges treat their law clerks poorly, while some less renowned judges are exceptional jurists who treat their clerks with deference and respect. Thus, you may not necessarily want to clerk for the judge who is the most famous and/or known for the greatest intellect. If at all possible, you will have to look beyond the robe.

In assessing this factor, you will be gathering information from other students, professors, attorneys in practice, and law clerks. However, in your zeal for the grapevine, be careful not to get caught up in rumors or unduly swayed by other students' perceptions of prestige. Always evaluate the nature of the information in conjunction with the credibility of your source. The *Almanac of the Judiciary* can provide a lawyer's perspective on most federal judges (although there is often very little information on the newer judges). The best source on this will be former law clerks, especially those who have clerked directly for this judge, as they will know what this judge is truly like to clerk for—a judge with a reputation among attorneys as a ferocious bear may be a teddy bear behind the closed doors of chambers in his dealings with his law clerks.

While reputation and prestige may be relevant criteria for you, do not let this eclipse the importance of the clerkship experience. As one law clerk advises: "Every law student should find a judge to clerk for regardless of what type of judge it is. It is essential to learn how lawyers are expected to behave and as a clerk there is no better way."

• **Mentor Relationship**

Judges vary as well in their attitude towards the role of judge and law clerk. The best clerkship experiences are the ones that are the most long lasting, with the judge as your lifelong mentor. Hopefully your judge will be someone who takes an interest in your career, advises you and follows your career and life in the future. You can ascertain this essential factor by subtly probing the relationship between the judge and his clerks and former clerks. Is there evidence that this judge maintains an extended family of past, present, and future law clerks, who share a common bond with periodic contact (*e.g.*, annual gathering, outing with families)? The additional benefits of this network continue long term far beyond your original clerkship year or years. I can attest to this fact from my own personal experience, as I have been extremely fortunate to have as a lifelong mentor my judge, along with our "extended family" of past, present, and future law clerks as well as court and chambers staff. Judge Brieant describes his ongoing relationship with his law clerks as follows: "I am very proud of my law clerks . . . I have more than 50 of them there. They've all been successful. We've stayed on friendly relations. We see each other occasionally, and I watch after their career progress. Occasionally they ask me for advice. I always give it. They never take it and then they come back and tell me how happy they are in their new job!"

An indicator is whether the judge maintains these relationships on a regular basis, such as through annual dinners or outings with his or her past and present law clerks. As a result, one clerk describes the significant benefits, "I have also stayed in contact with all of the judge's former clerks, including my two co-clerks (my senior clerk in my first year and my junior clerk in my second year), through our annual judicial clerkship dinners. Many of these talented former clerks have also served as my mentors during my career."

In addition, here is further corroboration from a former career clerk for the U.S. Court of Appeals on the importance of this factor: "I have tremendous respect for my judge. I will always view him as a mentor. I do know that in the past he had even become a father figure with some of his clerks, but that would not characterize my relationship.

He was also tremendously personable and a pleasure to spend time with in chambers or on our travels. He was thoughtful to include me in socializing while at sittings." Another former clerk for a Magistrate Judge explains, "You just become extended family. With my judge, I have gained a mentor for life who I frequently still converse with, and will always have a special relationship with. Also, I have gained new professional relationships with the lawyers that have clerked since I have left."

· **Demographic Characteristics of the Judge**

In your quest for the perfect clerkship, certain demographic character-istics may hold relevance for you, such as: race/ethnicity, gender, sex-ual orientation, or disability status of the judge. These personal characteristics of the judge may be important, particularly if you are looking for a mentor who reflects your own demographic background to add to your comfort level or bonding potential. If so, you can con-sult sources with biographical and background information on the judges, such as the *Judicial Yellow Book*, the Federal Judicial Center's biographical database (http://air.fjc.gov/history/judges_frm.html), and specialized resources such as the *Directory of Minority Judges* (for more places to find this type of information, look in Chapter 14 on Minorities, Women, and Clerkships, as well as in the resources chap-ter). Of course, only you know how relevant this factor will be for you, as it is a highly individualistic decision.

· **Clerkship Term—One year versus two years, one clerkship versus two successive clerkships**

Another criterion for many people is the length of the clerkship term, which is generally either one year or two years depending on the judge's preference. Only you can evaluate what is best for you in this regard, and whether financially or otherwise you are prepared to devote two years to a clerkship. Some students apply only for clerk-ships of a certain term, and for others the judge or clerkship experi-ence will be paramount in determining whether to apply for that clerkship. Generally flexibility as to the duration of the clerkship term increases the range of judges for whom to apply and, as a result, your ultimate chances of obtaining a clerkship.

When students ask what the ideal length of time for a clerkship is, I reply that it is a year and a half! There is an amazing learning curve of about two-thirds of the clerkship year before you can really start to look up, enjoy yourself and say, "I'm in a courtroom, oh, I'm not over-whelmed, look at this attorney's style" or that kind of thing; just as you start to appreciate the finer points of the clerkship experience, you find the year is over. So you leave a one-year clerkship feeling wist-fully that, "Oh, it was the best professional year of my life and it's gone." (The desire to recapture that unsurpassed experience is one rea-son I returned to my judge many years later as a Permanent Law Clerk, which is every former clerk's daydream but in actuality quite rare.) Typically in a two-year clerkship at about a year and a half, you may start to get a little fidgety at the perceived slowing of the learning curve and the anticipation of your post-clerkship employment; many law clerks at this point feel ready to wind down and move on.

Some students opt for two one-year successive clerkships, *e.g.*, for a District Court judge and a Court of Appeals judge. If a student can manage to obtain both (and I know many who have) the arrangement is ideal, because then he or she can really have the opportunity to learn more of a variety of information in an accelerated fashion with-out any kind of let-down of enjoyment. The clerkships can occur in either order, although more typically the first clerkship is for a Dis-trict Court judge, a clerkship that itself aided in the acquisition of the generally more competitive clerkship in the Court of Appeals. The added marketability of a second clerkship for a different court also exceeds the differential value to other employers of the second year of the same clerkship. (For instance, some law firms will only give a clerkship bonus or credit towards partnership for one year of a clerk-ship. *See* Chapter 9 on financial aspects.)

One clerk who pursued two successive clerkships in this manner explains his rationale. Christopher Sclafani Rhee clerked first for a judge on the District Court for the District of Columbia, and then for a second judge on the Court of Appeals for the same Circuit. "I chose to apply (very selectively) for a second clerkship for a few reasons. There is no denying that, as a general matter, appellate court clerkships are treated with a higher regard in the legal community. There are fewer judges, and the positions are more competitive. I was also very interested in pursuing a career in appellate litigation. A clerkship for an appellate judge provided a good vantage point and an excellent credential for that job." As an added bonus, he found clerking in the same circuit in successive years had its own rewards: "It was very interesting to track the progress of cases I had worked on. (Within my first month on the court of appeals, my judge was sitting on a panel reviewing the first opinion I had drafted in the district court. Fortunately, I passed.)" Yet he does recognize the drawbacks in clerking for two years: "Two years is a long time to serve as a clerk, even for two different people. Judges live an insular existence, largely because they are only at liberty to discuss their work with a small circle of people. For that reason, clerking is quite unlike any normal employment relationship. A clerk occupies an ambiguous role in the judge's life—you spend more time with them than anyone except their immediate family (in some cases more than their immediate family), but your job is to serve them. You are vulnerable to their mood swings and personality quirks. After a while, it is only natural that a clerk yearns for independence." However, if you are not in a rush to get to the "real world," this caveat probably does not apply to you.

Of course, if a judge who is ideal for you in all other respects only offers a two-year clerkship, take it! You may never again have such a valuable opportunity. Often the two years will vary somewhat as, depending on the structure in that judge's chambers, the second-year clerk may assume a different role and responsibilities as a "senior" clerk. One former District Court law clerk, Wendy Hufford, addressed these aspects of the two-year term positively: "Notwithstanding my initial reluctance to make a two-year commitment, a two-year clerkship was wonderful. First, I had a built-in mentor by having a senior clerk to work with in my first year. All of the stupid questions that occur in a new job were vetted through my senior clerk, who truly helped me learn my way around the courthouse. Second, I obtained mentoring and management experience myself by becoming senior clerk in my second year and teaching my junior clerk the ropes." She explains that the clerkship job at the District Court is sufficiently challenging that you only really master it by the end of your first year, and then use all of the good experience you have gained by serving a second year. Along the way, you further solidify your relationship with the judge. She adds that the most thrilling part of the second year of a trial level clerkship is seeing what happens on appeal to the cases you worked on during the first year!

Perhaps you are in no rush to the real world after all, and the second year gives you one more legitimate year to consider your options and plan your next career move. Then there are the growing group of "permanent" law clerks, who have discovered that there is nothing quite so wonderful as a judicial clerkship and choose, with their judge's permission of course, to remain there indefinitely!

· Special Status of Judge—Chief, Senior, New Appointee

There are a couple of things to note about the status of the judge, which may present nuances in the clerkship experience for that type of judge.

· Chief Judges

Each court has a Chief Judge (or Chief Justice), who is normally the judge who has served on the court the longest. In the federal system, for the District Court and Court of Appeals, the Chief Judge must be under age 65 at the time of receiving this designation, may serve a maximum of seven years, and may not serve in this capacity beyond the age of 70. In addition to their cases, Chief Judges have administrative responsibilities relating to the operation of the court, committees and so forth, which may or may not affect the job of the law clerk.

The first time I clerked for my judge he was the Chief Judge of the District Court for the Southern District of New York, which brought certain advantages in terms of additional opportunities to meet other judges, government officials, and court personnel at meetings as well as social functions. The extra prestige and added contacts had long-term benefits well beyond the clerkship year. At the same time, the types of tasks did not differ greatly from my second clerkship with him when he was no longer Chief Judge but an active District Judge with a full caseload. If anything, we had fewer cases to manage (a Chief Judge often carries less of a caseload), more pro se petitions to review (often one of the duties of a Chief Judge) and perhaps more speeches to help prepare. On a daily basis, the secretary handled most of the additional administrative tasks, but some Chief Judges may divide these responsibilities differently and delegate some of these functions to the law clerks as well. So it is something to consider if you are fortunate to clerk for a Chief Judge, but bear in mind that the distinction in the clerkship experience really does vary with the judge.

· *Senior Judges*

The judges on the U.S. District Court, Court of Appeals, and Court of International Trade have life tenure, and are eligible to retire if they are at least 65 years old and meet certain years of service requirements. However, despite the fact that they have the option to retire with a pension equivalent to their full salary, most of them continue to hear cases on a full or part-time basis as "Senior Judges." Thus, their love of the job must compel these judges effectively to work for free! In fact, Senior Judges typically handle about 15 to 20% of the appellate and district court caseloads.[2]

The clerkship implications of senior status vary tremendously with the judge. Some students are concerned that senior status means that judge is essentially retired and will not have enough work for them. However, typically judges on senior status hire only one law clerk, which may elevate that clerk's workload to the level of clerks for other judges. Before you exclude from your list Senior Judges, let me point out the possible benefits of this type of judge. Generally, fewer students apply to these judges and thus these clerkships are somewhat less difficult (relatively speaking, that is) to obtain. Yet the work level of a Senior Judge depends completely on that judge. Several of them have full caseloads and have accepted senior status mainly to open a vacancy on the court. It can range from that to a judge who wants to take a limited number of cases in his or her area of interest or perhaps avoid criminal cases entirely or decide to take only jury trials, which is a nice flexibility that only Senior Judges have. They have the option to decline the general random selection of cases and determine their own preferences. Their flexibility to work on law reform and special projects may add variety and unusual opportunities to the clerkship experience. They also have the chance to travel all over the country and go from courthouse to courthouse hearing cases by choice, if they arrange to do so. Depending on your own personal circumstances, this may be something that either appeals to you or would be unworkable for you. In any event, you need to try to ascertain this information before you apply for a clerkship with this judge.

Perhaps the principal benefit of a Senior Judge is the years of wisdom that judge likely carries and will share with you. If there is somewhat of a lower caseload, there may be more time to work with the judge on individual cases. On the other hand, the judge may work on a part-time schedule, with less daily contact with you. One federal appellate clerk described the benefits of clerking for a Senior Judge: "Because I was the judge's sole law clerk, the only other attorney with whom I had to consult was the judge. Needless to say, with his years of experience—as a former U.S. attorney, federal district judge, and his many years on the Sixth Circuit—he was a valuable sounding board."

Another former clerk told of his positive clerkship for a Senior Judge with over 20 years on the bench for the U.S. District Court: "He was less actively engaged in the minutiae of each case; but he had a breadth of experience and knowledge that allowed me to serve as an apprentice rather than strictly as an employee. On one occasion, I recall that my mind was completely made up about the law on a particular case, although I sympathized greatly with the plaintiffs. I set out to convince the judge that he would be harshly reversed if he ruled in the plaintiffs' favor. Much to my amazement, he devised a Solomonic outcome that gave the plaintiffs the relief they sought but also persuaded the defendants to settle rather than appeal."

As a Senior Judge, this member of the judiciary will be more of a known quantity with ample written information available as to his or her reputation, working style, and proclivities. Chances are, more of your people sources will have heard about this judge and be able to enlighten you as well. You should investigate further this particular judge beyond the status to see if his or her arrangement will work for you.

· *New Appointees*

Newly appointed judges are a key source of clerkships for students, particularly if you did not receive a clerkship in your previous application efforts. One disadvantage is the lack of information on this judge, beyond his or her previous work experiences (*e.g.*, government, private practice, or academia). However, even these prior work experiences may provide a meaningful clue as to his or her character and philosophies as a judge. Since there is less information out there as to ideology, or even treatment of law clerks, the risk is somewhat larger that you are entering uncharted territory with no way of knowing in advance how your clerkship experience for this judge will be.

Weighed against this risk are the infinite possibilities with this judge. Maybe this is somebody who has not been a judge before, but that presents a good opportunity to truly have an influence in setting up the chambers and the way the cases are handled. You can have a significant impact early on for this judge, and have a potentially longer lifetime of mentoring because there is more likely to be an extended time period for that person to be a judge. That can in itself be an enormous benefit that some people do not realize when they think of a new judge. There certainly will be even greater stature over the years and no relevancy that this judge was "new" during your clerkship. Another advantage might be the timing of the application for this clerkship, which is typically off-season as the confirmations occur. If you regularly gather up-to-date information as to confirmations (*see, e.g.*, special websites in the resources chapter), you may have the advantage of applying before other students are aware and thus benefit from a smaller applicant pool.

· *Supreme Court Feeders*

I have to say a word on Supreme Court feeders, somewhat reluctantly, as it can be a factor in choosing a judge. Some students are looking ahead to the next step and want to have a clerkship that they think can lead to a clerkship at the U.S. Supreme Court. As I discuss in the chapter on clerking for the Supreme Court (Chapter 11), it is really a second clerkship that almost always follows a federal appellate clerkship. In this "feeder" process, all judges and courts are not equal. It is a highly political process with certain judges who are known to be "feeders" with a history of supplying law clerks to the Supreme Court. (*See* Sample List of "Feeder" Judges in that chapter.) Be aware that the hiring decision is not necessarily based on the ability of the student as a law clerk because often this is a third year student applying before entering the first clerkship. This applicant may not even have begun the first clerkship, but the Supreme Court Justice has traditionally favored the law clerks from that judge, perhaps finding them to be trained to his or her liking by then. Clearly that student had top credentials to have been selected by the first judge. Keep in mind as well that the judges who are known to be "feeder" judges for the Supreme Court are also some of the most prestigious and competitive clerkships to obtain. If for no other reason, you should be aware of their status so as to not apply to them exclusively, if you want to maximize your chances of getting a clerkship at all.

The main thing I emphasize with students is that the first clerkship experience should be paramount. You may not be happy in a clerkship with one of these prominent judges, and there is no guarantee (indeed, the odds are still stacked against the possibility) that it would lead to a clerkship with the U.S. Supreme Court. So you should try to focus primarily on the clerkship year for which you are currently applying. Nevertheless, the information is valuable, and this consideration may be of fundamental importance to you.

· Connection to the Judge

For some students, one of the most significant factors in determining where to apply will be whether there is some sort of connection to the judge, either through their law school, their references, or their personal contacts. There is nothing wrong with this approach, since the goal is maximizing the chances for successfully obtaining a clerkship. If these avenues work for you, use them! Looking back years later, it will be unimportant how you initially came by your clerkship, so if one comes your way, grab it! However, be careful not to apply too narrowly to past pathways, as they provide no guarantees and may not be best for you—continue your self-assessment, do not be afraid to forge new roads and connections, and be open to where the wind may take you. Let's look more closely at this approach below.

· *Connections to Your Law School*

Perhaps the judge is a graduate of your school or the judge hired clerks from your school in the past. To discover this information, check the lists and resources at your school, including biographical sources on the judges and the law school backgrounds of the current clerks of the judge which may be of similar caliber to your school. (*See, e.g., Almanac of the Judiciary, the American Bench*, the *NALP Judicial Clerkship Directory*, WESTLAW® and LEXIS®, discussed further in Chapter 13.) You may then choose to seek out judges who have hired previously from your school or who are graduates of your school, among others. In your investigation, examine the background of the professors in your school to determine the judges for whom they clerked. In addition, you will benefit from talking to former law clerks who may be your friends and acquaintances, for general advice and possibly even an entrée to their judges. (Be careful not to attempt this with current law clerks with whom you have no prior relationship, as they represent an arm of the judge and as such will be interviewing you in all your dealings with them.) Depending on your school, this attention to connections may be the best approach for you in your quest.

One law clerk found this factor to be the most significant, and he advises: "Take the time to create an intelligently focused search. Personally, I did not even bother sending clerkship applications to judges who had no connection to [my law school]. It seemed like a waste of time. I mailed applications to judges who had either hired clerks from [my school] before and/or who had attended [my school] (including the judges' program) themselves. Then I narrowed it down to those whose judicial philosophies and geographical locations were compatible with my own (flexible) plans."

Note that, although you might have a better chance with them, you should not confine your applications only to these judges. In order to further maximize your odds, you should also forge new and different pathways from other students in your school who might be limiting themselves to these more "known" entities.

· *Connections to Your References*

Your references may have supplied law clerks to this judge in the past. As part of your ongoing dialogue with them, talk to your professors and employers who are serving as your references. Let them know that you are interested in this judge and/or that you seek a judicial clerkship in general and see which judges they recommend to you. Often this list will be the ones with whom they have had past connections. Depending on the professor, your reference may also take a more active role in contacting the judge on your behalf.

· *Personal Connection to the Judge*

Again, there is nothing wrong with this if you are lucky enough to be one of the few who actually has a personal connection with a judge, either through yourself, your family, or your friends. Now would be an appropriate time to contact that judge directly (asking the family member or friend first) for advice on applying for a clerkship in general, and in the process see whether that judge would be interested in hiring you. At the very least, you can express an interest and see what develops. Perhaps the judge will contact his or her colleagues on the bench for you. As long as you are polite, deferential, and not presumptuous or arrogant about the potential fruits of your relationship, this course of action would be appropriate.

By the way, this approach includes creating your own contacts by attending lectures or functions where judges will be in attendance, whether conducted by your law school, student groups, local bar association, or other organizations. Any opportunity you may have to mingle with, speak to, and even develop a relationship with a member of the judiciary will be a positive to your legal career as well as your application process.

From the judges' point of view, upon receiving hundreds of applications from faceless individuals who may be difficult to evaluate on paper, having actually met you and liked you in another context may be a welcome relief and help to them too. Often they do initiate this personal touch by contacting a reliable professor from your school or perhaps one of their former law clerks to see if they have any recommendations.

You may have a more remote connection to the judge of which you may not be aware. When you check the background of the judge, in particular look for areas you have in common (such as attending the same college or law school, affiliation with the same organization, or evidence of similar interests). You may then wish to highlight these areas subtly in your application materials or in the interview.

If you do not have personal connections to a judge, do not be discouraged from applying to that judge. Reflect upon the recent statistic from the National Judicial Clerkship Study that, despite student perceptions to the contrary, relatively few successful applicants actually had a personal connection to a judge. However, if you are fortunate enough to be one of the few who actually has or can build a connection with a judge, do not be afraid to do so!

MORE INTERESTING STATISTICS FROM YOUR PEERS

What factors do your peers consider the most important in deciding which judges to choose? The students and law clerks in the National Judicial Clerkship Study selected as the most important the reputation of the judge. Other significant factors rounding out the top four were: the length of the clerkship term (one year versus two year); the atmosphere in chambers/working conditions; and that the judge previously hired clerks from their law school.[3] While providing substantially similar responses to the students in most respects, the law clerks in the study ranked a mentor relationship with the judge more highly (almost one-third named this), and downplayed the significance of whether the judge had previously hired clerks from their law school (less than 10%). Considerably de-emphasized by the students, as well as the law clerks, were factors such as: personal connection to the judge; and race/ethnicity, gender, sexual orientation, or disability status of the judge. Geographic considerations appeared most often among the explanatory comments specified as their "other" reasons. Together the findings of these surveys shed some interesting light on the perceptions and factors most important to so many applicants in the clerkship process.

In addition, the study found that nearly two-thirds of the students who applied for a clerkship, and more than one-half of the law clerks surveyed, noted that their perception of their grades or another aspect of their law school record did affect their selection of courts and judges to whom to apply.[4] Accordingly, we should recognize that your grades and academic record may be a significant factor to consider in your own application process in shaping your selection of courts and judges. Again, upon your self-assessment of this factor, this does not mean you need to select yourself out of the process! Simply evaluate the competitiveness of these judges and consider broadening your list to more appropriate choices.

A FINAL NOTE ON THESE CRITERIA

Of course, only you know which of these factors will be relevant and most important for YOU in the clerkship application process. These factors are set forth here for your consideration as part of a personal assessment. Think of this as your customized lens through which to view and evaluate the courts and judges throughout the judiciary. You simply cannot apply to them all, and they would not all be right for you anyway! Choosing the courts and judges who will be best suited for you will be critical in deciding where to apply. Again, working backwards, the concept that you should not at the end of the process turn down an offer, will help guide you in how to apply. Beyond that caveat, strategically your own flexibility—both as to courts, including types and geographical location, and as to judges, in terms of ideology, prestige, and special status—can be your advantage. As general advice, one clerk offered, "Determine what you want out of a clerkship and cast as wide a net as possible during the application process." Considering and weighing these individual factors will help to direct you in your own quest for the perfect clerkship.

Notes

1. On work and pleasure, quoted by John Mason Brown "The Art of Keeping the Mind Refueled" *Vogue* 1 May 53.
2. According to the Administrative Office of U.S. Courts, *Understanding the Federal Courts* (1999).
3. *See* Table 36, NALP Report at 52. *See also* Table 56 at 71 for the detailed responses from the law clerks.
4. *See, e.g.,* NALP Report at 71 and 53 (Table 37 presents the responses of students by demographics).

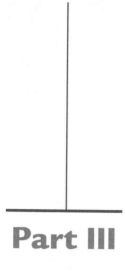

Part III

The Nuts and Bolts

CHAPTER Seven

Building a Successful Application

Many of the students surveyed in the National Judicial Clerkship Study found the clerkship application process problematic in several respects. Almost half of the students who applied for a clerkship reported experiencing difficulties with the mechanics of the clerkship process. Of this significant portion, the majority identified the primary difficulties as determining the application requirements and deadlines of each judge and the timeliness of the application. About a third of them had problems arranging or prioritizing the interviews, researching the background of the judges, and obtaining letters, of recommendation. Other mechanics such as assembling the application package and preparing the writing sample, cover letters, and resume presented some obstacles.[1] Hopefully this book will help you avoid some of these difficulties and pitfalls in your own application process.

THE TIMING OF THE APPLICATION

As discussed above, the timing of the application is a very tricky issue that currently varies by court and by judge. For federal court clerkships, the main sources to look for this type of information will be the Federal Law Clerk Information System, the *NALP Judicial Clerkship Directory*, any collections of letters from judges or other job postings available at your school, and on-line resources. (Check out Chapter 13 for more details on these and other resources.) Individual judges vary as to when they will begin reviewing applications. Generally, however, they are making hiring decisions at least a year and a half to two years in advance (*i.e.*, decisions will be made in the fall of the second year in law school for clerkships to begin after graduation in the fall). Some courts and judges are currently attempting to push their hiring to the fall of the third year (*see* Chapter 2). Note that in any event third year students may apply for federal clerkships but, depending on the judge, they may be starting the clerkship after working for a year post-graduation.

For state clerkships, the application dates vary by state, with some waiting until the fall of the third year of law school to begin hiring for positions beginning upon graduation. As a good starting place, I recommend the Vermont Law School's *Guide to State Judicial Clerkship Procedures*, which annually gathers clerkship information from all of the states and presents an overview of the procedures, salaries, and time frame for each state. You can also check with the state courts directly, including on-line listings for each court using the websites found in the resources chapter.

As a by-product of the absence of uniform application and interview dates, confusion is to some degree the norm. Even the judges are often uninformed as to when their other colleagues on the bench are reviewing applications and interviewing candidates. By calling chambers, you can seek out information as to when that judge is reviewing applications and setting up interviews, and try to get a sense of what his or her schedule and practice will be. Now more than ever the judges and their staff should be more understanding about additional phone calls to chambers without a negative implication that the applicant was somehow ignorant. Moreover, any opportunity to gain information and potentially make contact with someone in chambers could be advantageous. However, you should first check to see whether the particular judge has published his or her application date, requirements, and procedures in one or more of these publicly available sources. If not, a polite telephone call to chambers would certainly not be unreasonable.

THE ELEMENTS OF THE APPLICATION

The requirements of the clerkship application also vary by judge, so you need to determine each judge's rules and preferences first, to the extent that you can do so. If a judge has taken the time to post the position on a court website, to complete a form for the *NALP Judicial Clerkship Directory,* or to send a letter to your school, you should consider yourself on notice of its contents. Thus, you first need to consult these sources (and the Vermont Law School's *Guide to State Judicial Clerkship Procedures,* if it is a state court clerkship). If, on the other hand, there is no information posted by that judge, a phone call to chambers to inquire about his or her requirements is usually not necessary at this stage. Unless there is information from the particular judge to the contrary, the general rule of thumb is that the elements of the application consist of: a cover letter, resume, transcript, writing sample, and two or three letters of recommendation. We will discuss how to build each of these elements into a successful application, addressing as well the questions most frequently asked by your fellow students.

THE NUMBER OF APPLICATIONS

When I'm asked as to the ideal number of applications, I usually shift the focal point of the inquiry because you don't necessarily want to send out 40 or 50 or more applications. There is no magic number— and I have heard much larger numbers than these at times—but rather it all depends on where you are applying. My strategy is to try to broaden the range of where you are applying, similar to the college application process. Rather than only focusing on the number of applications (which statistically might also increase your odds of obtaining a clerkship), I also encourage flexibility to maximize your chances of success. If you are applying to Circuit Courts, maybe consider District Courts as well or other circuits besides the ones that you have selected so far, or even the state courts. If you have selected the most competitive courts and judges, consider expanding your list wherever possible to include some courts and judges who are more off the beaten path in terms of types of courts, judicial "prestige" level, and geographical location. In other words, look beyond the "big name" judges your classmates talk about pursuing. Your flexibility will work to your advantage for discovering the numerous other excellent judges and clerkship opportunities out there.

In your decision as to quantity do not forget quality. Remember to keep in mind my cardinal rule: never apply to a judge for whom you would not want to clerk. The appropriate number of applications depends on the student. Some students like to have a very focused search. They say, "These are the judges I want to clerk for, and if I don't get it I'm willing to accept that or maybe do another application process later." If you chose this more limited approach at the outset, remind yourself of that fact at the end of the process (as part of your reassessment), when you may indeed need to fall back on that second application process. Others blanket the judiciary with their applications and say, "I have to have a clerkship at all costs." Many of these students feel swept up in the frenzy of their classmates' application process and put themselves through considerable added turmoil and expense. For most students, the ideal number of clerkship applications lies somewhere between these two extremes (often 40 to 60)—but, once again, whom you apply to is more important than how many applications you send. Mindful of these strategies, the approach you favor is entirely up to you.

THE COVER LETTER

Regarding the cover letter, there are two schools of thought. I am a strong believer in a very brief cover letter. Some advisers, particularly many faculty members, will tell you that you should research the case law of each judge and discuss this with detailed legal reasoning in the cover letter as well as why you want a clerkship with this particular judge. Your letter would include an analysis of a fantastic case that came out of his or her chambers, why you are great for this judge, and all of your wonderful skills and abilities that you are going to apply to this clerkship which make you indispensable to his or her chambers. From my conversations with judges and the law clerks who often review these letters first, I have discovered that they really can be turned off by that approach. They are human beings with common-sense; if your letter does not seem credible or sincere, you may have supplied grounds to pull your application from the pile even before it reaches the judge. As Judge Winter cautions, "You probably ought not to write a letter describing how finely honed your legal talents are or how uniquely qualified you are for the job. It's enough to say, 'I am applying and I am enclosing a resume and a transcript.' It probably also doesn't help to say, 'I don't believe grades are of any importance and so I'm not sending you those'!"

My philosophy is to avoid dwelling on the obvious platitudes (such as why you desire the wonderful experience of a clerkship), and view your letter as essentially a conduit for your application materials. As such, it should simply state:

· Your status as a student at X Law School along with your year of graduation.

· The term for which you are applying for a clerkship in the judge's chambers.

· The items that are enclosed (*e.g.*, resume, transcript, writing sample).

· The names and phone numbers of the people who will be sending letters of recommendations to follow (if not included in your packet), as well as their relationship to you (*e.g.*, a professor for whom you work as a research assistant). As an alternative or in addition, you may prefer to supplement your cover letter and resume with a separate list of references (and in your cover letter identify this as an enclosure). Be sure to include their phone numbers as well as addresses. A judge may prefer to call a reference, particularly if operating on a quick timeframe.

· Your contact information (phone number, mailing and email address) as you would welcome the opportunity for an interview.

· If the court is located far from your law school and you plan to be in town at a particular time (*e.g.*, during a break to visit family and friends), do include these dates.

On this last point, note that generally judges are sensitive to travel expenses and may try to accommodate your schedule in arranging an interview; at the very least, you have subtly highlighted your geographic connection.

There are a few limited exceptions to this rule. If you have some genuine geographic connection to this court that is not readily apparent from your application materials (*i.e.*, you plan to practice law in that state), you may want to emphasize that fact directly. In the alternative, maybe you really do love this judge, you have had a life-long ambition to clerk for him or her—and you can express it in a very sincere way—then it might be appropriate to do so, but when in doubt keep it minimal and avoid the risk. A personal connection could also be mentioned deftly in the cover letter. A further exception might be warranted if you think that the judge has not hired law clerks from your school in the past and might need extra convincing to consider your application; you may need to demonstrate that something about your academic record and experiences makes you exemplary. Do not describe aspects of yourself in glowing terms, but instead briefly discuss your experiences. For example, the fact that you worked throughout law school to finance your education or did extensive research for a professor on a topic of interest shows your traits of reliability and diligence. If you did a judicial externship or internship, you can highlight this wonderful experience with Judge X and how it shaped your desire to apply for a judicial clerkship in the chambers of Judge Y. However, be careful not to overdo it with exaggeration, cliché, or the suggestion that the judge truly needs your contribution to chambers. You would not want to come across as insincere, arrogant, or presumptuous.

If you are applying to a specialized court, you may want to tailor your letter with your own corresponding particular qualifications. For example, if the clerkship is for a judge in the U.S. Court of Appeals for the Federal Circuit, you can accentuate your patent background and technical or engineering expertise, including any relevant coursework. Similarly, an expression of your strong interest in practicing tax law, or even past experiences in accounting or finance, would be appropriate for the U.S. Tax Court.

Correctly addressing your cover letter and envelope, with the proper titles, spellings and salutation lines, is crucial. In the address portion of the letter and on the envelope, all judges should be referred to as "The Honorable," followed by the judge's full name, court in which the judge sits, and address. For the salutation, you should use the appropriate title (*e.g.*, Judge, Justice, Chief Justice), followed by the judge's last name (*e.g.*, Dear Judge Jones). Note that judges on senior status should be referred to as "Judge" (not "Senior Judge") in the salutation. (*See* Appendix for specific examples of the proper manner of addressing a letter to a judge.)

As my sources at the Administrative Office of U.S. Courts advise, students should clearly mark the outside envelopes of the application materials and letters of recommendation with their contents, so that they do not get mixed in with the regular business of the court. It is also helpful to the judges for you to include your email address on your resume and in your cover letter, as chambers staff are now being advised to contact applicants through this route. Note that you should use your official law school (or employer) email address, rather than an unprofessional or downright weird personal email alternative! (Of course, if you ordinarily do not use that address as your preferred email, make sure that you now check that account on a regular basis.)

Above all, you must be careful to avoid the frequently fatal flaw— any grammatical or typographical errors in your cover letter or in any element of your clerkship application. Your letter should be clear, concise, and generally not longer than one page. It should convey the proper level of formality and professionalism, taking care to avoid being casual or chatty. As is the case with other job applications, you must present yourself at your best effort and abilities. The judge will want a law clerk who is meticulous in this regard, as the quality of his or her writing for the judge will largely depend on these traits. Judge Winter notes that with a word processor it is important to make sure that you change everything. "I once mailed back a letter to an applicant with a letter saying, 'I didn't know which Judge Ginsburg you wanted me to forward this to.' It had my address and then 'Dear Judge Ginsburg.' You have to watch that!"

A former law clerk for the U.S. Supreme Court and U.S. Court of Appeals for the Second Circuit, John Elwood, who has reviewed hundreds of cover letters in the hiring of law clerks for his chambers, echoes my philosophy. He believes that cover letters should be very short, essentially "Dear Judge X: [¶] I am writing to apply for a position as a law clerk in your chambers for [September/October Term 2002/2002–03/whatever]. I have enclosed a law-school transcript, a writing sample, and a copy of my resume. Please let me know if you would like any other materials. [¶] Thank you very much." He adds that if you have a particular reason to want to clerk for a judge (say, a friend recommended you, or you wish to settle in the location the judge works, or whatever), that might legitimately be placed in the letter, but with care:

> By all means, avoid using cover letters to tell what fine experience you have—that is the function of the resume. Cover letters as a whole tend to be useful only for making you look boastful or silly and, because they are inherently difficult and easy to ridicule, to highlight weaknesses in your writing, so keep them short and nondescript. I have been involved in the hiring of clerks for two clerkships and dozens of young associates and have never, EVER known of a candidate who was helped by his or her cover letter. Incidentally, a typographical or spelling error anywhere in your cover letter, resume, and (to a lesser extent) writing sample will often disqualify all but the best-credentialed candidates.

In sum, this is one of those not-so-rare cases where the less said, the better—but say it with perfect precision.

THE RESUME

As for the resume, it is not much different from a resume for any other employer, and need not be significantly altered for the clerkship application process. As such, the resume should be neat, professional, internally consistent, and free of typographical or grammatical errors.

A few key enhancements may be in order. Many of the students applying for clerkships have just gone through the process in the fall to obtain their employment for the following summer. One addition I recommend to that resume is to include your position for next summer, if known. Since you have not yet started that job, this might not otherwise occur to you. The proper etiquette is to use the phrase "Prospective Law Clerk" or "Prospective Summer Associate" or "prospective" whatever you're doing for the next summer. The judge may want to take that position into account, as it will be one of the experiences you will have had by the time you enter the clerkship. You should also emphasize your geographic ties to the judge here, such as including your home address or past employment in that city. You may wish to list your grade point average and class rank on your resume, if doing so would serve you well. In addition, any kind of activities, publications, or experiences that are law related are important to include, particularly research and writing endeavors of either a legal or non-legal nature, such as a judicial internship or the title of your prized journal note.

Rather unique to a resume for judicial clerkships is the opportunity to present more of yourself as a person, including relevant non-legal interests. For instance, if prior to law school you started your own business or developed a significant career unrelated to your current pursuits in the law, you should include this background information, which a judge may find adds an interesting dimension to you as an individual. Likewise be sure to list any interesting or unusual skills, experiences or activities such as foreign languages, musical proclivities, travel, or community service. These other aspects may spark the interest of a particular judge and may provide topics for an eventual interview. While an "interests" section is appropriate here, I do not recommend a "personal" section, as it tends to get *too* personal (*e.g.,* your spouse and/or children). Your resume should always be an accurate reflection of your current personal but professional self.

When asked if one should tailor the resume politically for the clerkship, I must say that I really do not believe in doing so. I might alert a particular student that his or her resume comes across very strongly in this political direction due to certain activities or work experiences, but that is usually the way that student would want it to be. Remember that it is a mutually selective process and very personal; if your political ideology has so strongly shaped your background that it is reflected on your resume, chances are it will be an important factor for you in your selection of judges to whom to apply. Moreover, you would want to be compatible with the judge for whom you clerk, and if this really is a critical factor for that judge you are better off finding out now. The converse is also true. Some judges may even prefer an enthusiastic law clerk who will occasionally challenge them with the opposite political views. As Judge Brieant states on the subject of law clerks and politics:

> I'm a believer that politics is a part of government. I have had many law clerks who belong to the opposite political party than I do and some that were quite vocal and quite extreme in their views, but I'd rather see somebody have some politics than no politics. And I think that people who have studied history and law owe it to the public to get out there and participate in the political process.[2]

Most times political ideology will not be a relevant factor for the student or the judge in the daily life and decision making in chambers. A politically neutral resume will be a natural reflection of that fact. Ultimately, honesty is paramount, for your sake as well as the judge's.

One more small (but not too small) point is, I believe, worth mentioning here. Occasionally I am presented with a student's resume with a size of print too small to read with ease. Rather than making the difficult editing choices that usually strengthen a resume (such as removing that fond old summer job from long before your law school days), some students opt instead to squeeze additional information onto their resume by ever decreasing margins and font size. This approach can be a mistake, as some judges (even older than myself) will be unable to read this precious information.

So, as general advice, think of your resume as a document that continually evolves with time—an ongoing scrolling off of some of the older, less relevant activities and employment (such as the burger-flipping post in high school) and a firm editing of the descriptive details (the eye will be drawn to the longer descriptions as what you have chosen to emphasize) as you build your primarily legal skills and experiences. By the way, if you are looking for an area to cut first, an "objective" section for clerkships can be too trite and unduly restrictive, and the phrase "references available upon request" is a further waste of space. Although most law students at this stage will have a resume that is no longer than one page, it might be acceptable to go beyond this limit if you have significant experiences or publications that legitimately fill a second page (not just a paragraph onto that page). You may have somewhat more page flexibility than for other employers; however, this should not be a substitute for the tight editing and tough choices that produce the best, most concise resume.

LETTERS OF RECOMMENDATION

References are of critical importance to judges in the application process. As one judge describes, "We get so many applicants that we cannot interview them all . . . So personal recommendations by prior law clerks or by faculty members of the law school—not just letters but actual person-to-person contact—is very important. You can't really tell much by a single interview or even two or three and you can't tell much by a transcript, but if someone vouches for the person and if their resume shows they've done something more than simply be a great student, that is very important."

• The number of references

The number of recommendations that will be required may vary by judge. As a result, you should check this element for each judge as part of your research of the application requirements (*see, e.g.,* Federal Law Clerk Information System, *NALP Judicial Clerkship Directory*, letters from the judges on file in your law school, discussed in Resources Chapter 13). As a rule of thumb, generally two or three letters of recommendation will be appropriate. If there are no published requirements to the contrary for that judge, you should aim for three strong letters. Particularly if the letters will be sent by the recommenders directly under separate cover, a third reference will help to insure that at least two will arrive in a timely manner and be matched up with the rest of your application materials. On the other hand, you would not want to inundate a judge with many more than that. The paper burdens on the judiciary are already voluminous, and quantity is no substitute for quality. The importance of these letters cannot be overstated. Accordingly, it will be more important to choose your references wisely and aim for the most meaningful two or three letters of recommendation.

· Who to Choose as a Reference

You should choose as a reference someone who you believe will write a strong letter of recommendation on your behalf. At least one or ideally two of your recommendations should be from a law school professor. Certainly the reference should be from someone in whose class you excelled. Most importantly, this person should know your legal writing well and be able to address your strengths in this regard. A judge will want to know first and foremost about your legal research and writing skills, as these are the most significant abilities you will need for your work in chambers. Your writing sample will also be of critical importance for this reason (discussed below). A professor for whom you took a small class, wrote a paper, or served as a research or teaching assistant would be best in this regard. While certain professors may be better "connected" with some judges than others, you should still choose the professors who have the strongest connection to you.

A visiting professor could be a suitable choice as one of your references, but keep in mind that it might be logistically complicated to arrange this once he or she has returned to the home law school.

Another appropriate choice might be a professor with whom you participated in a law school clinic. In addition to commenting on your legal writing, this professor could address other qualities such as: your ability to interact with clients and as a member of a team; your analytical and reasoning skills; your oral presentation techniques; your reliability and integrity; and your ability to work well under pressure to complete assignments in a timely manner with the utmost professionalism. Judges will also look to these aspects of your persona as relevant to a clerkship and the types of tasks to be performed in their chambers.

An employer or lawyer in practice from a summer job can also be an appropriate additional reference if this is someone who worked closely with you and knows your written work. This employer could also speak positively about other attributes such as work habits and character. There is an added benefit if this practitioner is a prominent attorney in the field or in the city or geographic area in which the judge is located. The credibility of such an attorney will carry substantial weight, and he or she may be more likely to have connections to the judge, which is always a plus. However, do not choose your reference based solely on the status of the attorney (or the professor); a strong positive letter by a senior associate who worked closely with you will have more impact than a lukewarm letter from a "big-name" partner. In addition, you should plan to use particular care to follow through with practitioners, as they may be especially busy and unaware of the critical timeframe for clerkship applications and recommendations.

Several students have asked whether they can use their former college professors for a letter to the judges. I generally discourage this choice as tending to be too remote chronologically and not as appropriate—this type of professor is usually unfamiliar with your more relevant *legal* writing and abilities. These concerns do not apply in the same way to transfer students, who can certainly use professors from their previous law school but should also try to find one from the current school, if possible. Of course, you do need to evaluate your own individual situation and select the strongest and most appropriate references available under the circumstances.

As reported in the National Judicial Clerkship Study, one-third of the students indicated that they experienced difficulties in finding people to provide these references and an even greater percentage (36%) reported problems with the content of the letters.[3] A large number of students expressed the concern that their professors did not know them well enough to write meaningful recommendations, due in part to the earlier timing of the application process. Moreover, some individual faculty members set their own limitations on the number of letters they will write per student. Accordingly, you will need to check the policies of your own law school and individual faculty members.

As John Elwood, former law clerk for the U.S. Supreme Court and U.S. Court of Appeals for the Second Circuit, explains:

> So long as you can get at least two letters of recommendation, stop worrying about quantity and focus on quality. Also, it is far better to have hyperbolic letters from a less-well known professor than tepid letters from a household name; you should ONLY have recommendation letters from people who will rave about you. If you have any questions about the tone of the likely recommendation, ask your recommenders at the outset if they would feel "comfortable" writing you a letter of recommendation: that leaves them an out if they expect to be less than enthusiastic. Incidentally, recommendations from professors carry more weight than those from employers.

So, how do you go about getting the strongest letters of recommendation available under your particular circumstances?

· **How and When to Approach Your Recommenders**

For all your references, I strongly suggest that you spend time early on (preferably *before* the clerkship application process) fostering a relationship with them and hopefully with your writing (which is beneficial for your law school career as well). You can do this by approaching them after class early in the semester to discuss legal issues unrelated to the clerkship process, engaging in class discussions, asking to write a paper in their class if this is an option, and/or serving as a research assistant. I also encourage students to use these professors as a source of information and advice about judges (including their own clerkship, if any) and their selection. Their input and suggestions as to judges may send you in other directions you had not previously anticipated in your search. Moreover, if they recommend a particular judge and court to you, chances are they have "connections" to those judges and courts. Directing your applications there will maximize your chances of obtaining a clerkship and will encourage your professors and other advisors to have a vested interest in your application process.

As a former law clerk for the Ninth Circuit Court of Appeals and Peer Advisor for his law school, Bart Epstein advises:

> Letters of recommendation are tremendously important. From day one in law school you should be developing relationships with a few professors you find interesting. Seek them out after class, do extra reading, and explore the complexities of the law that are not covered in class. This will not only enhance your chances of getting the clerkship you want, it will enrich your law school experience and help you develop your analytical skills even further. The letter you want is the one that not only says that you are one of the best students at your school, but explains why, in detail. Give your recommenders something to write about by getting to know them. If possible, take the same professor twice so you can really get to know him or her— and vice versa.

Be sure to approach your professors and recommenders early in the process, well before you are planning to send out your clerkship applications. Your fellow students will be soliciting their recommendations as well and, depending on the professor, there may be a limited number of students for whom he or she will write letters. Most importantly, you must give your professors ample time to prepare the letter on your behalf and to have their secretaries perform a mail merge and process the letters. The general guideline is to plan four weeks of advance time as a reasonable courtesy.

At the outset, it is particularly important to communicate with the people who may serve as your potential references. Be sure to ask your professor or employer if he or she knows your writing well enough to feel comfortable in writing a *strong* letter of recommendation on your behalf. Try to ascertain from the response whether the resulting letter will indeed be positive, enthusiastic, and supportive. As helpful background information, you should provide your professor/recommender with a packet of your resume, transcript, a writing sample, and possibly even a statement about your aspirations or other aspects of yourself. Anything that can assist your reference in writing you a strong letter—with specific information of significance for the judges—would be advisable. Some professors also prefer to have at the outset a list of the judges to whom you are applying, so they can tailor their letter accordingly and make it (and possibly even phone calls) more personal to the judges whom they know.

At some point after your initial contact on the matter, you will need to supply your professors with the names and addresses of these judges. In most cases, you will also need to provide this information on disk in mail merge format in order for the faculty secretaries to assemble the reference letters. Note that, like your cover letters, these letters must be personalized with the accurate name and address of each judge, as it is not appropriate to send letters that are addressed "To Whom It May Concern."

A few words on the mechanics: some law schools will collect the letters from the faculty for you and assemble the materials for your application packet. Most will leave the processing of the applications to you. If you do gather these letters directly, you should take care to maintain each letter in a sealed envelope with the author's signature across the seal. The fact that you have taken this additional step (even if the faculty member did not require you to do so) both demonstrates your integrity and enhances the weight or credibility of these letters. Either way, the judges do prefer a complete application package that includes the letters of recommendation; this helps to ameliorate the magnitude of their paper processing and the matching of separately arriving letters to their respective applications.

If your law school (or individual professor) requires the letters of recommendation to be mailed to the judges directly from their faculty, you should try to assist the judge by including the names of your references in your cover letter and indicate that their letters will be arriving under separate cover. Coordinate with your professors/employers to ensure that they do not send their letters of recommendation before you have sent your application to the judge. Ask your recommender to include on the outside of the envelopes a "re: your name" line (or do it for them if you are permitted to process the letters and envelopes for their signature). You may also want to consider adding an additional reference to offset the possibility that a letter may arrive late or be misdirected.

· Following Through for Timely Recommendations

Among the difficulties experienced by applicants, the national study revealed that almost one-third of the students experienced problems with the timely submission of these letters. An awareness of this common problem is important, to prevent this obstacle from hindering you.

Student comments on their issues concerning references included the following:[4]

- "If you have not worked for a professor [as a research assistant] it's hard to find professors that know you well enough to give you a recommendation."
- "It was hard to find professors who knew me well after only 2½ semesters of law school—most were large classes."
- "It would have been easier if the process was later when I knew more professors."
- "Professors tend to be very busy and to write many letters, so you have to jockey for a good position."

- "Some professors limit reference letters to one student per judge—thus you had to find professors early."

- "Some professors think (erroneously) that students they are recommending should limit their search to keep the recommendation letters from being diluted. This is true only for the very elite students. For the vast majority of us, we have to apply to 100 or more judges."

- "Although all my references readily agreed to mail letters on my behalf, I didn't know any professors who were well-connected to judges or the whole clerkship process, and I think that hurt me."

- "Sometimes people simply do not realize the importance of getting the letters turned in on time."

Further confirmation of this problem came from the observations of law school administrators, one-quarter of whom had experienced difficulty in getting the faculty to send letters of recommendation in a timely fashion. To rectify this problem, several schools described their informal efforts: the career service professionals' and the deans' multiple follow-up communication in writing and in person, offers of assistance, and strongly encouraging the students to follow up with faculty. In addition, some schools have implemented more formal procedures, including preparing letters through an administrator of the clerkship committee, keeping a log of requests with a procedure to remind faculty members, and a centralized process through the office of career services with faculty support.[5]

Since the timely submission of your letters of recommendation may be critical to your success, you may have to implement your own follow-up efforts with your recommenders, to the extent you can do so. Once again, communication is key.

THE WRITING SAMPLE

The writing sample is one of the most important elements of the application for a clerkship. Numerous judges have emphasized to me over the years how much they value those writing samples and look to this component as the key to a successful clerkship application, since the research and writing skills of a law clerk are essential. For example, Judge Cyganowski explains:

> The grades are obviously important, but for me probably the most important aspect of an application that I look at are the writing samples. I want to make sure that the person can write because that is critical. Whether it is communicating information to me or actually also writing or assisting in writing the decisions, the person has to be able to write and write cleanly, not esoterically, and not with too many footnotes although we have our share of footnotes. Clarity is probably the biggest component that we look for in writing.

As such, the writing sample must represent the best quality of your legal writing—meticulous, well organized, demonstrating your strong legal research and analytical skills. As Judge Smith emphasizes, "Law students who want to be considered for a clerkship should do everything possible to develop and improve their written work, because nothing is more important in the work that a law clerk does than drafting written opinions for the judge for whom the law clerk works."[6]

Some judges will want a writing sample sent in the initial packet of materials, while others will prefer to review your other materials first and receive it at the time of the interview. You may want to check the individual judges' requirements before including your weighty sample in your application. Doubts as to whether it is required by a particular judge should be resolved in favor of sending one. If you choose not to include a writing sample in your packet, mention in your cover letter that one is available upon request.

Students often ask two questions in connection with the writing sample: what type of writing sample is appropriate and how long should it be?

· **Type of Writing Sample**

The type of writing sample that may be appropriate depends on the court. For instance, if you are applying to a District Court you might be better off with something concrete such as a legal brief or memorandum rather than a historical, theoretical or policy-oriented article, for which there might be more latitude in the Court of Appeals, if at all. A memorandum or brief you wrote for a first year writing class might be suitable, but reread it first to make sure it still represents a good example of your best legal writing; your writing has most likely developed and improved since that early effort. For those of you for whom this earlier piece might still represent a rare or *only* piece of their writing to date, I offer a slight consolation. With the deadlines of some judges reaching to the beginning of the second year of law school, the first year writing is not from so far in the past, and thus may not appear quite as old! The operative word here is *legal* writing. An old paper from college, even if published and exemplary, would not be appropriate due to its age, content, and style. Moreover, a most recent sample of your writing would be best, as it would more likely demonstrate your current level of polish.

As an alternative to a paper written in law school, you might choose a memorandum or brief prepared during summer employment. It is very important though, and this is from the point of view of lawyers in practice as well, to always check with the law firm or other employer. If this was writing material from a previous summer's experience, it must be cleared with the employer to make sure that it is permissible to use as a writing sample and then indicate that authorization on the writing sample. Names of clients and identifying information will need to be redacted. This works out best by substituting fictitious names rather than crossing out or deleting the original names, which can make the facts difficult to follow; and be sure to add a brief statement explaining that you have done so. Confidentiality and proprietary considerations are essential to a judge and you will want to show that you have met that standard.

An extra word of caution is warranted if the employer in question was a judge and you worked as a judicial intern or extern. Certainly you must obtain and clearly state the judge's permission to use as your sample an opinion or decision written for that judge. You should also indicate that this is a draft of what you submitted to the judge, so that you are not representing that you wrote the final opinion. Even so, there are many judges who will disapprove of the use of an actual judicial opinion, either with the concern that it may not be a matter of public record or that you have broken the mystique of the work in chambers. As an unwritten rule, the judge is always the author of a judicial opinion, regardless of who assisted in its writing in chambers. For you to claim authorship may appear to be indiscreet.

As a general matter, it is always a good idea to make clear the purpose and context for which the piece was written (*e.g.*, Moot Court brief, law review note, employer memorandum). If you revise an earlier effort, you should describe the sample as "based on a memorandum I wrote for my seminar class on X." Depending on the format and content, you may need to set up the piece by providing a short preliminary statement of the facts and parameters with which you were presented—especially if this was a wacky law school hypothetical whose issues and facts were framed by the professor and not conjured up in your own mind! Similarly, if you are using an excerpt of a longer article (as discussed below), you may need to add a brief introductory paragraph of background details or other explanatory information to ensure that the excerpt makes sense on its own.

In any event, it is fundamental that this be your original and unedited writing. Co-authored pieces are not ideal as a representation of *your* work, unless your part is readily severable. A law journal article that has been finished and published may be questionable in that judges will be aware that it has been heavily edited in the process of preparing the article for publication; a more appropriate choice might be an earlier draft of the article as your original work (as long as it is sufficiently polished), with a reference to the final published version on your resume (again, you can always bring that one to the interview). Some judges will even question papers written for your professors as to whether they have been heavily edited by your professor. Some comments and suggestions along the way are fine (but not on the copy you submit), provided that the final work product has been created by your hands alone.

· **Length of the Writing Sample**

The writing sample should be long enough to allow you to present your analytic ability and organizational skills. I believe that the sample should also be relatively brief. How do I define brief? The precise number of pages depends on the writing sample, but as a very rough guideline (when prodded to offer an actual number) I would say generally not much more than 20 pages. Beyond that it starts to get very lengthy and potentially burdensome to the judge. The result might be that the judge either chooses not to read it, or picks a section of it to read which might not be the strongest one you would have offered. If you have a very lengthy, 50-page law journal article, I tell students you can always bring that with you to an interview and it will be on your resume, but you may not necessarily want to send the entire thing. Sending an excerpt of it is reasonable, if it can be separated and stands on its own; you would not want to leave the reader hanging, thinking whatever happened to the rest of the piece. For that purpose, you may need to add a preliminary and/or concluding statement to provide the context.

Some students have asked me whether an extremely short piece (*e.g.*, two to four pages) of writing is too little, and whether they can send an additional sample as showing a different aspect or type of their writing (*e.g.*, a memo and a brief). In general, I would say that would be fine if both samples are very small and together would provide a more complete picture of your writing without being redundant and adding up to a weighty bundle for judges already plagued with volumes of paper. However, my first instinct is to question whether such a short sample could show enough of your legal reasoning and developed analysis for that issue beyond your ability to be concise. Sometimes there is no substitute for reading the work directly before offering my final advice—you might need to ask an advisor or professor on site to review it for you. Before you do so, ask yourself: is this the best sample of my legal reasoning and writing? The ultimate test is the quality of writing rather than the quantity.

· Other Considerations

Finally, try to review your writing sample from the judge's perspective. Evaluate the subject matter for appropriateness and make sure that it will not be offensive to that judge in any way. Examples of this potential danger would include controversial content or politically charged positions; facts that were too silly or far-fetched (courtesy of your creative professor, no doubt) to support serious logical reasoning or legal discourse; and some arcane area of the law which might be soporific. Other pitfalls to avoid would include criticisms of appellate judges, personal disrespect for a judge, or maybe even open disparagement of the decision in a particular case authored by the judge to whom you are applying! Highly technical material that requires special expertise to understand should also be avoided, unless you are applying to a specialized court for which this subject matter would be appropriate. Moreover, it should go without saying that there must be no typographical or grammatical errors in your writing sample—use due care in the preparation as well as the selection of your work.

THE TRANSCRIPT

· Mechanics of the Transcript

Every judge will want you to include a current law school transcript. Typically an unofficial, photocopied transcript will be acceptable—and less expensive—unless the judge has specified that the transcript must be an official copy. Be aware that some judges will require an undergraduate transcript as well.

It may be necessary to attach to your transcript an explanatory note if your school has any unusual grading scales that are not included in a key. In addition, if you have any missing or incomplete grades, a note of explanation to the judge would be wise, particularly if there were extenuating circumstances that can be briefly conveyed without drawing more damaging attention to the situation. If the omission is due to a delay in the professor turning in your grade (which unfortunately is a very common occurrence), you must make it clear by attaching a note to your transcript stating that you have completed your work but the professor has not yet submitted your grade for the course. Judges do not like to see the label "tardy" or "incomplete." Their law clerks cannot demonstrate a failure to work with deadlines and follow through in their substantial writing for the court; and you would not want them to draw this negative inference from your transcript. By the way, as soon as these missing grades do make their way to your transcript, you should send a new transcript to the judge with a brief letter of addendum. In addition to being part of your continuing duty to update your application with new grades or information, this is also an excellent opportunity to remind the judge of your existence.

· **Courses to Pursue**

You may also wish to add a list of the courses you are currently taking, as they will not be reflected on your transcript and may be of interest to the judge. I am often asked the courses one should take in order to obtain a clerkship. What courses do the judges like to see? Of course, in addition to the standard first year curriculum, the basics such as Evidence, Federal Courts, Jurisdiction, Property, and Criminal Procedure will be helpful for your clerkship. Although you may not yet have had the chance to take these classes if you are applying for a clerkship early in your law school career, you should plan to tackle them as soon as possible, and certainly by the end of law school. (Keep in mind you may want to apply for a clerkship again, or for the first time, in your third year of law school and your transcript should ideally include them by then.) Do follow your heart and interests in your course selection, but also keep in mind how the courses, individually and in total, might appear to a judge. A sprinkling of the more "artsy" and perhaps interesting classes usually won't be held against you,[7] as long as you bolster them with some courses with more "practical" application to your legal career. Most practical of course are the clinics, externships, trial advocacy, Moot Court and the like. Law reviews and law journals provide excellent academic experiences in writing and editing appropriate for a clerkship as well, regardless of whether the journal is "the" journal that will also add an important credential to your academic record. I highly recommend these pursuits as benefiting your law school and legal career as well as strengthening your clerkship application.

· A Final Note on Grades

While grades are clearly a significant factor for a successful clerkship application, they do not portray the complete picture. Some judges look at grades more than others. Two true stories are worth sharing here for another perspective. One law school career development professional told me of his own experience with a student who had an entrepreneurial career prior to law school that was very successful, but in law school had very poor grades; so poor that the faculty clerkship committee would not write a recommendation as required by that school. Despite the considerable odds to the contrary, this student ended up with a large number of interviews because the judges found him to be an interesting individual.

I can add from my own observations and conversations with judges that having an interesting individual in their chambers for a year is often the prevailing factor for them. One District Judge emphasizes a common sentiment: "Compatibility of temperament is important. I like to see well-rounded people who have other interests in life than merely grades or merely books or merely the philosophy of law." Another judge for the U.S. Court of Appeals expressed his delight to me upon his selection of his latest law clerk, emphasizing the student's unique qualities, "He has long hair and he's a really great musician. Isn't that great? This is going to be such an interesting year in chambers!" I know of other compelling anecdotal evidence as well, such as a particular judge with an interest in classical music for whom a law clerk with talents in that area is an added plus. Then there's always the athletic bent of a certain Supreme Court justice, Chief Justice Rehnquist, who likes to challenge his clerks on the higher court in the building—the tennis court, that is!

So you never know what will be the deciding factor for a particular judge in the selection of a law clerk. It is a very individualistic decision. This is why I try to de-emphasize the grades somewhat. If there is a screening tool, then yes, maybe an applicant will not make the level for that particular judge—and it does vary by judge—but if the judge is looking at that individual's total application materials, there may be some interest or quality that sparks the judge's interest. Perhaps it will be in the interview phase that a certain chemistry will materialize. This is something that is so personalized for the judge that to have some really exciting and interesting law clerk in chambers may be all that judge really wants.

Notes

1. *See* Table 38 of the NALP Report at 54 for an assessment of their application process.
2. As always, best said by the Honorable Charles L. Brieant, U.S. District Judge for the Southern District of New York. (Yes, someday you too will find yourself continually quoting "your" judge's words of wisdom!) I have heard him express this view many times both during my clerkship terms and in the years since. This was true of our working relationship at times (although not too often), and we both greatly benefited as a result.
3. *See* NALP Report at 55, Table 21.
4. NALP Report at 54–55.
5. NALP Report at 38.
6. *See* Chapter 12 for further detailed advice on this and more from the Honorable Lisa M. Smith, U.S. Magistrate Judge, U.S. District Court for the Southern District of New York.
7. When I was a student in law school at Yale, one of my professors jokingly offered a course entitled, "Life, the Universe, and Everything." Amazingly, it became necessary to retract it officially, as so many students attempted to enroll! Then again, that was Yale, arguably at its best. I followed the more traditional route of building block courses, where they could be found!

CHAPTER

eight

Interviews, Offers, Acceptances, and Alternate Outcomes

THE CLERKSHIP INTERVIEW

The importance of the interview cannot be overstated. Unlike law firm interviews during on-campus recruitment, actually getting an interview is a major achievement. It is very difficult to get one, but once you do, you are almost there!

A few statistics on this may be enlightening for you. According to the National Clerkship Study, roughly one in 10 applications at the federal level resulted in an invitation to interview, and one in four applications at the state level did so. (It was noted, however, that the number of applications might effectively be higher than appears, since for some courts a student submits one application to a pool, which is then distributed to many judges in that court. These numbers may not accurately reflect that practice, which is more common in the state courts.) About one in three of the interviews with a state or federal judge resulted in an offer (even higher for state appellate courts, at 43%). (*See* Table 42, reproduced below, which illustrates in more detail the outcomes of the applications by type of court.)

Table 42. **Outcomes of Applications by Type of Court**

	Number of Applications Sent	% of Applications Resulting in Invitation to Interview	% of These Invitations Resulting in Interview	% of Interviews Resulting in Offer
Federal Appellate	8,948	10.0%	59.8%	36.4%
Federal District	16,085	11.2	50.0	33.6
Federal Other	1,240	13.2	66.5	33.0
State Appellate	1,571	24.9	74.7	43.2
State Trial	2,671	24.4	62.3	37.1
Local Appellate	13	46.2	83.3	20.0
Local Trial	556	19.1	52.8	14.3
Other	13	69.2	77.8	57.1

Based on 763 responses.
Note: Figures in this table provide a gauge of chances of success at each stage of the process. However, because of the variety of individual circumstances, such as instances of receiving a clerkship without going through the application process, having multiple interviews as the result of one letter of application to a pool of judges, and withdrawing other applications upon receiving an offer, these figures should not be viewed as precise quantities.

In addition, the law clerks in the study emphasized their belief that the interview was the most important aspect for a judge in selecting a judicial clerk. Since it is quite common for law clerks to review the applications, interview the applicants, and participate in the hiring decisions, their opinion on this holds substantial weight. Based on their past application experience and their observations as a law clerk, the vast majority of these law clerks (81%) identified most often as "extremely important" to the judge the evaluation of the interview; second in importance were personal character traits.[1] Their emphasis on the interview surpassed even the importance they placed on the academic record, although we must recognize implicitly the role that the academic record may have played in getting the applicant to the interview in the first place.

As explained by a candid former law clerk: "There are two parts to the clerkship search—getting the interview and getting the offer. The two most important factors for getting the interview are your law school and your grades . . . The better your grades are the less everything else matters. If you still have time, *work harder*." However, even this clerk acknowledged that there is more involved here than grades: "When it comes to the interview there tends to be a high degree of correlation between law school grades and the ability to perform legal analysis. That is one reason that judges look for students with top grades. That correlation, however, is not perfect. There are students with top grades without a lick of common sense or social skills. There are also plenty of brilliant and fascinating students in the middle of their classes."

At this point, your academic record or other factors may have gotten you to the interview, and now for many judges it is mostly a matter of chemistry, personality, and how well you get along with the judge and others in chambers. Of course this depends on the judge, as some have a more rigorous interviewing procedure based on case law analysis. You should research the interview type and style if possible through former law clerks or other students, alumni, or someone you know who has interviewed with that judge. You may also get an indication from the secretary or law clerk when scheduling the interview, *e.g.*, as to length of time to allot or with whom you will be meeting. However, you should be careful not to push or be overly aggressive in these conversations—remember that all contacts with chambers staff are part of the interviewing process and should be approached with caution and sense. This is part of your second round of research, which includes reading significant and recent case law of that judge. We will discuss each of these finer points in more detail below.

SCHEDULING THE INTERVIEWS

Once you have sent in your application, you may be hearing from a judge at any time thereafter, depending on the judge. (Again, check with your sources as to the timing of application deadlines and interviewing guidelines for each individual judge.) Generally the contact will occur as a phone call from either the secretary or even the judge directly, asking you for an interview. If at all possible, be there to receive the phone call. Of course you cannot sit by the phone waiting indefinitely. However, believe it or not, I have seen numerous instances where students purposely screened their phone calls from the judges and had them leave messages on their answering machine, so that they could wait to call back and schedule their top choice judges first. This strategy can often backfire, especially if the judge catches wind of it (suspiciously, no one from that law school was ever home)!

Needless to say, if you do receive a message from a judge, call back *promptly*. Failure to do so (*e.g.*, while you are still waiting for your "top" judges to call) carries the risk that all of the best interview slots will now be taken. Judges typically receive a few hundred applications for the one or two law clerk positions, but only interview between six and a dozen of these applicants; of course, these numbers vary greatly with the judge. There is a chance that the later interviews may be cancelled if the judge decides to give an offer to one of the earlier interviewees. Individual practices on this differ as well, but to maximize your chances of a clerkship offer, a wise strategy is to try to accept the first interview slot offered, even if it involves some inconvenience, short notice, or other difficulties for you to arrange.

Still, to the extent there is any flexibility in the application process, it occurs in the interviewing phase with the scheduling of the interviews. Some students follow a strategy of attempting to schedule interviews based on the ranking of a particular judge on their list. It goes like this: they hear from a judge and schedule the interview with that judge for a date further in the future, for example, on March 31, leaving open the earlier dates, say March 1, to wait for their number one or two choices. By the way, I mention this approach because it is not uncommon. Their reasoning is understandable. There is a natural human tendency to wonder "what if" I had waited for that other judge now that I may be presented with an offer from the first judge, which I must now accept (as we will discuss below). The process seems so random and students (particularly future lawyers used to strategizing and perhaps over-thinking) sometimes have a difficult time accepting the element of fate in all this. Yet I do believe that this attempt to control what otherwise seems entirely out of one's control can be a major mistake; a student should be happy simply to receive a call from a judge for an interview. Particularly if you have done your research ahead of time and followed the golden rule (only apply to a judge for whom you would want to clerk), any of these judges—whether number one or number 20 on your list—should potentially be an appropriate match for you. In addition, as I have indicated, this strategy does involve some risk. Your "top" judge may never in fact call, or may only have later interview slots open, and the later judge may then no longer have an open clerkship position. Keep in mind that this is not an exact science—can you really be sure of your initial ranking or know any of these judges so well at this point to ascertain with certainty which judge is perfect for you? Ultimately, you should do some soul-searching and determine for yourself if the measure of control outweighs the risk and is worth it for you.

Due to the lack of set timing guidelines, the temptation to adopt such a risky strategy should now be greatly reduced anyway, as the offers to interview will come in more randomly and be scheduled as they come. If you are fortunate enough to be one of the lucky ones to get such an opportunity, you will be less likely to be in the situation of turning down an interview with that prized, long-shot judge; chances are, he or she would have been one of the first ones to call you on the expedited schedule. And, as noted above, you can manage the process more through the timing of your applications, directing them in waves grouped by practices of the court, schedule of the judge, and to some extent your highest preferences.

Where there is a modicum of flexibility is in another proactive approach. Once you have scheduled an interview with a judge, particularly if you will be traveling to a distant location, you can seize the opportunity to parlay interviews with other judges in that area to whom you have applied. Let's say you are flying from the East Coast to the West Coast; you can call a number of those West Coast judges and say something like, "I'm coming out there for an interview with a judge in this circuit and I was wondering whether you are interested in seeing me while I'm here." That is perfectly acceptable from an etiquette point of view. Most judges are aware of the tremendous cost to a student associated with such long-distance travel, and will be understanding of your attempt to limit your costs and maximize your trip. In addition, there may be a benefit simply in providing a reason for the judge or staff to pull an applicant out of a large pile for another (or perhaps the first) review. Regardless of whether this strategy works in every case, it will generally not be held against you as long as you do so politely.

Regarding the scheduling of clerkship interviews, one former law clerk, Bart Epstein, sets forth this general strategy: "When you receive an offer for an interview, call all of your other judges and tell the secretary or clerk that you are putting together an interview trip and would like to see him or her if possible." He then takes the proactive approach one step farther: "While you'll obviously make these calls for judges in the same city as your interview, you should do this even for judges in other cities. Making that phone call gives the judge a signal that some other judge has evaluated you and deemed you worthy of an interview. Let other judges free-ride off of each other's interest in you. At the very least this will get your file percolating and in front of eyeballs. Don't be pushy, though." As another former clerk, Jeannie Sclafani Rhee, aptly advises: "You have to be aggressive to get a clerkship, as aggressive as is civil and polite."

However, in your zeal to strategically schedule your interviews, do not leave your integrity at the door. As always your ethical obligations as a future attorney will be of critical importance to a judge, and thus will impact your future potential as a law clerk. For many lawyers, the judges you will be coming into contact with are people you will be seeing again and again in your career, and any possible short-term gain you might obtain by any small untruth or misleading statement is far outweighed by the risk of detection. A former law clerk supplies us with anecdotal evidence of this point: "Finally, it should go without saying, but always turn square corners during your clerkship search. I personally know a candidate who misleadingly implied he had interviews with some members of a particular court of appeals in order to 'bootstrap' interviews from other members of that court. When one judge figured out what he had done, he informed all his colleagues, and he was basically blackballed from the entire court of appeals."

COMMUNICATIONS WITH CHAMBERS

When scheduling your interview, try to ascertain further information from the law clerk or secretary, such as the expected length of the interview, general format, or other people with whom you will be interviewing. This brings us to an important point worthy of additional emphasis. In all of your dealings with any of the chambers staff in setting up the interview or gathering information beforehand, use extra care to be professional and courteous. Each contact is an opportunity for you to gain key allies, or at least not antagonize potential comrades. All of these contacts with you will impact upon your chances of obtaining that clerkship. (We will talk more about the importance of chambers staff in the interview process below.)

PREPARATION FOR THE INTERVIEW

In your preparation for the interview, you should undergo a second round of research and information gathering for this individual judge. The first type of information to gather concerns the mechanics of the interview. The style, format, and substance of the interview vary greatly with the particular judge. Some judges will take a rigorous tack, grilling you on the substantive law or having you perform writing tasks on the spot. Others will have a more casual approach to see your personality and try to get to know these aspects of you.

Since the expectations and experience of the interview vary so greatly, this is very valuable information to have if at all possible in advance. You may be able to get a sense of the format and approach of this judge in your initial phone conversation with his staff to schedule the interview (*e.g.*, "Do you know how much time I should expect to allot for the interview with the judge?" "Will I be meeting with anyone else?" "Is there anything special I should bring to the interview?").

Again, tread lightly in your inquiry and be careful not to overstep your bounds with this potential interviewer. In addition, ask other people who have interviewed with this judge before to get a better sense of what to expect. It is particularly helpful to talk to former law clerks if you can, or third year students who have been through the process of interviewing with that judge and can indicate what type of procedure that judge has for an interview. To that end, consult whatever resources may be available in your law school regarding this judge and past interviews (*e.g.*, collections of feedback forms from other students and alumni law clerks, if available).

This is now the time to do some extra research and read some of the cases written by the judge, particularly the prominent past ones highlighted in the *Almanac of the Federal Judiciary* for that judge. A broad LEXIS® or WESTLAW® search of the most recent cases decided by this judge would be advisable in gaining an overview of the range of his or her cases. You can also use these resources (and web search engines) to determine whether anything interesting has surfaced about this judge and his or her cases in the media. It is possible that one of these cases or issues may come up in the interview. More likely, however, the style of the judge will be somewhat instilled in your thoughts by reading his or her opinions, which can help you "know" the judge in a more subtle way. If nothing else, you will enter the interview with more confidence since you have prepared to the full extent that you can. Before the interview, it is also a good idea to read through the *Chambers Handbook*, to get a flavor of the atmosphere, ethics and protocol in a judge's chambers, as well as some of the general tasks of a law clerk. (Don't forget to check the resources chapter for this and more.)

Make a packet of all the information you have gathered on this judge, including the biographical and background information gathered in your earlier research. Include in your packet additional copies of your own application materials, which you should also review and be prepared to discuss. If you have any updated information such as new grades, activities or honors, bring them to the interview, along with a list of references and their phone numbers. This can include your published law review article, or an additional writing sample, which you may have held back or not written until now; you may decide to offer it to the judge and possibly discuss it in the interview.

Take this opportunity to contact again the professors and employers who have served as your references, and tell them of your upcoming interview and your desire to clerk for that judge. They may have specific suggestions regarding this judge, or may even offer to call the judge as a follow-up to their letters. In the event that the judge now contacts your references, they will be alerted and prepared to offer additional positive information on your behalf.

DRESS CODE

Dress professionally, as if you were going to a law firm or other employment interview. A good rule of thumb is to view this as your appearance in court and dress accordingly. If the judge or chamber's staff indicates that the dress style in chambers is more casual, this may not apply to you as an applicant. (Moreover, determining the meaning of "casual" to a judge may be difficult; surely this does not include blue jeans, but may instead refer to business pants suits rather than skirts.) It is more prudent to err on the side of formality, as there is recognition that you are a job applicant so this will not be held against you. An overly familiar or casual style of dress, on the other hand, may convey the opposite result as appearing presumptuous or unprofessional.

THE CONTENT OF THE INTERVIEW

As noted above, there is no standard format or uniformity in the content of a clerkship interview. Depending on the judge, the length of the interview may range from 15 minutes to two or more hours. All of the general tips as to interviewing techniques do apply. There are basically two adages to remember here: "know thyself" and "know thy judge"—and be prepared to discuss both.

One important feature that distinguishes a clerkship interview is the highly personalized nature of the relationship between a judge and law clerk, which may be reflected in the interview. For this reason, do not be surprised if the judge asks you a question of a personal nature that might be improper for a law firm or other employer to inquire. Thus, it is perfectly acceptable for the judge to ask what does your father do for a living, or that kind of thing, to get to know you better on a personal level, look for a common interest or even a conflict. Asking about your political views or some other topic usually avoided will be fair game here. Of course, the standard questions about your interests, hobbies, and activities will likely be discussed, but unlike other employers where your answers are simply keeping the conversation going, the judge will truly be interested in your responses to see if one of these interests sparks a common ground for him or her (for example, classical music, cooking, tennis). Knowing these mutual interests first from your research on the judge will be a plus. At this point, the judge will almost certainly be looking for personality and fit—someone who will be comfortable to get along with and interesting to have in chambers, rather than just a brainy law student. Unlike any other employer, practically anything could come up in an interview, within reason, and you will react with more poise (rather than an instinctive alarm and defensiveness) if you are aware of this special nature.

On the other hand, the interview may hold a very legal, substantive discussion, which is why it is best to gather whatever information you can in advance as to the judge, the recent or prominent cases of that judge, and so forth, to enable you to address any of the big issues that may arise. It is not uncommon in the interview for a judge to ask you which of his or her opinions you found most interesting. The interview dialogue could include anything from your courses in law school or your law review topic, to controversial events in the news or important legal precedents. Bear in mind that the judge may be looking for someone who is not afraid to challenge him or her on these issues; this type of intellectual honesty may make you stand out from the crowd of the overly obsequious. Depending on the judge, the legal rigors of the interview could include a writing exercise or some other on-the-spot test of your critical reasoning and writing skills.

Here is some additional interviewing advice from a former law clerk: "Once you're at the interview, the most important factor is connecting with the judge." One way to do this is to read his or her major opinions and be prepared to mention them in casual conversation. "More importantly, if the judge has written anything substantive *read it thoroughly and be prepared to discuss it in depth*. Even if the judge doesn't bring it up, demonstrate that you've not only read his or her writing but that you understand it. The judge is looking for someone who understands and can implement his or her judicial philosophy." This means spending time before the interview learning about the judge and his or her philosophy, and possibly raising it in the interview. "Remember, it is better to be very prepared for five interviews than unprepared for 20."

The broad range of subject matter that could arise in a clerkship interview includes the sample questions listed below. Incidentally, many judges will ask you as well the names of other judges to whom you have applied or with whom you will be interviewing. Be prepared to answer this question directly (and without flinching). If you appear vague and unsure, the judge may draw a negative inference that perhaps you have applied randomly and do not have the conviction to be seeking a clerkship with him or her either. The judge may simply be looking for patterns in your preferences (political direction, geographic concentration) or judicial cronies with whom to compare notes.

SAMPLE QUESTIONS A JUDGE MAY ASK (BUT THE SKY'S THE LIMIT):

Personal Goals and Background

- Why do you want to do a clerkship?
- Why do you want to clerk on this (level and type of) court?
- Why do you want to clerk for *this* judge in particular?
- What are your future career plans for after the clerkship and where, geographically, do you plan to practice?
- What are your goals in life, and how does this clerkship fit within those goals? To that end, what do you wish to learn from this clerkship?

- What courses are you taking now and/or do you plan to take while in law school? What have been your most and least favorite courses?

- Have you participated in Moot Court, trial advocacy or other clinics?

- What has been your journal experience, if any?

- Describe your previous work experiences, and what you liked most or least about each position.

- What type of analytical research and writing skills have you demonstrated in your prior work experience and/or in law school?

- What are your hobbies or interests outside of law school?

- What are your family obligations and commitments (*e.g.*, marital status, parents)? What are the occupations of your parents?

- Where were you born and raised? Do you have any ties to this area (where the court is located)?

Substantive or Legal Topics

- Discuss your law journal note/article. Why did you choose this topic and what did you discover in your research and writing? What was your thesis or argument to the court?

- Be prepared to discuss your writing sample in great detail, including responding to any legal challenges raised by the judge.

- What type of law interests you the most?

- What are your views on [ANY] topic? (This may be a topic of a legal nature, a news item or personal politics.) OR/ What issues concern you most?

- Who is your favorite Supreme Court justice and why? (This is a perennial favorite among many judges.)

- What is your most or least favorite U.S. Supreme Court decision and why? How would you have decided the case differently? Some judges may ask you to comment on specific recent decisions, especially those pertinent to their jurisdiction.

Qualities as a Potential Law Clerk

- Describe your strengths and weaknesses. What qualities do you have which would make you an outstanding law clerk? (Be careful in your answers; the judge will favor an applicant who has traits such as commonsense, integrity, honesty, diligence, camaraderie, and loyalty, but reject one who admits to being a procrastinator, scatterbrain, loquacious, obstinate, or "high maintenance.")

- Are you comfortable under pressure and juggling many different types of tasks? Could you provide some examples from your own life as to these skills?

- How would you approach this case? If I ask you as a law clerk to write up a decision in a particular way and you disagree with the outcome, what will you do? (Note that your initial idea of the "right" answer to this question—"Anything you want, Judge"—may not be what the judge really seeks. Think carefully and respond honestly. For example, you may say that you would present your differing viewpoint to the judge and advocate your position vigorously, but ultimately of course prepare the decision according to the judge's directions.)

THE IMPORTANCE OF CHAMBERS STAFF

In all your contacts with chambers, be sure to be courteous and deferential to the secretary and law clerks—they are interviewing you too and may have the most weight in the judge's decision. Be sensitive to the egalitarian nature of a judge's chambers. Note the critical importance of being a "team player." The judge's secretary will usually have been with the judge for many years and will have a term of employment far beyond any one law clerk. As a result, the judge will most likely consult the secretary in this hiring decision to avoid burdening the secretary with a difficult or demanding clerk.

Sometimes the judge will include the secretary and/or law clerks in the actual interview, while other judges will have this process occur less formally through your interactions with them in chambers. Yet even this apparently casual information and chemistry (whether good or bad) will funnel directly into the judge, to whom the clerks owe the ultimate loyalty. One of the elements they will be looking for is your ability to get along with the others in chambers. So, remember that every member of the chambers staff is an extension of the judge and act appropriately. I have heard of numerous instances of applicants arriving with an attitude of arrogance towards the chamber's staff, or taking a law clerk aside with over-familiarity as to the real "scoop" on this judge. This type of approach essentially guarantees you will not get that clerkship.

In contrast, I still remember my own interview process, chatting with the judge's secretary at length when I arrived (as I naturally do with everyone!) and finding an instant bond with her. It turns out that she sat alongside the judge in the actual interview, which was really quite brief and uneventful. As I discovered later, she had a great deal of influence and an active role in chambers. Her positive words in the judge's ear could only have helped!

Another law clerk describes the importance of this deferential approach to chamber's staff in the interview:

> When you get to the interview treat every member of the judge's staff as if he or she has veto power over your offer. My judge always asks his secretaries what they think of every applicant. Clerkship interviews are not law firm interviews. In a healthy economy a top student from a top law school can probably do 20 half-assed interviews and get 18 offers from big firms. If you go into your clerkship interviews sporting the "I'm in demand" attitude that you developed during firm recruiting you're going to be very disappointed. Two words: thorough and humble.

This clerk further recommends that you "pay attention" in your interviews with the law clerks. "If they like you they often try to telegraph to you what is important to the judge. Also, don't be afraid to ask them what things are most important to the judge. Be yourself, but emphasize those things that the judge is looking for. The clerks are looking to see if you are something special." Thus, taking care not to offend the secretary and law clerks, and if possible developing a rapport with them, can be a sure route to the judge's heart.

Of course, you may still ask a few intelligent and discreet questions of the judges and the law clerks, and indeed, it is generally a good idea to do so to show your thoughtfulness and interest. I have included some suggested questions below. Try to divide them up among the people you talk to, or select only a handful of the ones most compelling for you—don't bombard the judge with too much of an inquisition!

SAMPLE QUESTIONS TO ASK THE JUDGE OR AREAS TO INVESTIGATE WITH THE CLERKS (TACTFULLY OF COURSE):

- What is the typical day like for a law clerk?
- How hard do the clerks work and what hours? (Some work most weekends and many evenings, and others almost none.) If there is weekend work, is the judge working there too, by your side?
- What is the division of labor/cases, including the different types of tasks? What are the primary responsibilities of a law clerk?
- Does the judge believe in all written opinions or does he or she make oral decisions from the bench? This will affect the workload (more if all opinions are formally written) and pace of work (faster and more intense if bench memos must be of a level that the judge can rule from the bench) for the law clerk.
- How do opinions get written? Does the judge or clerk write the first draft? How many drafts does the judge usually require? Does the judge heavily edit the drafts or not at all? Sometimes you would prefer to have a judge who will edit your work and improve upon it, rather than leave you with the tremendous burden of knowing your work will be filed and published directly without much written input from the judge.

- Does the judge work closely with the clerks on cases on an ongoing basis or only periodic more formal meetings?

- As a corollary of this, how accessible is the judge to the clerks? Do the clerks communicate with the judge predominantly on paper or in person?

- How much time do the law clerks spend in the courtroom? Do the law clerks attend oral argument or settlement conferences with the judge?

- How much contact do the clerks have with the attorneys? Do they have the authority to give extensions or to resolve disputes between the litigants by phone?

- Does the judge take an interest or get involved in the clerks' personal lives (for good or bad)?

- What are the judge's outside interests and commitments, and how does the law clerk figure into those? This includes tennis, judging Moot Courts, and giving (i.e., writing) speeches. (You might also be able to get a sense of these interests from evidence in chambers and be able to convey your observations.) At the very least, the lack of such activities may indicate that the judge spends the bulk of the work day (and night?) working in chambers.

- Does the judge take the law clerks when traveling to other courthouses, events or conferences? How often does the judge sit elsewhere or have additional travel?

- Are there contacts, periodic outings with present and former clerks—the maintenance of an "extended family"? If so, this can be an indication of a good long-term mentor relationship with the judge.

- Be observant and try to get a sense of the atmosphere in chambers. Do the law clerks look tense and overwhelmed, or like they are enjoying themselves? How does the judge interact with them?

- Take note of the physical layout of the law clerks' offices and their proximity to the judge. Are they all confined to the same space? Does this hamper effectiveness or contribute to a good working environment with a sense of camaraderie and an ongoing exchange of ideas?

- How many other clerks (or judges) are there in the building? Do the law clerks have a great deal of working contact (or socializing) with the clerks of other judges, or is there a sense of isolation within chambers and the courthouse?

- What are the types of cases and what is the size of the docket? Look for signs of big case backlog (*e.g.*, if there is a motion table, check out the size of the piles).

- How well organized does the chambers seem? (A lack of order can significantly impact the daily clerkship experience.)

- Regarding the hiring of law clerks: What qualities does the judge look for in a law clerk? What is the judge's timetable for making a decision?

In addition, you can ask the judge about his or her opinions in specific cases that you have read, and how he or she reached these decisions. Your interest in the job can also be conveyed by asking about the role of the law clerks in reaching the decisions and assisting with the opinions. If the interview is following an intellectual track, a thoughtful discussion might ensue from an inquiry into his or her favorite case, most difficult decision or most surprising jury verdict. A query about the judge's longest and shortest trial and whether they were typical in this regard might give you a sense of the flow of cases as well as some interesting war stories. (Hint: Judges typically like to talk about their cases and their views on a variety of topics.) Aside from information gathering, your goal should be to appear enthusiastic, pleasant, and articulate—in short, your best professional (and personal) self.

As the Honorable Lisa M. Smith, U.S. Magistrate Judge for the Southern District of New York, advises, an applicant should prepare for the interview by researching the judge through a plethora of sources, and demonstrate that preparation:

> Any candidate should also think about some questions that would be appropriate to ask the judge—one question to ask a

Magistrate Judge would be what percentage of the caseload results in trials, as the answer will be different from judge to judge—because the judge will probably give the candidate an opportunity to ask questions, and a failure to ask any questions will give the appearance that the candidate is not fully prepared. These are just a few suggested ways to prepare for an interview with a judge. Every judge likes to think that an applicant has prepared for the interview, and is organized enough to have found the time to do so.

Finally, be prepared when you go into that interview to accept an offer if you are fortunate enough to have one extended to you. (Incidentally, this may happen on the spot, as we will discuss in a few moments.) If you have done the necessary research before this point and up to now, you should be walking into an interview with a judge for whom you would be happy to clerk. Hopefully you have weeded out any judges from your initial list for whom you would not want to clerk *before* you sent out your applications, or before the interview. If something unusual or offensive does arise in the interview and you suddenly discover you do *not* want to clerk for that judge, there is a protocol you must follow to withdraw your application promptly. Generally, you do not have to do this directly to the judge on the spot, but should call chambers immediately upon your return. In withdrawing your application with that judge, you need not furnish a reason. Although often the feeling of a negative interview will be mutual, do not wait to see first if you will receive an offer from that judge; this might put you in a difficult situation of turning down an offer from a judge, which is taboo. The intricacies involved in the timing of the offers and acceptances will be discussed below.

THANK-YOU LETTERS AND FOLLOW-UP

As a practical matter, the timing of the process may not give you the opportunity to send a thank-you note or letter before the judge has made a decision. However, if at all possible in terms of timing, you should follow the etiquette of sending a brief follow-up letter very promptly. Since judges typically do not send you a formal letter on the status of your application, you may need to make a diffident follow-up call to chambers to ascertain this information. Take this opportunity for a casual chat to reiterate your interest in the judge and/or your pleasure in meeting the secretary/law clerk; hopefully your potential ally may be able to tip the scale in your direction with the judge. (However, do not call the chambers repeatedly; I have witnessed an occasional applicant do so, be labeled by the secretary as a nuisance, and summarily dismissed by the judge.) Additionally, if you do have the good fortune to receive and accept an offer, you must send a letter to all of the other judges withdrawing your applications for a clerkship with them.

COSTS OF THE APPLICATION AND INTERVIEWING PROCESS

It should be acknowledged that many students experience financial burdens in the course of the clerkship application process. This may occur to some extent from the cost of calling judges' chambers and mailing application packets, but is more likely the result of the interview process, where they are often called upon—if they are among the lucky ones, that is—to fly across the country on short notice with high plane fares and hotel bills. As a result, some applicants may adjust their application strategies to apply only to local judges or employ other tactics to limit their interview expenses.

While a few judges, especially in remote places, may interview you by phone, most judges will require an in-person interview. Unlike other employers, judges cannot pay for your visiting them to interview for a position. If selected to interview, you will likely bear all the costs associated with that visit, including airfare, hotel and/or rental car. If you do need financial assistance in order to apply for a judicial clerkship, be sure to check with your school to see what forms of financial help are available. Although over 40% of career services offices provide no financial assistance to students in connection with the clerkship application and interview process, almost one-quarter supply phone access for long-distance calls, and some cover postage for applications, or "other" expenses, including copying, fax, travel loans for interviews, computer and printer use.[2] You should of course investigate which of these services and subsidies, if any, may be offered by your school.

According to the National Clerkship Study, the financial burdens of applying for a judicial clerkship did not appear to be as burdensome for students as had been commonly believed.[3] For example, when students were asked to assess their total clerkship interviewing costs (*i.e.*, airfare, lodging), *exclusive* of costs that would have been incurred anyway such as travel home during a school break, the vast majority (73%) responded that these costs fell in the lowest cost level ($0–500). (However, these students may have practiced some of the cost-saving measures suggested below.) As with their selection of courts, the financial factor did not appear to be their most significant concern during the application process. Yet others in their general comments did point to the expensive nature of the clerkship application and interview process as a reason for their dissatisfaction:

- "I am very happy with the clerkship I got, but the process was an expensive, unorganized nightmare."
- "The only difficulties are the personal expense and lack of structure to the process. But I feel it was worth it."
- "Some students who are very deserving of clerkships have spent $3000-$4000 and gotten nothing. Something needs to be done about the costs. Many judges could cooperate in their interviewing and do regional 'interview weekends' so students wouldn't have to make so many trips."

When asked whether the costs related to the application process affected their choices, the majority (67%) of the law clerks surveyed responded that costs did not affect their choices during the application process.[4] A relatively small percentage, 17%, applied to fewer judges as a consequence of the cost, 16% applied or interviewed primarily with local judges, and 6% accepted fewer invitations to interview. Others complained of the expense and difficulty of arranging their travel for interviews on short notice.

While this may seem a bit overwhelming, there are ways to reduce expenses. If you apply early enough, you may be able combine an interview trip with a trip home for the holidays or to visit friends and relatives, minimizing airfare and hotel expenses. You may avoid car rental costs if the court is located in a metropolitan area; you can stay near the judge's chambers and plan to walk, take public transportation, or a short taxi ride to the interview. It may help to know that, in recognition of the difficulty of interview costs, many judges are receptive to your efforts to schedule your interviews in one city together. For this reason, you may include in your cover letter the dates during which you will be in that town, *e.g.*, for a school break to visit family and friends. A phone call to chambers politely informing the judge's staff of your plans to be in the area on certain dates for other interviews may also be favorably received (if that city is relatively far from your law school, that is)—and, remember, may confer the added benefit of encouraging the judge to pull your application off the pile to review!

Finally, as with any other expenses associated with law school, you should view this as part of the cost of investing in your legal career. For most students, these short-term expenses will be far outweighed by the long-term benefits—and thus well worth the ultimate prize.

OFFERS AND ACCEPTANCES

Offers and acceptances may occur very quickly, depending on the judge. Some judges will present an offer to an applicant on the spot at the interview or call soon thereafter. (Notice again that this would mean the applicants scheduled for later interviews might have the clerkship evaporate for them before they have an opportunity to interview. To avoid this risk, you should take the earliest interview slot offered with that judge.) Others will wait until they have interviewed a few of the other candidates first. They may give you an idea of their procedure and expected timeframe at your interview. In any event, the judge will usually call you personally to make the offer.

Most importantly, know that this is not like any other process you have ever gone through. It is not like applying for a position at a law firm, for instance, where you collect up all of your offers and then look at them, make inquiries or go back for more information, reevaluate, and then decide where you want to go. It is not like that at all.

THE RISK OF "EXPLODING" OFFERS

Judges vary as to the timeframe they will allow for your response to their offer. It is not uncommon for a judge to expect you to give an immediate, enthusiastic acceptance of their offer for a clerkship. Some will be more sensitive to your need to run this by a spouse or significant other, and perhaps give you 24 hours or more to decide. For a time, this minimum 24-hour window was strongly urged in a letter to the federal judiciary by the law school deans, but there have never been binding guidelines on this required of the judges (*see* Chapter 2 for some background on the timing issue).

However, you should be forewarned that many judges give what has been called an "exploding offer," meaning that he (or she) who hesitates is lost. Some judges will really react negatively to being told, "Sorry, I have to think it over," or "Can I have until tomorrow?" or even, "Can I have until the end of the day?" If one of these judges perceives hesitancy or reluctance on your part instead of an immediate acceptance, said judge may be offended and rescind the offer forthwith. Unfortunately, this puts a great deal of pressure on the student who may love this judge, but may have some other personal factors to consider. If you need to consider some special issues, plan to do so in advance. While I am not saying this practice is followed by a majority of judges, students have to be very careful going in to the interview that this might be that kind of situation, and be alerted to the danger. You may be able to determine through your earlier research the practices of a judge in this regard, or may gauge a sense of the judge's attitude on this at the time the offer is presented. In any event, being educated on this practice and prepared to give your response will save you from potential disaster. Most students do accept the first offer they receive.

Fortunately, we now have some statistics as to the prevalence of this experience. Students in the National Judicial Clerkship Study reported that judges generally give applicants more time to respond to clerkship offers than has been widely perceived. While the time period can range from "more than 1 month" to "on the spot," depending on the judge and circumstances, the response time most often described—identified by approximately one-third of the students—was "2 days to 1 week." Still, students frequently reported "on the spot" responses to offers as the least amount of time given, and often even as the most amount of time given. Some students expressed frustration with the time pressure they experienced in scheduling their interviews and responding to an offer. Many of the students did not answer this question, noting that they chose to accept the offer on the spot and withdraw all other applications.

For several students, the time pressure in responding to the clerkship offer negatively impacted their application experiences, as illustrated by these sample comments:[5]

- "I had under 24 hours to decide, had to cancel interviews and make my decision before knowing what my other options would have been. Also, because of the timing issue my year was total chaos."
- "I found the lack of any deadlines very frustrating, as did many students. I was also disappointed with the short amount of time judges give to make up your mind after they extend offers. I had two appellate court interviews scheduled, but had to withdraw my applications because I was offered a district court clerkship and did not have time to interview with the two appellate courts."

Again, this process is like no other. Thus, you should not expect to experience a smorgasbord of interviews throughout the judiciary. At this point, take your interviews and offer(s) as they come.

THE ETIQUETTE OF ACCEPTANCES

Now I am not saying that you could *never* turn down an offer from a judge, but you need to have a *very* good reason in order to do so, and to be alerted in advance to the potential consequences of your action.

Most law schools will tell you not to turn down a clerkship offer from a judge, and this is generally sound advice. Keep in mind their institutional reason for this policy as well, since your actions may jeopardize the chances of other students from your law school (because "those students from X law school are too arrogant or misadvised"). How you conduct yourself in this process reflects on your school as well as yourself. One can never tell how far the wrath of a judge scorned will extend and exactly what the consequences will be, for you or for others. For instance, many judges are acquainted with judges beyond their court, and may communicate with them. At the very least, if you turn down a judge, you can pretty much assume that you will be persona non grata on his or her entire court. Such a rejection for them occurs relatively rarely, and the judges do talk (particularly if offended or angered). In fact, once an offer has been made, many judges on the same court will refrain from making that applicant an offer to avoid stealing a clerk from a colleague. Loyalty of course runs high among judges, because while a law clerk may come and go, they will be sharing the bench with their colleagues for numerous years—for many, a lifetime. As a result, most judges would not risk offending one of their own, or placing themselves in an awkward position by hiring that law clerk for the year.

Once again, this potential dilemma is the ultimate reason that you must research and choose carefully at the outset. If you do your investigation diligently in advance, you will avoid applying to a judge for whom you would not want to clerk. Moreover, as noted above, if something comes up in your interview and you realize belatedly that clerking for this judge would be out of the question, the proper etiquette is to withdraw your application. This action circumvents the uncomfortable situation of having to turn down an offer. As one wise former clerk for the U.S. Court of Appeals and U.S. Supreme Court cautions, "Applicants should take care to choose carefully in deciding which judges to apply to. Some judges can be ogres to work with. If judges offer you a clerkship, it is very difficult to decline without being blackballed among some of their colleagues. Thus, it is advisable to learn as much as possible about them beforehand, and only apply to judges with whom you actually would be willing to work." In a variation of the wave theory, he recommends applying to the judges you most want to work with first, and wait until later to apply to judges who would come farther down your list. "That way, you won't find yourself turning down a judge you would have preferred to work for because you had no alternative to accepting an offer from a judge you didn't like as much."

The National Clerkship Study confirms the universal belief that most students do not decline the clerkship offer.[6] Over two-thirds of the student group, 68%, did not decline any clerkship offers. Of those who did decline offers, the predominant reason given by 82% was that the student had accepted an offer from another judge. (It was noted that most the law schools instruct their students to withdraw all other applications upon accepting a clerkship offer from a judge.) In that extensive student pool, a handful of students gave as their reason that they did not want to clerk for this particular judge, and a few that they had decided not to do a judicial clerkship after all. Only one student identified financial constraint (*i.e.*, educational and consumer debt) as the reason for declining a clerkship offer. Thus, simply turning down a judge is not something any of them would have done lightly.

If you do find yourself in an untenable position and must turn down the offer, do so with extreme care and hope for the best. No one can force you to work for someone whom you simply cannot tolerate or for some other compelling reason would find working for impossible. However, do not take this action without due consideration or merely as a matter of strategy. You need to enter the process knowing that it is unlike any other you have experienced—certainly not comparable to the law firm interview process with its structured timing guidelines and the weighing of multiple offers. A clerkship interview and offer are much more personal and seldom bestowed; as a consequence, this process requires more forethought and care. If you attempt to play the game of parlaying your offer, or waiting for an offer from one of your more "highly ranked" judges, you do so at tremendous peril. Judges do not appreciate such crass attempts at maneuvering. You should weigh against the possible benefits that you could gain by asking for time to decide whether to accept an offer, or rejecting an offer hoping that something better will come along, the tremendous opportunity you might miss. In hesitating to accept an offer on the spot, you may have tossed away your chance of a valuable judicial clerkship. At the very least, you will now be aware of the risk.

Hopefully, though, you will have avoided this problem by following the ample advice throughout this book and by doing your research well. Some element of fate will do the rest and bring you to this moment. If so, you should be thrilled to receive an offer to work for this judge and have set the stage for a positive clerkship experience!

By the way, as noted above, once you do accept an offer for a clerkship, the established protocol requires you to withdraw all of your applications with other judges promptly. This is not only for the sake of the other applicants, but to avoid potential embarrassment for those judges and yourself (*i.e.*, so they will not subsequently call and present you with an offer that you must decline). In addition, you should confirm your acceptance with the judge in writing (with thanks, appreciation, and a note that you are looking forward to a wonderful year, etc.). Of course, your law school and your references will also want a timely report of this positive outcome.

ALTERNATE OUTCOMES: ENCOURAGING ANOTHER TRY

If at first you don't succeed, I would say first check to see if you really haven't succeeded. Oftentimes the grapevine is running rampant; everybody is talking about clerkships and a student feels completely left out, lamenting, "I haven't had a call, I haven't had interviews, it's over and I don't have a clerkship." This is not necessarily sound reasoning. Unless you have called the chambers of the judges where you have submitted applications, you cannot be sure it is truly over. Unlike other application processes, the judges do not routinely send letters informing you of the status (or even the rejection) of your application. Rarely in all this does a judge send a letter stating, "I'm sorry, I've hired someone else." If you schedule an interview with a judge and that judge extends an offer to someone else who accepts the offer, then you will receive a letter or phone call from chambers informing you that your interview has, as a consequence, been canceled. If you have not reached that stage, however, you may not even hear from the judge at all. Some of the uncertainty may be a reflection of a later timeline for some judges and areas of the country, particularly given the current state of fluctuation as to individual judges' deadlines and procedures. So I encourage students to call chambers and find out if these judges are still considering applications, scheduling interviews and so forth. That is the first step to conclude whether in fact it is "over" for this round.

THE EVALUATION PROCESS

Next comes an evaluation process to assess the possible reasons for this less-than-stellar outcome. The evaluation process is a personal assessment first of yourself to see if maybe, under the circumstances of your academic record, you aimed too high and applied to only the most competitive judges and courts. Perhaps one of the elements of your application lacked a necessary quality, such as errors in your cover letter or a deficient or inappropriate writing sample. The fault may lie in the process itself. Examine the facts to determine, for instance, whether all of your professors sent in their letters of recommendation on time. Sometimes it is something of a mechanical nature like that, which can be very frustrating, or a recommendation letter may have been weak; these facts are important to ascertain so that you can know whom to avoid in the future in asking for a reference. Accordingly, you should try to gather this information and feedback, if at all possible (even from the judge's law clerks), to see which if any element of your application was the cause to overcome in the future.

On the other hand, if you did receive invitations to interview, perhaps the outcome was determined at the interview stage. Of course, if you never had the opportunity actually to go to the interview due to a cancellation by the judge, it may simply have been "dumb luck" and the misfortune of the interview schedule. (If you can next time, try to schedule your interview in the earliest available slot.) If you did receive and attend several interviews, none of which panned out, chances are your application itself was successful in that it led you to that point. You will need to reevaluate the interview itself, to determine whether you felt prepared and conveyed a true sense of your personality and merits. If not, try to practice and work on that for next time. Maybe you simply did not find a chemistry with any of these judges, but there are more out there with whom you may strike a better match.

THE RANDOM FACTOR / ELEMENT OF FATE

The other thing is what I call the random factor, or the element of fate, because sometimes you are a wonderful candidate for a clerkship and it just fails to happen this time. There is a lot of uncertainty in the process, and with so many applicants, the judges simply may not review all of the applications in depth. One never knows what will catch the attention of a particular judge and pull that applicant from the pile. Once someone has met a certain academic threshold, it could be a particular interest or common background with the judge. Or maybe an applicant's phone call sparked an interest by chambers staff or the judge. Some of it is political and happenstance, such as which professor happens to be that judge's good acquaintance and which student does that professor recommend. Perhaps a professor or colleague called the judge on that day (or vice versa) and recommended someone on the interview schedule. That really could be all it is.

It might help somewhat to look at this process for a moment from the perspective of a judge. One prominent Circuit Court judge noted that he receives 300 applications that arrive in parts with separate envelopes, amounting to roughly 1200 pieces of paper, during a very short period of time. "So there is an arbitrariness of the process that simply cannot be helped. We don't stop hearing cases to assemble 1200 pieces of mail." He explained to students, "You have to understand the process if you think you are being treated overly curtly. There is no way to write a good letter saying 'I'm not even going to bother interviewing you,' and I would be writing over 280 such letters every year! It is a process with a lot of arbitrary aspects in it and there isn't much we can do about it."

Of the students in the National Judicial Clerkship Study who were unsuccessful in their clerkship applications, over half believed that the reason was the arbitrary nature of the application process. One student lamented: "I really do not know why I was rejected. That, I think, is the worst part because I thought I had all the right qualifications."[7] There may be nothing you have done wrong, but it simply did not work out for you with these judges under these particular circumstances. If this is the scenario, the random element may work with you the next time to determine your fate with a more positive outcome.

This factor is important to recognize and, to some extent, to accept and hope for the best. You can only control that which you can control; the rest is out of your hands and perhaps even out of the hands of the judges. Do what you can—and try not to fret about the rest! With the increased uncertainty from the lack of uniform guidelines, this random factor is likely to increase. In the current trend of earlier application dates, judges are hiring up to two years in advance students who have not had much of an opportunity to develop an academic record, law school activities or significant professional work experience. This means that they cannot possibly know that they are hiring the "best and brightest" clerks. One can only hope that, if this hiring decision based on the unknown begins to impact negatively on the judges' pool of law clerks as they ultimately begin their clerkships, additional reforms may succeed. Meanwhile, one can view the arbitrariness, in an odd way, as *somewhat* of a universal equalizer. With this book in hand, however, you will have the best chance of mastering the application process!

CHANGING YOUR OUTCOME: RENEW YOUR STRATEGY AND APPLY AGAIN

Maybe there is another clerkship opportunity out there that you previously did not consider or one that has just become available (*e.g.*, a newly confirmed judge, or unforeseen circumstances causing a law clerk to leave or withdraw his or her acceptance). Perhaps this is the clerkship that you were meant to have and is right for you. Keep exploring the sources discussed previously for other types of clerkships and courts. For instance, you can search by application date the web databases (*Federal Law Clerk Information System, NALP Judicial Clerkship Directory* on-line at LEXIS®), the letters from judges posted at your school, and web sources for new confirmations, as well as the links in www.judicialclerkships.com. Consider applying for state court clerkships, which often have later application dates (check state court websites, Vermont Law School's *Guide to State Judicial Clerkship Procedures*, or call the court or judge directly). In addition, let your contacts (career center, professors, attorneys in practice, friends who are currently clerking) know that you are still looking and to be on the alert for new clerkship openings. Update and revamp the elements of your application so that you will be ready to reapply as soon as one of these clerkship positions surfaces.

Depending on the timing, your secondary application process may take the form of a second "wave" of applications, or a few select applications as new positions arise. As we discuss in more detail below, you may even choose to apply for a clerkship again in your third year of law school or later, for a position that starts one year or more after graduation. At that point, your application will likely be stronger, with additional grades and activities, more work experience, and professors who know you better. Note also that some judges and courts do select as late as the third year of law school for clerkship positions in the same year, *i.e.*, commencing immediately upon graduation.

The story of one former law clerk might be illustrative here. Josh Cohen was in the spring of his third year of law school with a law firm job lined up, but felt somehow that he had let the clerkship boat pass him by. He saw a posting for a position at the Ninth Circuit Court of Appeals for a "Court Law Clerk" (a predecessor for "Staff Attorney," as they are now called) for the *upcoming* fall and decided at the last minute to go for it. As he told me at length with enthusiasm, this position quite unexpectedly turned out to be an exciting and unique experience. The clerks rotated through the court doing the substantive work of a law clerk, but for all of the judges. Occasionally, a judge would ask for the same clerk and "adopt" him or her; this happened for him, and he found himself working face to face with two very different and quite prominent judges—at that time, Judge Anthony M. Kennedy (before he was appointed to the U.S. Supreme Court) and Judge Harry Pregerson (who was of the opposite political persuasion). Working behind the scenes for them was indeed remarkable. (He could have kept me entertained for hours with his stories about his work for them and the court, but unfortunately it was time to leave that dinner party!) Now 20 years later, even as a successful non-litigation attorney in New York City, he still raves about his experience as a Court Law Clerk as the best! Three lessons can be learned here: (1) it is never too late to grab a clerkship; (2) even if you pick a clerkship that is lesser known or different, you may be surprised by how great the experience will turn out to be; and (3) you don't even have to be a litigator!

So reevaluate your particular situation—your application process and experiences, and anything you have learned if you were fortunate to get feedback from the judges, law clerks, or fellow students along the way—and try again! You certainly have nothing to lose; years down the road, the application process will be but a dim memory while your ultimate clerkship experience will stay with you forever.

CLERKING A YEAR OR MORE AFTER LAW SCHOOL

I have decided to devote an entire section to this subject because it is an alternate path worthy of emphasis yet so often forgotten. For those of you who are no longer in law school—or third-year students contemplating being in that situation when you would begin your potential clerkship—take heart. The possibilities of a judicial clerkship can still be yours.

In fact, there is an increasing trend towards judges preferring clerks with post-graduation legal experience. Many judges are very receptive to having somebody coming out of private practice, public interest or government employment. As one federal District Court judge told me he has discovered about the desirability of clerks with a year or two of such experience: "They know the discipline of an office. They are responsible, and they have their feet on the ground."

Certain types of federal judges, such as Magistrate and Bankruptcy Court judges, are more likely to follow this approach or to hire permanent clerks (another trend), since they are only allotted one law clerk, or in the alternative, may opt for a second law clerk instead of a secretary. An experienced law clerk for them would be most beneficial. In addition, many state courts do not accept students straight out of law school but actually require prior work experience; many of those state judges as well follow the trend of maintaining permanent law clerks.

This practice is particularly common with newly appointed judges, who often recognize the benefit of compensating for their own inexperience as judges by taking on a law clerk who has prior experience in law practice or as a law clerk for another judge. Note that judges appointed from the private sector will often take with them an associate from their law firm for that first critical year. In general, both law clerks and judges are becoming progressively more aware of the value of having some experience in a law practice prior to entering a clerkship.

I can verify the benefits of this trend from my own personal experience, having done it both ways, first directly after law school and then several years later as a Permanent Law Clerk for the same District Court judge. As is typical, I found having a clerkship right after law school to be very overwhelming for quite a while, when you realize how much the judge is relying upon your work and how little you seem to know. In contrast, when I went back to my judge years later it was genuinely refreshing. After my time in private practice as an associate in a large New York City law firm, I had gained a greater appreciation of the ability and freedom to have such a large role in the decisions and an impact upon the law, without feeling unduly burdened by this responsibility. I could now roll up my sleeves and delve through a huge stack of papers, cutting right through it to the fundamental essence of the issues and solutions. To this day, I am not sure whether this difference in my reasoning and perceptions was age, maturity, or just plain experience. Moreover, I have had co-clerks who were in practice first for a year or two before entering their clerkships, and I felt very appreciative of their generally higher abilities, confidence, and skill level in comparison to my co-clerks who came straight from law school. Over the years with my judge, I had the pleasure of working with a total of five co-clerks, so I have a personal yardstick to measure the fact that such experience truly made a considerable difference.

Why pursue a clerkship later? Oftentimes students were unaware of the value of a clerkship during the prime application season in their second (or third) year of law school. Either they realize the desirability of a clerkship in their third year, after watching their friends go through the process, or even once they have entered a law firm (for the summer or post-graduation) and observe the premium placed on judicial law clerks there. Perhaps they have heard that clerkships are great, regret they did not do it, and choose to look for one after all.

Some pursue this path for financial reasons, choosing to work for a year or two for a more high-paying employer, and then come in at a higher clerkship salary by receiving credit for the additional work experience and possibly receiving the benefit of the federal salary matching program (*see* Chapter 9 on financial aspects). On the other hand, if you wait too many years, you may not want to leave the increased salary or partnership-track advancement of your law practice. Depending on your law firm or other employer, the support you receive for such a decision may wane with the years. (Many of the same firms who will support your leave of absence for a clerkship in the early years of your association with them, when they would benefit most greatly from your experience as a judicial clerk, would discourage such an action years later when they have invested more in your legal training, plan to scrutinize your work in the remaining year or two towards partnership, and would be risking more if you failed to return to the firm.)

Some attorneys choose a later clerkship for an entirely different reason—to transition from a career path that they are seeking to leave (thus "saving face" and raising fewer questions as to why they left their law firm). Or, perhaps they wish to change geographic areas entirely. I have had several experienced attorneys call me for advice in obtaining a clerkship when desiring to leave their law firms or to explore another city or region. A judicial clerkship may offer them the best opportunity to get to know the local laws and procedures, as well as the attorneys and employment opportunities in that area. The added credential of this clerkship then aids in the acquisition of their post-clerkship employment.

You may even choose to apply for a clerkship again in your third year of law school or even after graduation, due to an improvement in your academic record or overall credentials. Regardless of whether you applied for a clerkship previously (*e.g.*, as a second year law student) or came to this decision later, the farther out you are in your law school career, your application will likely be stronger, with additional grades and activities, more work experience, and professors who know you better. Pursuing this clerkship and having it on your resume may even help you obtain your first post-graduation employment. Conversely, if you have (or will have at the time you enter the clerkship) a year or two of law practice under your belt, this will make you even more attractive to a judge.

Then there are those who return to clerking again and again as an alternative to other forms of practicing law. I found interesting the story of Patricia DeJuneas, who pursued three successive clerkships—first in state appellate court, then in federal court for a Magistrate Judge, after practicing in a law firm and government work for two years in between, and next for a judge in a District Court across the country. Reflecting upon the issue of clerking years out of law school, she had this to say: "I have enjoyed both clerkships tremendously and found them to be VERY different experiences . . . The variety of cases and issues keeps the job very interesting and challenging even though I'm now four years out of law school. I think that having had the opportunity to practice for a couple of years has made this experience much more valuable to me than if I came here right out of law school." After being in law practice, she appreciated the fact that clerking at the trial court level gave her a great overall view of litigation and exposed her to all levels of litigation practice. She explained, "I have participated in everything from informal chambers conferences and mediations to jury and bench trials. I have been able to improve upon not only my research and writing skills, but I have also acquired better judgment in assessing cases and developing litigation strategies." She commented on the value of these clerkships in terms of a law practice: "I think the first clerkship [for a state appellate court judge] helped me with private practice to the extent that it improved upon my research and writing. I think the second one would prove to be more valuable than the first, however, in terms of private practice. The pace of this one is much more akin to that in a firm and there are so many different aspects of litigation that I deal with on a daily basis."

Addressing the issue of prior work experience, Ms. DeJuneas confirmed my observations: "I have also found that many magistrate judges preferred experienced candidates—most are only allowed one law clerk and there is not much time for training. I'd highly recommend such a clerkship to a lawyer who has been practicing for a year or two. The experience is undeniably an asset to anyone who wants to continue to practice." Yes, in case you are curious, I did ask her why she had pursued another clerkship and whether she seemed destined to clerk forever. Here is her response: "I did a second clerkship because I don't particularly care for private practice. I like the objectivity of this job as opposed to being an advocate. And I hate billing!!"

Another law clerk spoke highly of the sequence she pursued, entering private practice for a year before her clerkship. Sherene Hannon applied for and received her clerkship during her third year of law school and, after practicing in a law firm for the first year after graduation, took a leave of absence from the firm to pursue her clerkship. Although she was aware of the prestige associated with being a federal clerk, she was hesitant about leaving the firm because she felt that such an interruption could have negative implications. "Despite my temporary misgivings, however, all of the associates and partners at the firm, particularly those who had clerked themselves, were extremely encouraging about my clerkship. Everyone expressed the value which they believed I would add upon my return from my year as a clerk." She discovered as well the lasting impact of gaining a judicial mentor and contacts that boost your legal career. "The network of colleagues which a clerk develops is extremely beneficial as the clerk's career progresses. Every law clerk becomes part of an established tradition and a judicial family of law clerks and judges throughout the country."

So, keep in mind the option of applying (or reapplying) upon gaining some valuable work experience after law school, and pursuing a non-traditional path. Remember, it's never too late to do a judicial clerkship!

Notes

1. NALP Report at 68–69, Table 53.
2. NALP Report at 40; Table 23.
3. *Id.* at 55.
4. *Id.* at 71. *See also* Table 57.
5. *See* Table 43, NALP Report at 58–59.
6. NALP Report at 59, Table 44.
7. NALP Report at 48. *See* Chapter 2 for a further discussion of the keys for success.

CHAPTER
nine

What Do Clerks Earn?

A word on the financial aspects is called for here. Much ado has been made about the financial sacrifice of a judicial clerkship, as this has generally been considered the biggest disadvantage of clerking. One must recognize the existence of a financial differential between a clerkship salary and other post-graduation employment such as large law firms. This salary gap, in combination with a considerable educational debt, may deter some students from applying for a judicial clerkship in the first instance. We will look more closely at each of these aspects and explore the avenues that might be available to assist you in surmounting your financial constraints. So, what do clerks really earn?

CLERKSHIP SALARY

· Federal

For federal clerkships, there is a salary range that depends upon the law clerk's legal work experience subsequent to graduation from law school and bar membership, as well as the degree to which each individual judge will interpret the qualifications of the law clerk in executing the appropriate paperwork. By the time of appointment to a law clerk position, the candidate must be a law school graduate or be certified as having completed all law school studies and requirements and merely awaiting conferment of degree. Generally, federal law clerks who begin their clerkships directly upon graduation from law school qualify for a JSP–11 level salary under the federal government judicial pay scale. For current clerks, this level corresponds to a minimum of $43,326.[1] The salary for federal law clerks entering their clerkships after one year of legal work experience post-graduation is typically in the JSP–12 range; currently this level corresponds to a minimum of $51,927. This salary level would also apply to the second year of a two-year clerkship. If a law clerk has post-graduate work experience as a federal judicial law clerk, the salary could range between $51,927 and $94,862. There is also an advantageous salary matching program—if you worked for a year at a law firm before clerking and made $100,000 or more, you may be able to boost your clerkship salary to the $65,000 to $70,000 area. Keep in mind as well that the federal pay scale increases every year by cost of living allowances and periodic raises; accordingly, the exact dollar equivalents of this scale will be proportionately higher by the time you enter your clerkship.

However, it actually gets a little more complicated than that. Here is some of the additional minutia in the salary determination. There are locality pay differentials added for areas in which the cost of living exceeds the national average; so, depending on the location of your clerkship, a certain percentage increase based on the local cost of living may be added to these base numbers. These figures represent the minimum step within each level. Each grade has 10 steps, and law clerks directly out of law school generally start at the first step within the grade. Law clerks appointed for more than one year who have at least one year legal work experience, bar membership, and a current salary higher than the first step of the appointment grade may be eligible for a higher salary within the appointment grade. For instance, in the discretion of the judge, law clerks can receive a salary increase along the scale once they are admitted to the bar.

Certain educational criteria may be substituted for one year of legal work experience.[2] Now, if you *really* want to know everything on this subject, it works like this. Technically, graduating from law school with no previous years of legal work experience falls into the category of JSP-9. However, most new graduates entering their clerkships directly from law school will find that their judge considers certain "educational substitutions" to be applicable and thus will be eligible for the level JSP-11. For example, you will be considered to have qualified for JSP-11 if you have standing within the upper third of the class from a law school on the approved list of the American Bar Association or that of the Association of American Law Schools; or experience on the editorial board of a law review of such a school; or graduation from a law school on the approved list of the American Bar Association or that of the Association of American Law Schools with an LLM degree; or demonstrated proficiency in legal studies which, in the opinion of the appointing judge, is the equivalent of the above. The following are examples of criteria which are considered as equivalent:

(1) Publication of a noteworthy article in a law school student publication or other scholarly publication; or

(2) Special high-level honors for academic excellence in law school, such as election to the Order of the Coif; or

(3) Winning of a Moot Court competition or membership on a Moot Court team that represents the law school in competition with other law schools; or

(4) Participation in the legal aid or other law school clinical program sanctioned by the law school not for academic credit; or

(5) Summer experience as a law clerk to a state or local judge or law clerk experience on a continuous basis (either full or part-time)

in a private firm while attending school, *i.e.,* "working the way through college," not for academic credit.

Moreover, in determining work experience subsequent to graduation from law school, credit may be granted for bar examination preparation courses.

If you are confused by all of this, don't worry about it (but welcome to the federal government)! You will probably not need to concern yourself with this level of minutia anyway, as the judge and his or her staff will already have figured it out for you. If you are concerned, you may safely assume, if you are coming straight from law school, that the clerkship salary will be in the general vicinity of JSP-11 plus the current cost-of-living increases and whatever locality pay differentials apply to that area. Of course, ultimately you will need to check with the judge as to your exact anticipated salary.

The compensation for federal judicial law clerks also includes other financial benefits. "Term appointment" law clerks, appointed for a term of less than four years (generally one or two years), are covered by Social Security and are eligible to participate in health and life insurance programs including long-term care insurance, and pre-tax health and dependent care supplemental insurance programs. "Career judicial law clerks," appointed for four or more years, in addition can participate in the federal retirement system and the Thrift Savings Plan (which augments the clerk's investment income with matching funds from the government). Each judge has the discretion to determine the vacation and sick leave that will be available to a law clerk. At the time of your clerkship, you will need to check with the judge and the personnel office of the court for the current compensation and benefits plans.

· State

For state court clerkships, the salary varies substantially by the state and court, ranging from the low $30,000's to the upper $50,000's. Many courts give judicial law clerks a small raise, even during the first year of a clerkship, if the clerk passes a bar exam. While state law clerks on average earn slightly less than their federal counterparts, a few state courts pay higher salaries than federal courts. At the upper end of the scale, the New York Court of Appeals (the highest appellate court in that state) currently offers as starting salary, for both Judges' and Central Staff clerks, more than $57,000 per year plus state employment benefits. Judges' clerks who must travel also receive a travel and meal allowance while attending court sessions in Albany.[3] Since individual states will differ so greatly, you must check with the courts of each state for information on specific clerkship salaries and benefits. Some state courts will have this information on-line (available also through the court links in www.judicialclerkships.com). For an overview of state court application guidelines, as well as salary information, *see also The Guide to State Judicial Clerkship Procedures* (published annually by Vermont Law School).

· **Citizenship Requirement**

Occasionally a student asks me whether one needs to be a citizen of the United States in order to be employed as a judicial law clerk. For federal clerks, here is the latest word on this from the Administrative Office of the United States Courts: Pursuant to the Treasury and General Government Appropriations Act, 2000, Public Law No. 106–58, section 605 (September 29, 1969), "any judicial employee assigned in the continental United States compensated with federal funds must be a United States citizen or otherwise eligible for federal employment within the United States. A non-citizen of the United States may be employed by the federal judiciary to work for courts located in Puerto Rico, Guam, the Virgin Islands, Northern Mariana Islands and Hawaii."[4] Thus, judicial clerkships fall within the general restrictions on the use of appropriated funds for payment of federal salaries to individuals who are not citizens of the United States. Note that these restrictions do not apply to employment outside of the continental United States; hence you may pursue a federal clerkship in the islands listed above. Other exceptions may be applicable, both statutory and by treaty with certain countries. For additional information regarding the employment of non-United States citizens, you are advised to consult the United States Office of Personnel Management website at http://www.opm.gov/employ/html/non_cit.htm or call the Office of General Counsel at the Administrative Office of the U.S. Courts at (202) 502-1100.

For state clerkships, the citizenship requirements hinge upon the laws of the particular state. If you are not a citizen of the United States, you will need to check directly with the individual state court on this matter.

FINANCIAL DIFFERENTIAL

When compared with salaries in government and public interest positions, the judicial clerkship salary is relatively competitive or even higher. However, the clerkship salary is substantially lower than the typical salary offered by large metropolitan law firms for that year (or two) of your clerkship. If your clerkship is located in an area of the country with a lower cost of living than that big firm, the effective salary differential may be less than you think. Keep in mind as well that a portion of the salary differential would be reduced by the correspondingly higher income taxes. In general, though, this short-term differential is admittedly a disadvantage of pursuing a judicial clerkship. Although you may be foregoing the higher pay of the private sector, there is more than the short term to consider.

A substantial number of students in the National Clerkship Study cited the financial differential of a clerkship salary as a component of their decision not to apply for a clerkship at all. More than one-third of the students who did not apply for a clerkship cited the lack of the finances to consider a clerkship, emphasizing as a deterrent the financial differential of the clerkship salary given their considerable educational debt.[5]

If this is the direction you are heading, you should first explore the possibility of financial assistance and/or loan deferral, choosing a shorter clerkship term, or even working elsewhere for a year first. In addition, you should take into account as well the long-term financial and non-economic benefits. All of these will be discussed briefly below.

FINANCIAL ASSISTANCE AND LOAN DEFERRAL

Financial assistance in connection with the clerkship application and interview process is limited at best. The National Clerkship Study found that no law schools offered any other financial assistance for the judicial clerkship term except for a few schools that include clerkships within their loan forgiveness programs.[6] However, the study set forth initiatives that included encouraging the law schools, in the strongest of terms, to address these financial concerns, stating that some form of financial assistance or loan deferment from law schools is imperative: "Such assistance might facilitate applications for those who could not apply due to the financial factor (salary differential and educational debt burden), thereby increasing the diversity of the applicant pool and law clerks and expanding the availability of clerkships to all who are otherwise qualified. There is no readily ascertainable reason why judicial clerkships, which are a form of public service, cannot be treated like other public interest jobs, evoking eligibility for financial assistance, loan forgiveness or deferral programs."[7] Since that time, more of these recommended measures may have been implemented by the law schools, other organizations, and even the judiciary. For instance, the federal government is currently considering a proposal to grant to federal law clerks deferral on their federally insured student loans during the term of their service for a period of up to three years.[8] Some state courts have similar programs, such as Texas, which has a student loan repayment program for its law clerks.[9]

Most lenders will not allow you to defer student loan repayments during your clerkship. However, often the repayment obligation for these loans does not go into effect until about six months after graduation, or potentially halfway through your clerkship. Moreover, you may be able to consolidate your loans or make other arrangements to service your debt while you are clerking. You should talk to the financial aid office of your school about your options.

Shorter Clerkship Term

If the financial factor is a serious concern for you, this factor may be a determinative one in guiding your choice of judges by clerkship term. Perhaps you should choose a judge with a one-year term rather than one for whom your clerkship would be two years long. The benefits of a clerkship would still be yours without the added strain of the salary differential for a second year.

Working Elsewhere for a Year First

If all else fails, consider as an alternative to forgoing a judicial clerkship and missing this valuable experience the idea of working for a year first. Currently a trend is emerging towards waiting a year after graduation (*i.e.,* applying in the third year of law school or later) and working elsewhere first to pay off some debt. An added benefit of this approach is the fact that this additional work experience generally allows you to be eligible for higher clerkship salary, JSP-12 and above. Provided that the judge agrees and completes the requisite paperwork, you may have a considerable boost to your salary for the term of your judicial clerkship.

Most employers will be supportive of this option as well. The premium placed on hiring a judicial law clerk and the knowledge that you will bring back to them this added value usually surpasses the risk of losing you after the clerkship year. You must be up front with the other employer about your plans to clerk, and depending on the timing may need to seek the firm's permission. If you successfully apply for a clerkship during your third year of law school for the second year after graduation, you may even find having that prospective clerkship on your resume assists you in obtaining your first post-graduation job.

CLERKSHIP BONUS

As a consolation, consider also that many law firms do offer substantial clerkship bonuses for law clerks to entice them to their firms and compensate them somewhat for the financial differential of their clerkship year(s). Depending on the law firm and level or type of clerkship, this bonus can vary from $10,000 to $35,000 per clerkship year; at present, most of these fall within the $10,000 to $20,000 range.[10] Note that many firms do not give an additional bonus for the second year of a clerkship; but for those that do, the bonus is generally double the amount of the one-year bonus, or at least a substantial increase over that figure (*e.g.*, $25,000 for two-year, compared to $15,000 for a one-year clerkship). The bonus given after a clerkship for the U.S. Supreme Court may be the same or significantly higher (currently as much as $60,000), depending on the firm. Some of these issues may hinge on the firm's consideration of the individual circumstances and the particulars of the clerkship.

Recently a number of states have raised the issue of the propriety and ethics of offering and accepting a bonus between a law firm and a judicial law clerk. For example, in Texas the possibility was raised that the longstanding practice of several firms that offered clerkship bonuses could fall within its penal code prohibiting bribery of public officials. After an extended controversy, the Texas Supreme Court released new ethics rules forbidding its clerks from accepting bonuses from law firms that express interest in hiring them after they leave the court.[11] Few states have a written policy on clerkship bonuses. One that does, Delaware, provides in its Code of Conduct for Law Clerks that, although clerks may be reimbursed for interview expenses from law firms, a clerk "may not accept the payment of any bonuses or moving expenses until the end of the clerkship." In Arizona, the Judicial Ethics Advisory Committee of the Arizona Supreme Court concluded that an appellate law clerk cannot be employed by a law firm while working at the court or accept payment of bar dues by the firm, even after the clerkship ends. The committee stated that, "This limitation is intended to avoid any appearance that the payment is related to the service as a law clerk . . . It is immaterial whether the payment is made during or after the clerkship."[12] It remains to be seen how this issue will be resolved in the future on a state-by-state basis; but be aware that, if you plan to clerk for a state court and consider such perks from a law firm, you will need to inquire as to the current policy of that state.

For federal clerks, the bonus issue resulted in an advisory opinion (No. 83) by the 1998 Committee on Codes of Conduct of the Judicial Conference of the United States, which states that since the rules apply only to employees, bonuses paid before or after clerkships are acceptable, but payments during clerkships are not. The opinion suggests that clerks check with judges, since individual judges may follow their own more stringent policy.

Similar issues have been raised with respect to bar exam or review course fees. To avoid any appearance of a conflict or impropriety, some law firms will not pay for these expenses if you accept a judicial clerkship; however, most will reimburse you once you join the firm. Note that law firms also differ on whether an employment offer can be deferred or will remain open during a judicial clerkship.

As always, check with your judge regarding his or her policies on the matter. (Hopefully by now this is a familiar mantra for you.) Individual judges vary on whether you can accept a permanent offer from another legal employer, such as a law firm, before or during the clerkship. Even some judges who permit their clerks or future clerks to accept employment offers prohibit them from accepting any signing or other bonuses from the firm. Others allow their clerks to accept a clerkship bonus either before or after, but not during, the clerkship. Of course, if you do accept a position for after the clerkship, you must notify the judge and follow the judge's instructions, which will probably translate into not working on matters in which your future firm is involved. (*See* ethical considerations in Chapter 10 on Preparing for Your Judicial Clerkship.)

SENIORITY CREDIT AND ADVANCEMENT

Regardless of whether they offer a clerkship bonus, most firms will give law clerks credit for that clerkship year or two, along with the corresponding higher salary, and advance them to the next level of seniority among the ranks towards partnership. In addition to joining the firm as a second or third-year associate (depending on the length and stature of your clerkship), you may advance more quickly than your colleagues who did not have the opportunity to clerk. As I noticed from my own experiences in a law firm, I was frequently sought after for litigation strategies and advice, given a higher level of work than some of my colleagues, and generally treated with a higher level of respect and credibility, due at least in part to my clerkship experience. Of course, there are added benefits in the long term as well—both financial (translating into a more successful law career) and non-monetary.

NON-MONETARY BENEFITS

One approach is to view a judicial clerkship as another year of law school. As such, it is somewhat of an expense—although far less than one year of law school—but one that gives you in return a learning experience, an honor, and a permanent boost to your career. A clerkship is a valuable opportunity to do public service, make a contribution and impact upon the law, while at the same time receiving enormous personal satisfaction and advantage. One law firm openly states the benefits of clerking in its attraction for judicial clerks: "Yes, many of our attorneys have completed judicial clerkships. The research and writing skills as well as the exposure to the trial and appeal process have proven to be valuable skills in the professional development of these attorneys."[13]

A clerkship may open the door to an employment option or job that would not otherwise be available to you. As one insider from a firm replete with clerks describes: "There are lots of people walking around the office who interviewed for the summer program, but didn't get in. They went back to school, got clerkships, and now work here."[14]

This short-term financial sacrifice of sorts endows lifelong benefits, as we discussed at the outset. A former law clerk describes the weighing of these competing interests first in financial terms, as follows: "The substantive experience of a clerkship is unquestionably rewarding, but with first-year associates now making $125,000 the pay gap may give some students pause. As a law clerk I made $43,000. Even with the $15,000 clerkship bonus from my firm there was an opportunity cost to clerking of $67,000 before taxes. Was it worth it? Absolutely. Instead of being a first-year associate at a large law firm, I spent my time working closely with one of the most interesting and important people I will ever know. I also developed a tremendous friendship (with my co-clerk) that will endure for many years." He went on to describe more of the non-monetary benefits:

> The work I did for [my judge] was far more interesting, substantive and important than anything I could have done as a cog in a large firm. I worked on important cases from beginning to end. It will be many years before I have another opportunity to be directly and centrally involved in so many issues of public importance. I would go back and do it again in a second. The clerkship credential stays with you for the rest of your life and clients want lawyers who have clerked. That's a nice side benefit to a wonderful experience.

So, think of this as an investment in your career, for a judicial clerkship will bring you many professional rewards that far exceed your initial opportunity costs.

Notes

1. Figures and salary and benefits supplied by the Administrative Office of U.S. Courts for the year 2002. See *Law Clerk Employment Information*, January 8, 2002, https://lawclerks.ao.uscourts.gov/employinfo.htm.
2. For a further description of "legal work experience" and more on these "educational substitutions," see, e.g., *FMJA Law Clerk Information*, January 8, 2002, http://www.fedjudge.org/content/lawclerks.htm.
3. *Clerkship Opportunities at the New York Court of Appeals*, January 8, 2002, http://www.courts.state.ny.us/ctapps/clrkship.htm.

4. *Law Clerk Employment Information,* January 8, 2002, https://lawclerks.ao.uscourts.gov/employinfo.htm.
5. *See* NALP Report at 15, 50; Table 34 at 51.
6. *Id.* at 11, 40; Tables 23 and 24.
7. NALP Report at 17. *See also* Strauss, Debra M., "Empowering the Participants: Initiatives from the National Judicial Clerkship Study," *NALP Bulletin,* Vol. 13, No. 12, December 2000.
8. Section 205 of the Federal Courts Improvement Act of 2001, H.R. 2522, was introduced in the House of Representatives on July 17, 2001. This bill has been referred to the Committee on the Judiciary and the Committee on Education and the Workforce for consideration.
9. *See, e.g.,* website of the Texas Judiciary, www.courts.net/tx/index.html (7/29/01).
10. *See Supplemental Information on Salaries and Bonuses,* March 11, 2001, http://www.lawjobs.com/surveys/supplement.html.
11. This issue was variably addressed in Texas by its Supreme Court, legislature, Governor and Ethics Commission. *See* Texans for Public Justice, www.tpj.org, and the Texas Ethics Commission, www.ethics.state.tx.us (Ethics Advisory Opinion No. 441, 1/14/02). *See also* Robbins, Mary Alice, "Legislators Enter Texas Court Clerk Bonus Brouhaha," *Texas Lawyer,* March 12, 2001; Amon, Elizabeth, "Texas Messes With Clerk Perks," *The National Law Journal,* Feb. 23, 2001.
12. Amon, Elizabeth, "Texas DA Probes Clerk Signing Bonuses," *The National Law Journal,* Jan. 23, 2001.
13. Haynes and Boone, LLP, *Frequently Asked Questions—Judicial Clerkships,* March 10, 2001, http://www.hayboo.com/recruit/faq_judicial_clerk.htm.
14. *Williams & Connolly,* March 11, 2001, http://www.lawjobs.com/career/vault/firms/williams.html.

CHAPTER

ten

Preparing for
Your Judicial Clerkship

The most important thing to know is that the world of the judicial clerkship is the judge's world. As such, it is like no other you have experienced. It encompasses its own culture, players, rules, and ethical considerations. Before you embark on your voyage, you will need some tools and a little orientation to help develop your inner compass and the proper state of mind. If you enter with the appropriate attitude and awareness, the rest will follow in time, with your judge as your guide to a successful clerkship experience—and beyond.

You are entering what promises to be, or at least has the true potential of being, the best professional year or years of your life. (When was the last time you heard that? Probably when you were entering college, and looking back at some distant point in the future, you will most likely believe that to be true. Well, this is even more so.) Of course this depends in large part on the judge, and on your chemistry with the judge, but hopefully if you have been successful in the application and interview process, with researching the judge and the like, you have already set the stage for a positive experience.

Yes, this is undoubtedly a good credential. But it is also much more than that, as you are about to discover. This is one of your best opportunities to see the inside of a courtroom and the behind the scenes of a judge's chambers and the courthouse (clerk's office, pro se office, administrative offices). You will especially have an amazing, if not downright scary or overwhelming, impact and influence on the law through your judge's decision-making and opinion writing. For this reason, don't be concerned if you are two-thirds through the first year of your clerkship before you feel comfortable with this role—this is typical. At that point, you will finally be able to look beyond your own tasks and appreciate the finer points such as the level of lawyering you are witnessing and the points of law you are learning. Believe me, when you are a new associate in a law firm, or wherever else your next stop is, you will realize for perhaps the first time just how much you did, saw, and absorbed.

Throughout your legal career, you should try to maintain contact with your judge, co-clerks, and network of previous and future law clerks—whether through phone calls, advice-seeking, holiday cards or an occasional note attaching something of interest to the judge personally or professionally. Make every effort to attend whatever functions your judge arranges; some hold annual clerk gatherings. These relationships will be an important professional (and personal) asset for you. Hopefully the benefits of your clerkship will be long lasting— in a special bond with your judge as your lifelong mentor.

WORKING RELATIONSHIPS, ATTITUDE, AND ATMOSPHERE

First and foremost, I advise a positive attitude toward chambers and court staff. Be nice, not arrogant. This may seem like commonsense, but it is particularly applicable to the intense, personalized setting and relationships in chambers. Don't expect much in the way of support staff and library help, and you won't be disappointed. For instance, depending on the practices of chambers, you will probably be typing up your own memos and opinions on the computer, as well as reshelving books and maintaining the library in chambers. (At this stage in your career, this aspect will probably be relatively easy to get used to, since you have just been students and you have not yet been spoiled by the big law firms!)

Keep in mind that the atmosphere in a judge's chambers is egalitarian, unlike a law firm. It is of critical importance to be a team player, especially with co-clerks and staff. I'm sure you all know to be respectful to and professional with the judge, but you should also be aware that his secretary will probably be someone who has been with him for years, while his law clerks come and go. I have seen an occasional law clerk undermine his or her relationship with the judge through an arrogant attitude towards court staff and particularly the secretary. The secretary is also a great conduit between you and the judge, if you want to check with her about the judge's practices and preferences first rather than bother the judge with minor matters or maybe even appear foolish; and the secretary can be a great ally if you ever want to lobby for some change of an age-old practice (but of course don't go in there trying to "rock the boat").

The Deputy Clerk is another key player. In most chambers, he or she (but sometimes also the law clerks) controls the judge's calendar, which is of critical importance in scheduling conferences, motion return dates, trials, and even vacations. Note that you will probably be scheduling yours around the judge's schedule, depending on the judge's policies in this regard. In a trial court, the Deputy Clerk also swears in the witnesses, takes appearances from the attorneys, and marks exhibits during a trial. Depending on the judge and court, the law clerk may at times help with all of these tasks except the swearing in of witnesses, which can only be done by the Deputy Clerk or the judge.

The Clerk's Office staff and the Court Reporters are also important people to be (and after your clerkship, remain) on good terms with. They will be your source of case files, docketing of specific court papers, and general inside information as to the inner workings of the court system. One former clerk echoes the importance of always being polite and respectful to the judge's courtroom staff and other staff including the secretary, office assistant, and the court clerks. "Most of these individuals have dedicated, and I mean dedicated themselves, to working for the judge or in the courthouse for many years and know the judge much better than you ever will. If any personality conflicts arise, you may find yourself on the losing side of the argument because they are there to serve the judge for the long term." She also found on occasion that new lawyers may think they know the law better than some court personnel because they attended law school and passed the bar. "That is until they must prepare a file and the paperwork for certifying an appeal or prepare the paperwork for the grand jury's return on an indictment." Then the law clerks realize that the court personnel should be some of their "new best friends" for their clerkship term (and beyond).

While we are on the subject of court papers, *never* bring the original documents home with you—use "courtesy copies" provided by the attorneys for this purpose or make your own copies. A clerk's worst nightmare is a story told to us (and hanging through the halls of the courthouse ever since) about a former clerk who took a court file home with him and accidentally left it on the subway! Also guard your own notes and work product with your life, as you are protecting the integrity and respect of the court!

You should be aware that the Pro Se Office handles questions and problems of litigants who are not represented by an attorney, so you can refer some of your "crazy pro se" callers to them; and any papers they file will come from that office. Do not under any circumstances give these litigants legal advice, or you will find yourself "adopted" (*i.e.*, hounded) by them, as happened with one of my co-clerks; he was even followed by that wacky but harmless individual to his subsequent law firm, as he had somehow been naïve enough to let the firm name slip. In addition, the Pro Se Office acts as a screen of the most dubious cases that its staff determine to have absolutely no merit— they draft orders of dismissal, which are then reviewed and signed by the Chief Judge.

Hopefully, you will also get to know the law clerks, judges, and staff of other chambers. This is particularly true for clerkships with the Court of Appeals, where the judges are more likely to be working together on case decision-making and opinion writing, although the chambers life may be more isolating. In the District Court, you may work as well with the Magistrate Judge, as your cases are referred to him or her for pretrial matters, discovery disputes, and even for jury or non-jury trials.

THE LAW CLERK'S BIBLE

An important resource for law clerks is the *Chambers Handbook for Judges' Law Clerks and Secretaries ("Chambers Handbook")*, which contains very accurate, and rather condensed, useful information on many topics, including the role of a law clerk, the judicial code of conduct, civil and criminal procedure, federal court structure, and chambers and case management. This manual for law clerks originated in the Federal Judicial Center, with reprinted versions by West Publishing. However, as a caveat, West last reprinted this manual in 1994 and the Federal Judicial Center has no immediate plans of revising it, at least as of this writing. (Note however that beginning with the fifth printing, its appendix contains the Code of Conduct for Judicial Employees adopted by the Judicial Conference in September 1995, replacing the original Code of Conduct for Law Clerks that was included in the first printing of this publication. We will discuss this Code below.) So, you should be aware that some of the specific rules or information may have changed by the time you enter your clerkship, but the general guidelines will remain sound.

In addition, you should always check with your judge and the Clerk's Office of your court, which often publish local rules and practices. Most judges will have some sort of written instructions for incoming law clerks, as well as special rules for attorneys for trials, conferences and other pretrial matters, with which you must be familiar. As always, the judge's rules are supreme—whatever he or she establishes (including work hours and approach), you follow—and there is no appeal!

ETHICAL CONSIDERATIONS

Integrity and discretion are the key benchmarks of a successful law clerk. Your loyalty to your judge should be paramount and lifelong. Most people are unaware that there is a special code of ethics for federal law clerks. The Judicial Conference of the United States (the governing body of the federal courts) adopted the Code of Conduct for Law Clerks in March 1981 and has amended it several times, with the latest version, the Code of Conduct for Judicial Employees, adopted by the Judicial Conference in September 1995. It is presented along with some explanatory detail in the *Chambers Handbook*. You should read it on your own and become thoroughly familiar with its rules. For your handy reference, I have also included a copy of the most recent Code of Conduct for Judicial Employees in the Appendix to this book. Reviewing it prior to your clerkship (or even your clerkship interview) will give you an appropriate mindset and a good sense of your important role as a law clerk. As an example, the kinds of restrictions or sensitive matters include limitations on political activity and concerns regarding the confidentiality of cases. At all times, you are a representative of the court, as well as your judge, and must conduct yourself accordingly. In addition, some states have their own code of conduct for law clerks (*e.g.,* Delaware) or advisory opinions from a judicial ethics committee (*e.g.,* Arizona), which may apply to you as a state court clerk.

    I caution law clerks to always be careful in elevators, hallways, and in your outside life as well—you never know who may be listening—litigants, attorneys, jurors, witnesses, and even family members or friends of the parties involved. The same is true of your conversations with the law clerks, judges, and staff of other chambers—remember not to divulge any confidential information about the practices of or the cases in your judge's chambers. Sometimes the limits of this principle can be tested, such as the time I went away for the weekend to the Catskills and found myself sitting at the same table with the defendant's family; I had to endure three meals a day hearing how their relative had been "mistreated" by my judge, without saying a word on the subject in response!

Another point of emphasis concerns law clerk involvement in cases connected with a law firm in which an offer for employment is pending. Practices regarding this matter vary with the judge. Most judges will restrict your involvement with such cases. It is important to know his or her policy and communicate any possible connections or conflicts of interest promptly to your judge.

LAW FIRM OFFERS AND BONUSES

Judges also differ on whether you can accept a permanent offer from another legal employer, such as a law firm, before or during the clerkship. Even some judges who permit their clerks or future clerks to accept employment offers prohibit them from accepting any signing or other bonuses from the firm. (*See also* Chapter 9 on the Financial Aspects, including a discussion of the ethical issues raised by a clerkship bonus and other firm perks.)

In any event, if you do accept a position for after the clerkship, you must notify the judge at once, particularly since you will most likely need to refrain from working on cases in which your future firm is involved.

BAR EXAM AND GRADUATION REQUIREMENTS

There are general requirements for employment as a federal law clerk that must be satisfied by all appointees. By the time of appointment to a law clerk position, the candidate must be a law school graduate or be certified as having completed all law school studies and requirements and merely awaiting conferment of degree.[1]

However, most federal courts do not require that law clerks be licensed to practice in the jurisdiction. In addition, clerks usually do not have to take a bar examination before beginning a clerkship. Many students who accept federal judicial clerkships wait to take the bar exam until deciding the state in which they wish to practice.

A few courts do require clerks to take a specific bar exam. Aside from the official requirements of the court, individual judges vary on their preferences in this regard. Some judges will want their law clerks to take the bar exam *before* the clerkship. As general advice, if you know the state in which you plan to practice, it is beneficial to take the bar exam for that state during the prior summer when you have more time to study and attend traditional bar courses; in the process, you will learn valuable practical law and procedure that is helpful to know for your clerkship. As a further benefit, once you pass the bar exam and are admitted to the bar of a state, you may be eligible for an increase in your federal salary grade level. (For more on salaries, consult the financial chapter.) Note also that state courts often require the clerk to take and pass the state's bar examination within a certain period. Well before the beginning of your clerkship, you should check with your judge and follow his or her policy.

Research and Writing Tips

The *Chambers Handbook* includes a section on research and writing for judicial clerkships. Other key reference materials for law clerks include: the Federal Rules of Evidence, Federal Rules of Civil Procedure, Federal Rules of Criminal Procure, Federal Rules of Appellate Procedure, U.S. Bankruptcy Code, state substantive law and procedural rules, and the Blue Book (although the judges don't all follow it as religiously as do law students). Another interesting but lesser known source is the *Judicial Writing Manual*, published by the Federal Judicial Center in 1991, which is designed to help judges organize opinions and improve their opinion writing; it offers advice on writing tailored to the needs of the federal judiciary, which makes it useful for law clerks as well. *See also Judicial Externships: The Clinic Inside the Courthouse* by Rebecca A. Cochran (Cincinnati: Anderson Publishing Co., Second edition 1999). This instructional text, designed for the classroom component of a judicial externship, includes materials on the role of the law clerk, judicial ethics, and opinion writing. Lastly, read over the published opinions of your judge to get a flavor of his or her style and technique.

On law clerk writing, I urge students to be practical, concise, and reach a definite conclusion—remember these are real people with real factual disputes that need to be resolved justly on a case-by-case basis. Deadlines for a judge are of critical importance. You simply can't tell the litigants in court you aren't ready or you need an extension of time. In some form, you are a representative of the judge, and need to preserve the dignity of the court. Be prepared, mentally if nothing else, to be juggling many cases and be ready for a great deal of on-the-spot decision-making, particularly if you are clerking on the trial court level.

It is important to sit in at trial and oral argument as often as possible, so try to resist the urge to stay only in chambers or the library to get your work done. Observing the attorneys perform orally as well as in their written briefs will help you to understand all elements of a case. Also, it is vital to hear the judge's questions and/or comments to the attorney presenting a matter, as the issues develop and interact. To see the complete process and the judge's ruling allows a new lawyer or even an experienced one to have a "macro" view of the case. A new lawyer might not have this exposure and vital information for several years at a law firm.

In the writing process, one of the most valuable benefits is the continual guidance and advice you receive from "your judge." Your judge will be very honest with you about your work, and frank critiquing only improves the quality of the final product. As an experienced jurist who is most likely a top member of the legal profession, the judge is in the optimum position to teach you the best—and it will ultimately be his or her name and reputation at stake. Accordingly, you should leave your ego at the door and listen to the judge's advice!

In addition, I recommend taking advantage of LEXIS® and WEST-LAW® training classes for judicial law clerks, if these are available to you, to learn how to research legal issues and check case and statutory citations. As a caveat on computer research versus the books—and I believe this is good advice for your general law practice as well—be sure you are comfortable using both forms of research. Some of the judges are old-timers and trust the books more; they may want you to run into chambers during a trial, pull out a couple of pertinent cases (*e.g.*, on rules of evidence or an on-the-spot legal issue) and run back into the courtroom to hand the books up to the judge on the bench. Also, you might have a situation where one or the other source is unavailable to you; if you are in a satellite courthouse, you either may not have LEXIS®/WESTLAW® access or your book library may be incomplete due to expense and space constraints. So, you must be able to master both modes of research—and not get overly reliant on either the books *or* the computer.

As general advice, another former law clerk instructs, "Just be prepared to work very hard and long hours. Not because you are forced to, but because you realize that you want to do your very best effort for the judge and the legal community. Nothing gives a clerk greater satisfaction than when a judge comes to your desk and tells you you did a fabulous job on your assignment for the case and it seems you know more about the case than either lawyer for the opposing sides."

FEEDBACK FOR OTHERS

Once you do enter your clerkship, feel free to participate in the forum for law clerks on my website, www.judicialclerkships.com, which provides an opportunity to share your clerkship experiences, as well as offer information for fellow law students. In addition, your law school or individual students may contact you to provide feedback on your clerkship. If so, remember that people sources were probably the most valuable source for you (in addition to this book, that is)—and now you can share your wisdom with others!

Notes

1. According to the Administrative Office of U.S. Courts. *See Law Clerk Employment Information*, March 9, 2001, http://www.lawclerks.ao.uscourts.gov/employinfo.htm.

CHAPTER
eleven

The Ultimate Prize:
Clerking for the U.S. Supreme Court

As job guru Kimm Walton has called it, of the ultimate dream jobs, clerking for the U.S. Supreme Court is really the "plummiest of the plum."[1] In a five-month study on the effect and growing influence of law clerks, *USA Today* found that eight of the nine Justices now routinely allow their clerks to write the crucial first drafts of the opinions they write, and eight Justices also give the clerks the key job of making the initial review of incoming cases. The study concluded that the law clerks of the Supreme Court are "the most powerful, least known young lawyers in America . . . For an intoxicating year, 36 young men and women quietly screen most of the cases that come to the nation's highest court and write most of the words that come out."[2] The professional impact of this highest clerkship carries with you for a lifetime.

Since a clerkship for the U.S. Supreme Court is highly sought after, rare and prestigious, it is extremely competitive. First and foremost, a candidate must have an exceptional academic record, including top grades, law journal experience, and strong work experience. Most are also graduates from top tier law schools, although occasionally a Supreme Court clerk will come from a less highly ranked school (only if truly outstanding and usually with some prior connection to the Justice). Beyond that, the personality traits and background of the applicant that appeal to a particular Justice will vary. One thing almost all successful applicants have in common is a prior clerkship with a federal appellate judge.

FEEDER JUDGES

A clerkship for the U.S. Supreme Court is a second clerkship that almost always follows a federal appellate clerkship, but all judges and courts are not equal. It is a highly political process with certain judges who are known to be "feeders" with a history of supplying law clerks to the Supreme Court. (*See* Sample List of Feeder Judges, below.) Many of them are judges for the U.S. Court of Appeals for the D.C. Circuit, where the circuit judges are likely to have more interaction with the Justices. The feeder judge has a personal relationship with one or more of the Supreme Court Justices, which results in that judge's recommendation for a law clerk carrying more weight than the recommendation from a judge who does not have this connection. However, from time to time another judge emerges as a feeder to the Supreme Court, so do not select yourself out of the process if you did not clerk for one of the judges commonly known to have supplied clerks in the past. If you have top credentials, you may still have a shot at a Supreme Court clerkship!

Sample List of Supreme Court Feeder Judges

Here are some of the judges who in recent years have had several law clerks go on to clerk for Supreme Court Justices. Note that this list is not intended to reflect all judges who have ever sent a law clerk to the Supreme Court, and is a partial list only.[3] Moreover, additional judges occasionally emerge. You can also check the lists of Supreme Court clerks for the year or two prior to your application process to see where they clerked previously and to note any new feeder judges.

U.S. Courts of Appeals:

First Circuit

· Chief Judge Michael Boudin

Second Circuit

· Judge Jose A. Cabranes
· Judge Guido Calabresi
· Judge Amalya L. Kearse
· Judge Pierre N. Leval
· Judge Jon O. Newman
  (Senior, former Chief Judge)
· Chief Judge John M. Walker, Jr.
· Judge Ralph K. Winter, Jr.
  (Senior, former Chief Judge)

Third Circuit

· Chief Judge Edward R. Becker

Fourth Circuit

· Judge J. Michael Luttig
· Judge Paul V. Niemeyer
· Chief Judge J. Harvie Wilkinson, III

Fifth Circuit

· Judge Patrick E. Higginbotham

Seventh Circuit

· Judge Frank H. Easterbrook
· Chief Judge Joel M. Flaum
· Judge Richard A. Posner
  (former Chief Judge)

Eighth Circuit

· Judge Morris S. Arnold
· Judge Richard S. Arnold
  (Senior, former Chief Judge)

Ninth Circuit

· Judge James R. Browning
  (Senior, former Chief Judge)
· Judge Alex Kozinski
· Judge Dorothy W. Nelson (Senior)
· Judge Diarmuid F. O'Scannlain
· Judge Stephen Reinhardt
· Judge Pamela Ann Rymer
· Judge J. Clifford Wallace (Senior, former Chief Judge)

Tenth Circuit

· Judge David M. Ebel
· Chief Judge Deanell R. Tacha

D.C. Circuit

· Judge Harry T. Edwards
  (former Chief Judge)
· Judge Merrick B. Garland
· Chief Judge Douglas H. Ginsburg
· Judge Louis F. Oberdorfer (Senior)
· Judge A. Raymond Randolph
· Judge Judith W. Rogers
· Judge David B. Sentelle
· Judge Laurence H. Silberman (Senior)
· Judge David S. Tatel
· Judge Stephen F. Williams (Senior)

Post-Clerkship Work Before Applying

Another option that can be advantageous is to apply for a Supreme Court clerkship after working for a year or two after your first clerkship. Some of the Justices prefer as law clerks someone who has had a year or two of work experience. This post-clerkship employment could be either in a law firm or in the public sector, particularly in a government position. In general, there tends to be a close relationship between government employment and any kind of clerkship, which is actually a form of public service. At this early stage in your legal career, however, experience in a private firm is also highly valued by the judges, as you will gain some practical skills, knowledge, and added maturity.

Apply More Than Once

A key strategy is to apply more than once for that shot at a clerkship for the U.S. Supreme Court—as a third-year student with your upcoming federal appellate clerkship on your resume, during your initial clerkship, and upon entering your post-clerkship employment. There is certainly no penalty for doing so, and I know of several students who received a Supreme Court clerkship upon a second (or even third) application attempt.

How to Apply

The term for a Supreme Court clerkship is one year, encompassing the term of the Supreme Court but beginning well before that first Monday in October. Depending on the preferences of the individual Justice, the clerks usually begin work in the middle of July and end the middle of the following July (but individual Justices vary on this starting date from as early as the last week in June to as late as mid-August).

Even among Supreme Court Justices, the timeframe for applications and interviews varies greatly. For instance, the current range in timing spans from Associate Justice Sandra Day O'Connor, who looks at applications beginning in December more than one and a half years before the term for which she is hiring, to Associate Justice David H. Souter, who waits to review applications until January of the year in which the clerkship begins and selects his clerks in the late spring (*i.e.*, for a clerkship beginning that summer). Most Justices hire their clerks about a year and a half in advance. However, you should aim not to wait until the "due date" for a particular Justice, as it is never too soon to send in your application materials. Thus, it would be reasonable to send them all in at the earliest deadline, or around December of the year before the term for which you are applying (*e.g.*, December of your third year of law school for a Supreme Court clerkship to begin directly after your first clerkship). Plan continually to update your applications with new grades, honors, activities and so forth. Since you may not be hearing from the Justices for quite a while, also remember to send them new phone numbers, addresses and other contact information during that time period.

You should apply directly to each Supreme Court Justice. Application materials generally consist of: a cover letter, a resume, three or four letters of recommendation (or a list of references if the letters of recommendation will be sent directly to the Justice), a law school transcript, and a writing sample. Believe it or not, most Justices prefer the cover letter and writing sample to be short and concise! The Justices will look for a letter of recommendation from your lower court judge and will give it substantial weight. In your resume, be sure to include your first clerkship (as "prospective" if it has not yet commenced), any published writing, and especially your activities, hobbies, and outside interests. (*See also* Chapter 7 on Building a Successful Application, and Chapter 8 on Interviewing, which pertain here as well.)

Some Justices prefer the clerks of particular judges or law schools. Others are drawn to a well-rounded clerk, or a common background with or special interests of the clerk (*e.g.*, for Chief Justice William H. Rehnquist, it is playing tennis and/or coming from his home state of Arizona, while Justice O'Connor looks for interesting extracurricular activities and often does aerobics with her clerks). One can discover these patterns by looking at the critical background information of the Justices and the past and current clerks, and through consulting the resources on the Supreme Court Justices listed below.

Customarily the etiquette is to apply to all nine of the Justices and any retired Justice(s) (*see* below). (Fortunately, there are not so many as to be unduly burdensome anyway.) Despite the differences in their general timeframes, you may apply at one time (advisably the earliest one, as noted above), whether they will take action on your application now or later. To make distinctions in your application strategy based on ideology could be viewed as arrogant and presumptuous. You should have the intellectual capacity to clerk for any of the Justices, represent his or her points of view, and consider this rare opportunity to be an honor regardless of the identity of the Justice. Some Justices shy away from offending their fellow Justices by accepting as a law clerk someone who did not even apply to their own colleague.

By the way, this includes applying to any senior Justice who is hiring a clerk. Although you may be concerned that the Justice is "retired," this term may be somewhat misleading, as the Justice may be involved in some active cases, other projects, or sit by designation on the Court of Appeals. While the role of this jurist may be more limited, the role of the law clerk is not. First, a retired Justice has only one law clerk, in contrast to the other Justices; most have four clerks, although a couple (Chief Justice Rehnquist and Associate Justice John Paul Stevens) select only three clerks. Thus, there may be an especially close relationship with the retired Justice as the only law clerk. Second, a law clerk for a retired Justice may rotate as well to other Justices or work closely with another one in particular. So, there can be more exposure for that law clerk to additional Justices. For those students who are unaware of this fact, that clerkship with the "retired" Justice may be *slightly* less competitive but certainly amply prestigious. Do not, though, rely too heavily on that proposition. After all, a Supreme Court Justice is a Supreme Court Justice! Even with the best of credentials, acquiring a clerkship for the Supreme Court may be a long shot, but certainly worth the effort to apply—imagine the possibilities . . .

Forms of Address:

The Honorable William H. Rehnquist
Chief Justice of the United States
The Supreme Court
1 First Street, N.E.
Washington, D.C. 20543

The Honorable Ruth Bader Ginsburg
Associate Justice
The Supreme Court
1 First Street, N.E.
Washington, D.C. 20543

Dear Chief Justice Rehnquist:

Dear Justice Ginsburg:

COMMENTS FROM A SUPREME COURT CLERK

On clerking for the U.S. Supreme Court, here is some sound advice directly from a former Supreme Court clerk, John Elwood:[4]

It's a once-in-a-lifetime opportunity to work closely with one of the best lawyers in the country (*i.e.*, the Justices) with some of the brightest recent law grads in the country (*i.e.*, the clerks) on some of the most important questions in the courts. Afterwards, I don't know if it gives you entrée to new opportunities, although it certainly hasn't hurt me. At a minimum, the networks will be ringing your phone off the hook the next time a presidential election is thrown into the courts.

Candidates should apply to all the Justices. It's no big deal working with a judge who is not of your political leanings. In the old days, Justice Blackmun supposedly wouldn't hire people who didn't apply to all the Justices. I think he didn't like the idea of the clerk making that choice based on ideology.

As for timing, people should start applying to the Supreme Court in late December of their third year of law school. That's when the earliest of the Justices (*i.e.*, Justice O'Connor) starts to pick her clerks. People also shouldn't hesitate to reapply a second time, especially if they've had a recent achievement that has made them a more attractive candidate.

Finally, to the extent there are retired Justices still around the Court who are still taking clerks, people should consider applying to them as well. Those clerks are usually loaned out to an active Justice's chambers, and you get the same experience.[5]

THE ROLE OF THE SUPREME COURT CLERK

For Lawyers, Clerkship Is Ultimate Job[6]
Year of work in top court brings unrivaled access
By Tony Mauro, *USA TODAY*

It often is called the best job a young lawyer can have. For some, after serving as a Supreme Court law clerk, it's downhill from there—a job they spend the rest of their careers trying to match.

The work is terrifying, exciting and exhausting, all at the same time.

For a year, they become seven-day-a-week laborers, confidants and as close as family to the nine justices they work for-the same justices whose court they have been taught at law school to revere.

Each justice is allowed to hire four clerks every year, though William Rehnquist and John Paul Stevens often take fewer.

"It spoils you for any other legal job in the country," says Laura Ingraham, a former clerk for Justice Clarence Thomas who now is a CBS News commentator.

The signs of the exclusivity and cachet are everywhere. At the court, the clerks lunch in a separate room, built especially to prevent outsiders from eavesdropping on their conversations.

They are sworn to secrecy at an initiation tea given each fall by the chief justice two weeks before the term.

A legendary 90-second rule used to prevail at the court: Any clerk seen talking to a journalist for more than 90 seconds would be fired.

Their access to the justices is unrivaled. By custom, each justice goes to lunch at least once with the clerks of all the other justices—the clerks pay—except Sandra Day O'Connor, who recently decided the tradition was too fattening.

Clerks have been known to play tennis with Rehnquist, shoot baskets with Thomas, jog with Anthony Kennedy and do aerobics with O'Connor.

O'Connor cooks lunch for the clerks when they come in Saturdays. Thomas, still spurned in some academic circles, wins praise from clerks for engaging them in wide-ranging intellectual debate.

The clerks even get to poke fun at their justices—the ultimate emblem of acceptance. At an end-of-term event attended only by justices and court employees every year, clerks caricature their justices in skits. In one memorable skit, after Kennedy changed his mind in key cases, clerks played the theme song from the TV show *Flipper* at the mention of his name.

Clerks are the eyes and ears, and often the mouthpieces, of their cloistered justices, shuttling between offices to negotiate changes and concessions in opinions.

"It's almost an ambassadorial role, trying to pick up information behind the scenes," says Martha Minow, a former clerk for the late Thurgood Marshall and current Harvard law professor.

The access to research materials, clerks say, also is heady. Former clerk Mark Haddad recalls musing aloud about the meaning of the word "privacy" in the 18th century; he called the court library and within an hour, a rare original Samuel Johnson dictionary was placed on his desk, opened to the appropriate page.

A recent best-selling thriller, *The Tenth Justice*, adds glamour to the job. It focuses on a Supreme Court clerk who violated court secrecy and resorted to ever-more dangerous strategies to cover his tracks.

"I went to the topic because I was fascinated that so much power rests in the hands of people who are so inexperienced," says Brad Meltzer, a lawyer who interviewed clerks before and after writing the book. "I talked to clerks who wrote opinions outright. It's the most prestigious job any lawyer can get."

Whitewater prosecutor Kenneth Starr is a former clerk, as is Warren Christopher, President Clinton's first secretary of state, and ABC News president David Westin.

Lawrence Lessig, named recently as a special master to sort out the government's antitrust charges against Microsoft, is a former law clerk, as is Joel Klein, the Justice Department official who is pursuing Microsoft in court.

For most of the last 20 years, three of the nine justices have been former clerks-Rehnquist, Stevens and Stephen Breyer among the current nine.

"It's a very strange mix of awesome responsibility and complete subservience," says Columbia law professor Michael Dorf, who clerked for Kennedy. "It's more responsibility than you'll ever have again."

Supreme Court clerks at work

More than 7,000 people and companies a year take their cases "all the way to the Supreme Court" by petitioning the court to review a lower court ruling they don't like. The 35 or 36 law clerks for the nine Supreme Court justices play a key role in the process.

1. Clerks do the initial screening of petitions. The clerks for eight of the nine justices participate in a "pool" in which they divide up the cases and write a single memorandum about each that is sent to the eight justices. Justice John Paul Stevens does not participate in the pool. (Stevens, who has chosen to stay out of the pool, says he does not read most petitions either. He says his own clerks dispose of most cases without sending him a memo. For the rest, his clerks write memos or he reviews the petitions himself.)

2. The pool memos summarize the facts and the issues and often recommend whether the case should be accepted by the court for review. In most cases, the justices who receive the pool memos dispose of the cases without further study.

3. Based on the clerks' memoranda and occasional independent research, all nine justices meet privately to decide whether to accept or deny a petition for review. If four of the nine justices say a case warrants review, it is docketed for oral arguments. Fewer than 100 cases are accepted each term.

4. Before a case is argued, some justices have clerks write a "bench memo" that summarizes the case and may also suggest questions the justice could ask during oral arguments.

5. After a case is argued, the justices meet in private to take an initial vote and assign the writing of the majority and dissenting opinions. Clerks usually write the first drafts.

6. Drafts are circulated to other justices for editing and revision. Clerks are often the conduits for communicating and negotiating between justices about the final wording.

7. When the opinions are finished, they are handed down under the names of the justices. Clerks are never mentioned.

A NOTE ON THE JUDICIAL FELLOWS PROGRAM

While we are discussing the U.S. Supreme Court, another opportunity to consider there is the Judicial Fellows Program. Following a clerkship at the district or circuit court, if you are interested in further study at the highest level of the federal judiciary, this one-year position "offers a unique opportunity for outstanding individuals to apply their talents and interests to the administration of justice at the national level."[7] These fellowships are one-year appointments, typically commencing in August or September (with applications due the previous November). Fellows work at the Supreme Court, the Federal Judicial Center, the Administrative Office of the United States Courts, or the United States Sentencing Commission on various projects concerning the federal court system and judicial administration. Founded by Chief Justice Burger in 1973, the program provides fellows the prospect to study first-hand both the administrative machinery of the federal judiciary and the dynamics of inter-branch relations.

Candidates must have at least one post-graduate degree, two or more years of professional experience with a record of high performance, and multi-disciplinary training and experience, including familiarity with the judicial process. For more information about this highly competitive program, call 202–479–3415, or check out the website for the Judicial Fellows Program at http://www.fellows.supremecourtus.gov/ (provides program information, candidate instructions and even a downloadable application via the Internet).

INFORMATION ON THE SUPREME COURT AND JUSTICES

In gathering information on the U.S. Supreme Court and its Justices, it may be helpful to check with the career services office of your law school for lists of alumni and faculty who have clerked for the Supreme Court. As always, you should consult these valuable people sources. You may also contact the U.S. Supreme Court directly at 202-479-3000, for the most recent lists of Supreme Court clerks (including their law schools and prior clerkships), as well as specific information from the chambers of the individual Justices. In addition, you can conduct your own research using the principal resources listed below.

On-line:

- *U.S. Supreme Court official website* (includes information about the court and biographies on the Justices)—
  http://www.supremecourtus.gov/about/about.html
- *Legal Information Institute: Supreme Court collection* (gallery of the Justices, including pictures, biographies, and lists of decisions by the current and former Justices; Supreme Court cases; information about the organization and rules of the Court)—
  http://supct.law.cornell.edu/supct/
- *The Oyez Project Northwestern University* (contains Supreme Court cases, a virtual tour of the Supreme Court building, audio clips of court proceedings, and profiles of current Justices)—
  http://oyez.nwu.edu/
- *Jurist* (contains scholarly articles and news pertaining to the Supreme Court and links to various other Supreme Court sites)—http://jurist.law.pitt.edu/clerk.htm
- *Findlaw: Supreme Court Center* (current term Supreme Court docket, orders, briefs, argument calendar, and more)—
  http://supreme.findlaw.com/Supreme_Court/resources.html

- *Alliance for Justice* (profiles and political positions of the Justices)—http://www.afj.org/jsp/supremecourt/home.html
- *USA Today Supreme Court Site* (a comprehensive listing of Supreme Court related news stories)—http://www.usatoday.com/news/court/nscot000.htm

In Print:

- Cushman, Clare (ed.), *The Supreme Court Justices: Illustrated Biographies, 1785–1995* (Congressional Quarterly, Inc., September 1995) (detailed biographies of each Justice who has served on the Supreme Court, including major issues and cases).
- Jost, Kenneth, *The Supreme Court Yearbook 2000–2001* (Congressional Quarterly, Inc., June 2001) (annual publication of cases and trends from the most recent term and preview of significant cases scheduled for the upcoming term).
- Lazarus, Edward P., *Closed Chambers: The First Eyewitness Account of the Epic Struggles Inside the Supreme Court* (Crown Publishing Group, March 1998) (insiders book by former clerk to Justice Harry Blackmun).
- Martin, Fenton S., Coehlert, Robert U., *How to Research the Supreme Court* (Congressional Quarterly, Inc., January 1994) (provides descriptions of a variety of sources, ranging from printed to database and compact disc products).
- Perry, Barbara A., *"The Supremes": Essays on the Current Justices of the Supreme Court of the United States* (Peter Lang Publishers, November 1999) (intriguing stories of the nine justices of the current U.S. Supreme Court through portrayals of each justice's biography, judicial philosophy, and personality).

Notes

1. *See* Walton, Kimm Alayne, *America's Greatest Places to Work With a Law Degree* (Harcourt Brace, 1999), pp. 109–114. See also her entertaining discussion of the reasons a

judicial clerkship is a job she has recommended to more students than any other (*id.*, pp. 915–917).

2. Mauro, Tony, "Justices Give Key Role to Novice Lawyers," *USA Today*, October 4, 1999.

3. These judges sent two or more law clerks to the U.S. Supreme Court during a six-year period through the October 2001 term. Most of them have had numerous clerks go on to the Court through these years.

4. John Elwood, Yale Law School 1993, clerked for Supreme Court Justice Anthony M. Kennedy after clerking for Judge J. Daniel Mahoney of the U.S. Court of Appeals for the Second Circuit (now deceased). He went on to practice law at the D.C. firm of Miller, Cassidy, Larroca & Lewin, now Baker Botts LLP.

5. *See also* the comments of another one of my students from Yale, Rick Garnett, describing the thrill of his experience clerking for Chief Justice Rehnquist, in Kimm Walton's book, *America's Greatest Places to Work With a Law Degree* (Harcourt Brace, 1999), pp. 111–114.

6. Reprinted with permission from Mauro, Tony, "For Lawyers, Clerkship is Ultimate Job," *USA Today*, March 13, 1998.

7. Press release, "The Supreme Court Judicial Fellows Program," 5/31/01, Washington, D.C. (http://www.supremecourtus.gov/publicinfo/press/pr_05-31-01.html).

twelve

Lessons and Advice
Directly from the Judges

I have gathered some special stories and advice from a few prominent judges, who bring a unique perspective as they share their thoughts on the positive impact a clerkship can have on your life. Each of these essays is golden—due to a combination of what they are saying and who is doing the talking! Together they present quite a compelling picture of why clerking will have a lasting value for your career regardless of what future career path you follow.

First, we have the moving words of the Honorable Stefan Underhill, U.S. District Judge for the District of Connecticut. Judge Underhill speaks in the most glowing terms of his own clerkship experience—a tribute to his judge, the Honorable Jon O. Newman, formerly Chief Judge and now a Senior Judge for the U.S. Court of Appeals for the Second Circuit—which led him ultimately to follow his path as a federal judge and serve as a role model for his law clerks. Judge Underhill presents a dual perspective both of his experiences as a law clerk and as a judge in a daily relationship with his own clerks. Next is an enlightening essay from the Honorable Lisa Margaret Smith, a Magistrate Judge for the U.S. District Court for the Southern District of New York, who has taken the time to present you with some hands-on description of the role of a law clerk, and even the nuts and bolts of applying for a clerkship from an extremely valuable judge's perspective. With her gentle and sensitive advice, Judge Smith shares her personal experiences with clerkships, including the fact that she regrets never having done one herself! The concluding passage was contributed by the Honorable Melanie Cyganowski, who is part of my extended family as a former fellow clerk of the Honorable Charles L. Brieant (District Judge, formerly Chief Judge, for the U.S. District Court for the Southern District of New York). After several years in private practice at the prominent New York firms of Sullivan & Cromwell and Milbank Tweed, she is now a fine judge herself on the U.S. Bankruptcy Court for the Eastern District of New York. Judge Cyganowski echoes my sentiments about clerking for Judge Brieant, of course, and adds a glimpse into the impact of that experience on her future law practice both as a litigator and as a judge.

Lessons from a Clerkship
By the Honorable Stefan R. Underhill
United States District Judge
U.S. District Court for the District of Connecticut

"I am clerking for the greatest judge in America." For one memorable year, that was how I responded when asked where I was working. In retrospect, I realize that I must have sounded both naïve and arrogant, but the statement was an honest one. During my clerkship year, I was immensely proud of the man for whom I worked and proud of the work I helped him perform.

The "greatest judge in America" was Jon O. Newman, who sat on the United States Court of Appeals for the Second Circuit. Judge Newman earned his unofficial title by personifying the qualities I wish every judge could: a brilliant intellect, a deep and accurate sense of fairness, remarkable patience, an intense productivity, constant courtesy and a respect for language that resulted in thinking and writing of unusual precision and clarity. Prior to becoming an appellate judge, Jon Newman had worked as a Congressional aide, a federal agency counsel, a lawyer in private practice, the United States Attorney for the District of Connecticut and a United States District Judge. The variety of these experiences permitted Judge Newman to view legal issues from an unusually broad perspective.

By faithfully applying these personal qualities and varying experiences to the legal disputes before him, Judge Newman consistently rendered justice of the highest quality. Indeed, he often did so without assistance from his clerks. Although he was entitled to hire three clerks, Judge Newman hired only two, because he worked so hard himself. "Do you want me to prepare a draft opinion, Judge?" "No. I know just what I want to do with this one," he would reply. Then he would sit hunched over his manual typewriter for hours, hunting and pecking with two fingers, oblivious to anyone who wandered into his office to retrieve briefs or to borrow a book. The first drafts Judge Newman produced in this way were rarely touched. They came out of the typewriter and went directly into the *Federal Reporter* without need for revision or correction.

These performances inspired, but Judge Newman taught not merely by example. He instilled his sincere concern for precision in writing, in research, even in grammar and citation style, in each of his clerks. Judge Newman ate lunch with us almost every day, and our lunch discussions would range from recent Supreme Court decisions, to William Safire's latest "On Language" column, to the editorials in *The New York Times*. The questions he asked during these discussions— and whenever hearing oral argument of an appeal or when reviewing a clerk's work—focused uncannily on the critical fact or issue on which the outcome depended.

Clerking for Judge Newman was a heady experience. We worked hard, but the work was all done in furtherance of justice and thus was much more satisfying than most other work that can be done with a law degree. Spending a year with a man of such exceptional talents was itself a privilege, but the clerkship also brought with it instant prestige. I was a Newman clerk, so my resume was instantly stronger. Was and is. I am still known, I am sure, as a Newman clerk—and rightly so. The one year I clerked for Judge Newman shaped me more distinctly than my three years in law school. I knew even then that clerking was the best job I would ever have—unless I became a judge myself some day.

No doubt in part because I was a Newman clerk, I have recently been given the opportunity to serve as a United States District Judge. One of the many satisfying aspects of my new job is the relationship I enjoy with my law clerks. These talented lawyers work tirelessly on the many procedural, evidentiary and substantive problems that arise before and during trials in the District Court. They are the only other people who work directly in my chambers and the only lawyers with whom I have frequent professional contact. We have developed a wonderfully close relationship.

I depend on my clerks constantly. On the District Court, with hundreds of pending cases and scores of pending motions, we can function effectively only if we work as a team. My clerks and I together review the factual and legal issues we anticipate each time before I take the bench to preside over a trial or to hear argument of a motion. They prepare first drafts of nearly all of my written opinions. The back-and-forth editing process results in both of us learning from the other. I find our discussions of legal issues to be invaluable to the process by which I arrive at decisions, and I have come to trust my clerks' judgment as a helpful double-check of my own instincts.

I do sometimes wonder whether I am providing the same quality guidance to my clerks that Judge Newman provided me. As a District Court Judge, I must deal with many times more issues, and decide them much more quickly, than a Circuit Court Judge. Imposing precision often seems a luxury, and merely avoiding chaos a necessity, at the trial court level. I certainly have many more interactions with my clerks each day, but those interactions often seem less meaningful, than Judge Newman had with me. I do not expect to be the intellectual giant to my clerks that Judge Newman was to me. Still, I believe that, through it all, my clerks have come to understand the ideals that underlie every decision we make. Together we do whatever we can—whatever we need to do—to reach the right decision and to ensure that all perceive that justice has been done. If my clerks learn only that lesson, I believe that they will long cherish the time we worked together.

For many years I have kept a photograph of Judge Newman by my desk. Although the words he wrote on that portrait have all but faded away, the lessons I learned when clerking for him never will. I try always to apply those lessons to my work on the court. If I can do so faithfully, then one day a group of exceptional lawyers will be proud to say that they were Underhill clerks.

Clerking in the Chambers of a Magistrate Judge
By the Honorable Lisa Margaret Smith
United States Magistrate Judge
U.S. District Court for the Southern District of New York

Next month I will celebrate the sixth anniversary of my induction as a United States Magistrate Judge for the Southern District of New York. During that time I have had seven law clerks, including the two currently in chambers. I have already hired a law clerk for this coming fall, to replace my outgoing senior law clerk, and as I write this, I am in the process of interviewing candidates for the law clerk position available in September, 2002, when my junior law clerk reaches the end of her term. As I focus on the hiring process, it occurs to me that it would be extraordinarily easy for the process of selecting a law clerk to become all-consuming. First, the number of law students applying for clerkship positions is increasing at a geometric rate every year; this progression has been furthered by the advent of easily available and affordable word processing systems, lists of judges that are available through the Internet as well as from more traditional sources, and the increasing awareness among law students of the variety and value of clerkship opportunities. Second, the unique nature of the relationship between judges and their law clerks is one that most judges treasure—my law clerks are truly my extended family. In order for those relationships to continue to be of value, I must spend sufficient time in the selection process to be sure that I choose the most appropriate person from the huge number of candidates who apply. Of course, I can never know if someone I did not select would have made a better law clerk than the person I chose. It would only be if a law clerk did not work out (which situation has not occurred in my chambers) that I might question the selection process I have developed for choosing my staff.

The relationships that have developed between my law clerks and me while they are in chambers provide the chief value of the clerkship experience, to them and to me. I believe that I have succeeded in mentoring my law clerks, and in helping them to achieve at least some of their professional aspirations. The experience has caused them to hone their writing and analytical skills, as well as to give them a broad introduction to many of the issues that arise in federal court. This has helped them to define their future employment goals, and to take steps intended to achieve those goals. I am proud of the achievements of my law clerks, and delighted to have had such a bright and hard-working group of young people in chambers.

A Magistrate Judge's chambers is slightly different from a District Judge's chambers, because we are allotted only two staff people, in addition to a courtroom deputy (who is technically employed by the Clerk of Court, not the individual judge). Recently, many Magistrate Judges, including this author, have opted to hire two law clerks rather than a law clerk and a secretary. While this provides additional legal skills, it does mean that certain administrative and clerical tasks must be performed by the law clerks, and so my law clerks handle incoming telephone calls, deal with the mail, make photocopies, file documents and shelve new books. This part of the task, however, is minimal compared to the legal work that they do.

The law clerks who have been a part of my chambers have provided an invaluable service, by carefully and thoroughly researching legal issues in cases before me, and by helping me to maintain an organized and efficient chambers. When a case is assigned to me, that case is randomly assigned to a law clerk, with an effort to maintaining an even caseload between them. The assigned law clerk has the responsibility to prepare a bench memo before the first conference, which summarizes the crucial information about the case, including the crux of the factual allegations, the names of lawyers, time schedules and deadlines already set in the case, and, sometimes most importantly, identifying any omissions, such as failure to file pleadings or notices of appearance. As the case proceeds, the law clerk is responsible for researching issues presented by motions, and may draft a decision or a report and recommendation (*see* 26 U.S.C. §636(b)(1)) on the motion. The law clerks regularly discuss the cases for which they are responsible, and share the knowledge that they have acquired with their fellow clerks, and we often discuss particularly knotty issues in order to determine which way I think the matter should be decided, sometimes revisiting the issues in light of additional information or case law. During the first few months of a law clerk's term, I am extremely careful to check every citation, every quote, and every reference to the record, to make sure that the law clerk's work is careful and accurate in every detail. Within a few months, I find that law clerks are able to adopt my idiosyncrasies and writing preferences, and that they have learned to be appropriately careful in their use of the record and the case law. When I review the work of law clerks who have achieved that ability, I am able to focus completely upon the substantive analysis, and fine tune the written work. My reliance on my law clerks for drafting some of my decisions and reports and recommendations frees me to spend my time in court, either in conference with attorneys, conducting settlement negotiations or presiding at hearings or trials.

When a case is ready for trial, the assigned law clerk is responsible for making sure that counsel have submitted the required pretrial documents, and for using the submissions of the parties to prepare a proposed voir dire for my review and use in jury selection, as well as to prepare proposed jury instructions and verdict sheets for use at the conclusion of the case. My law clerks are encouraged to sit in on any proceeding in which they have a particular interest, and we have an intercom system that permits them to listen to trials or other court proceedings while continuing to work at their desks.

Every federal judicial district, and even every separate courthouse within a district, has a different approach to the utilization of Magistrate Judges. I am fortunate that the practice in my courthouse is for litigants to consent to the jurisdiction of the Magistrate Judges in a large percentage of cases (*see* 28 U.S.C. §636(c)), and I therefore have an opportunity to preside regularly at trials. In some districts Magistrate Judges have even greater numbers of consent cases and trials, and in some districts my colleagues have few if any trials. I do believe that the opportunity to assist in preparing a case for trial, and to see the trial itself, is a major part of the learning experience for law clerks.

Another difference from district to district and courthouse to courthouse is the variety of cases that make up a judge's docket. In the courthouse in which I work, in the Southern District of New York, a substantial percentage of our cases are civil rights actions, employment discrimination cases, contract actions and tort claims. We also have a significant number of petitions for writs of habeas corpus from petitioners convicted in the state courts, and some Social Security appeals. The caseload also includes environmental actions, brought both by the Government and by private citizens or groups, cases filed under the Individuals with Disabilities in Education Act, admiralty cases, and cases brought under ERISA. For the most part, Magistrate Judges in this courthouse see few securities cases, and have little responsibility for class actions, but in most other respects our caseloads mirror the caseloads of the District Judges. The wide variety of cases that come before a federal court present a constant challenge to the judge and the judge's staff to be up-to-date in many areas of the law, and to have the ability to learn new areas very quickly. It certainly is the case that we are rarely bored!

As a Magistrate Judge I also have responsibility, on a rotating basis with my fellow Magistrate Judges, for preliminary criminal matters. In that role I issue search and arrest warrants, and pen registers and other orders by which the Government can obtain telephonic and computer information. I conduct the initial appearance and determine bail for an arrested defendant, as well as detention hearings and preliminary hearings when necessary. I preside over selection of the grand jury, and take returns of indictments from the foreperson of the grand jury. I take felony guilty pleas upon the consent of the parties, and then report to the assigned District Judge my recommendation as to whether or not the guilty plea should be accepted. I also may preside over misdemeanor cases, upon consent of the parties, although it is rare in this courthouse for a misdemeanor case to proceed to trial; I do have occasion to take misdemeanor guilty pleas and subsequently to impose sentence on a defendant who has entered such a plea. Finally, I conduct hearings on motions to revoke or modify bail, and on violations of probation and supervised release. The criminal part of my duties takes a relatively small amount of my time, and does not require the assistance of my law clerks.

As noted earlier, I consider my law clerks to be an essential part of my chambers, and they have become an important part of my personal life as well. The time and care that I take in selecting a law clerk reflects the position that each law clerk holds. Any student interested in applying for a clerkship should consider taking the same time and care in deciding which judges they wish to apply to, and how to go about presenting themselves to those judges in the most positive manner.

The selection process that I undertake is personal to me. Although there are undoubtedly similarities between judges' hiring practices, every judge also has unique criteria and concerns that the judge must address and consider during the selection process. One of my considerations is the value of training attorneys for future work in this District, for this community. Thus, I ordinarily do not consider the "mercenary" candidate, who has no apparent ties or connections with the Southern District of New York or its environs. Additionally, because of my background in public service, I give weight to a candidate's demonstrated commitment to serving the public, either by volunteer positions, internships or actual employment in public service, whether legal or non-legal. However, the most important criteria that I consider is the quality of the written work, in both its legal analysis and its presentation (including such niceties as spelling, punctuation and grammar). I believe that most judges consider the ability to write a succinct, reasoned analysis to be a primary criteria for a law clerk.

Law students who want to be considered for a clerkship should do everything possible to develop and improve their written work, because nothing is more important in the work that a law clerk does than drafting written opinions for the judge for whom the law clerk works. A law student who is seriously pursuing a clerkship should take the chosen writing sample (preferably one that has not been edited by a professor or other editor) and carefully edit it; the student should not simply print out another copy of a paper that earned an "A" grade, without reviewing it in order to correct previously missed errors, or to hone the writing. Even a well-written document can be improved when the author considers it outside the pressures of the class or other assignment deadline. The law student should also ask a friend or colleague to read it carefully for any errors in spelling, punctuation or grammar. In addition, the student should re-read the writing sample before the interview, because the judge may use the contents of the writing sample as a way to stimulate conversation. Finally, if the writing sample being submitted is more than a few months old by the time of the interview, the student should look at other, more recent writings, and select a newer writing sample to bring to the interview. There should be an opportunity during the interview to offer the updated writing sample to the judge, or the judge may actually request a more recent sample of work. Having a newer writing sample to offer when asked can only reflect positively on the student.

Being prepared for an interview in other ways will help any candidate for a clerkship. In addition to the updated writing sample, a candidate should also take to the interview an updated transcript and resume (or additional copies if there is nothing to update), and a list of references, including phone numbers. A candidate should also review all available resources that may provide information about the judge. The placement office or clerkship committee may have information about the judge, including the judge's stated criteria for law clerks; various directories contain biographical information about the judge, and may identify the law school from which the current law clerks graduated; for clerkships with federal judges, there is a website which may be viewed to provide specific information about available clerkships (*see* www.uscourts.gov, click on "Federal Law Clerk Information System"); legal research may reveal written opinions of the judge, or appeals from trials held before that judge, all of which may be enlightening; finally, there may be alumni who have clerked for that judge, or have clerked in the courthouse where that judge sits, and having a conversation with such a person may add to the plethora of information which will prepare you for the interview. Any candidate should also think about some questions that would be appropriate to ask the judge—one question to ask a Magistrate Judge would be what percentage of the caseload results in trials, as the answer will be different from judge to judge—because the judge will probably give the candidate an opportunity to ask questions, and a failure to ask any questions will give the appearance that the candidate is not fully prepared. These are just a few suggested ways to prepare for an interview with a judge. Every judge likes to think that an applicant has prepared for the interview, and is organized enough to have found the time to do so.

I mentioned references, and this is one area where a student may have limited choices and little control. However, a student who is seeking a clerkship should consider the need for references at an early stage of legal study. The student should make efforts to connect with one or two professors, either through extra efforts at class discussion in a field of particular interest, or outside contact with the professor. The student should also keep in mind that professors can only reveal academic achievement, whereas a person for whom the student worked, either as an intern or employee, will provide a different and usually valuable perspective on the student's work ethic. Thus, every student should remember that every job, no matter how simple, can be important in that it could provide a resource that the student will want to use as a reference sometime down the road.

Of course, a student cannot (and should not) know the content of a written reference, but a student can (and should) (1) make sure that the person asked to write the reference actually knows something about the student (after all, a reference which says, "Ann wrote an A exam but I know little else about her," is not very valuable), (2) specifically ask the reference if he or she feels comfortable writing a reference, and if it will be a positive reference—by asking these questions, the student may avoid having a lukewarm reference, or a reference that mirrors every other reference being given (I have frequently seen the exact same referral letter for more than one student, and in those instances I disregard the reference), (3) provide a current resume and transcript to remind the reference of things about the student's history, interests and achievements, (4) ask the reference if he or she would like you to provide postage, pre-addressed envelopes or mailing labels to assist in the process, especially if you are asking for more than just a few letters, and (5) every time you have an interview, alert the reference that they may be hearing from someone about your application—when I call a professor who does not remember the student until after reviewing that student's file, I am likely to discount any reference the professor might give.

One of the most useful ways of preparing for an interview is to practice. Many law schools have facilities which permit a student to undergo a practice interview, and then to be critiqued, perhaps even while viewing a videotape of the practice session. By utilizing this service—or creating your own version of it—a student might learn the value of avoiding such phrases as "I think it would be cool to work for a government agency" and "you know what I mean." Both of these phrases were used by an otherwise worthy candidate in a recent interview I conducted, and it is unfortunate for that student. One or two practice rounds, and especially a videotaped practice interview, would probably have taught the student not to use such colloquial phrases, which detracted significantly from the student's otherwise appropriate presentation. The opportunity to undergo a practice interview also gives the student a chance to think about various ways to answer questions, and to prepare answers to difficult questions.

I once received an application letter for a clerkship in which the writer expressed that he would make an excellent law clerk because he was meticulous. However, this very careful person had incorrectly addressed the letter, sending it not to Lisa Margaret Smith, but to Lisa Marie Smith. As you might expect, this student's claim of being meticulous was immediately destroyed, and the student did not receive an interview with me. Another recently received resume listed a school address and a "permanant" address. These kinds of sloppy errors reflect poorly on a candidate for a clerkship, because much of a law clerk's job involves making sure that what is presented to the judge is absolutely accurate. Thus, if a clerkship candidate cannot (or does not) take the time to double check or proofread the documents being submitted to the judge, then the judge is unlikely to take the time to consider that student for a clerkship. A student who is serious about applying for a clerkship must put the same time and effort into the task as she or he would expend in any other competitive enterprise, such as competing for membership on a law journal, or for a spot on a Moot Court team.

All of these suggestions were made to me, in one form or another, when I was seeking employment following law school, and for the most part I ignored the advice. I hope that those of you who are making use of this book will not follow my path, which was mostly one of ignorance. I thought that I was busy in law school, and that I did not have time for some of these tasks, but I have learned that a student's schedule is nothing compared to the schedule of a working judge, especially one with a young family. I have also learned that these things do matter in the process of obtaining employment. After sitting on my side of the desk, I realize that I was mistaken to ignore the advice I had been given—I hope that each of you will take the advice to heart, and will be successful in obtaining a position in a judge's chambers.

Finally, even if you do not obtain a clerkship while you are still in law school, do not lose heart. If you are truly interested in pursuing a clerkship, the opportunity may still be available to you after a year or more in practice. Three of my law clerks had significant careers in law before returning to serve in a clerkship, and their experience helped them to be extremely valuable in their positions in my chambers, because they had the maturity and understanding to quickly grasp the issues and problems in a given case. Several of my colleagues on the bench have expressed a preference for experienced attorneys as law clerks. A candidate for a clerkship who has not obtained a position immediately upon graduation should continue to utilize the resources at a law school's placement office, and the myriad other resources regarding clerkship opportunities, and should submit an application after achieving sufficient post-graduate experience that the candidate will be even more attractive to a judge. That post-graduate experience should consist of something that the candidate feels strongly about, and in which the candidate can excel—the experience is particularly valuable if it enhances the existing resume, and if it results in even more effective references.

My recommendation to continue to apply for a clerkship is also based on my personal experience. When I was in law school I had not considered applying for a clerkship (only the very top students were advised by the law school's placement office to make such applications), but six years after graduation, as a result of the referral of my supervisor, I applied for and was offered a clerkship with an Associate Judge of the New York State Court of Appeals. Although it was a very hard decision for me, for personal reasons I turned down the offer, which would have required me to split my time between Albany and New York. Now that I am a judge, and I have law clerks who work closely with me, I particularly regret having missed out on the experience of a clerkship (though I have no doubt that the decision that I made was right for me at the time). From my experience, however, I can assure every prospective law clerk that there are opportunities that are available, if you wish to pursue them. In addition, even if your resume and transcript in law school are not sufficiently attractive to merit application for a clerkship, the ambitious student can find a way to pursue a challenging and interesting legal career, and find ways to improve that resume so a clerkship application will be possible in future.

If you are not successful in obtaining a clerkship, however, keep in mind that there are plenty of people, like me, who have successful and worthwhile careers even without that experience. There are many more qualified applicants for clerkships than there are clerkship positions available, and it is not possible for every applicant to be successful. The most important things to do as you move forward are to make maximum use of every employment opportunity; to foster relationships with those who can teach you and guide you; and to find something, whether as an employee or as a volunteer, which gives you fulfillment and a sense of personal pride. I wish you the very best in your efforts to obtain meaningful and worthwhile work in the law.

On the Impact of a Clerkship Experience
By the Honorable Melanie L. Cyganowski
United States Bankruptcy Judge
U.S. District Court for the Eastern District of New York

Graduation from law school leaves you believing that, on one hand, you know so much and yet, on the other hand, so very little. Then, if you are as fortunate as I was to begin employment as a law clerk, you quickly find yourself in a judicial chambers seeing how the law is actually administered, both publicly and behind the scenes. For me, I was honored to have been chosen to serve as a law clerk to the Honorable Charles L. Brieant in the United States District Court for the Southern District of New York. It was an experience that has stayed with me for life. And, you will find the same to be true for you. It molds you as a lawyer, it molds your thinking, and certainly, upon having the honor and good fortune of being appointed to serve as a federal bankruptcy judge, it was an experience upon which I thought back all the more.

How does the law clerking experience impact your life? It's one thing to say globally that it impacts you in every way, but it truly does. When you're a law student, you're looking at cases that reflect decided issues. Casebooks are filled with decisions by judges, rendered after trial or significant discovery. By the time that you read a case, the issues have been identified, narrowed, and isolated. As a law clerk, particularly if you are clerking for a trial court, you have the opportunity to observe litigation as it is unfolding and taking place: you are able to see the litigants, see the faces of the parties, see the facts as they are being presented, see what evidence is being excluded or admitted, and then, perhaps the most interesting aspect, is watching the judge assimilate all the information that is being presented. In my case, I was able to watch Judge Brieant undertake credibility analysis of the witnesses who were testifying in court, observing which witnesses he thought were more credible than others, and what evidence he thought was more persuasive than another. Particularly as I reflected upon my clerkship experience in later years, I had not realized how much impact on me it was to simply observe him shift and sift through the evidence. Later, when I found myself as a young litigator at Sullivan & Cromwell being confronted with a client asking me "what should we do," I found myself almost instinctively being able to weigh whether certain evidence or arguments would be more persuasive, whether certain arguments were better presented at trial than at a pre-trial stage or whether other arguments should be explored and better developed. I also found myself more able to objectively consider our case and assess where the weakness in our argument lay and whether a witness was as credible as another.

A clerkship experience impacts you in other ways as well. Above all, you have the opportunity to observe the way in which a judge makes a determination and then renders a decision. You may also have the opportunity to participate in the decision-making process. The technique of rendering a decision, in and of itself, is not an easy task. For anyone who has tried to dictate a memorandum of law, you realize quite quickly that speaking in a complete sentence that has a subject and verb and fits within a paragraph is a skill to be learned. Not only does a judge become quite skilled in speaking in open court, but he or she becomes a master at pulling together findings of facts and rendering conclusions of law that flow from them.

Another skill that becomes honed for a law clerk is your writing skill because, whether you are writing a bench memo or assisting in the draft of a decision, you are learning to say things clearly and persuasively in order to review the point as easily as you can. Similarly, it is not unusual for a judge to play "devil's advocate" with the law clerk and require the law clerk to articulate one of the parties' arguments as if they were being presented in court. Whether by dealing with the lawyers or being called upon to argue in this fashion, the law clerk is encouraged to use oratory skills in a way that will serve the clerk well in the future.

All of these skills and experiences serve a law clerk as a future lawyer in the profession, regardless if the clerk becomes a litigator, a corporate lawyer or an in-house lawyer. Can they be learned elsewhere? Probably they can. But, somehow in a judicial clerking experience, where the surroundings are more limited with only a judge and perhaps another law clerk or secretary, the experience is far more concentrated than in a law firm. To be sure, a law firm teaches a lot and a young lawyer learns many skills in a firm that are not learned in a clerkship. But, nothing replaces the experience of a clerkship and nothing sets you off on a nicer foot in your future career than clerking.

The best of all benefits is that you get to stay in touch with the judge for whom you clerked. It was a real joy for me that when I was appointed as a bankruptcy judge, Judge Brieant was one of the speakers at my investiture. Not only have we stayed in touch, but we have also maintained contact with the other members of the "judicial family" as we call it. We have quite a network of all the many clerks that have been part of Judge Brieant's family over the years. We stay in touch annually if not every couple of years, and particularly as we all grow older in the profession, it is fun to say "I knew her when" or "I knew him when." We all have this common link knowing we can call on each other for advice and support.

In closing, I cannot be more enthusiastic in urging you to apply for a clerkship if the opportunity is presented and to take one if it is ever offered, no matter what the court. I think you will find that wherever the court, the experience will be one that you will treasure throughout your career.

Part IV

Resources for Prospective Judicial Clerks and Their Law Schools

CHAPTER
thirteen

Tools For Research: Where to Look for Information on Courts, Judges, and the Like

A large part of the application process is a research project. No one source will have everything you need regarding every judge, and different types of research are required at different stages.

When you are initially forming your list of judges to whom to apply, it will usually be adequate to research geographic information on the court and biographical or background information on the judge. Several of the directories are a good starting place because you can get an overview of what courts and judges are out there, and your school may have a computer database as well of names and addresses to help out in the mechanics of preparing your letters and submitting your clerkship applications. Gathering information about the reputation of the judge and what it is like to clerk for that judge, you may consult a variety of people—law clerks, lawyers in practice, faculty, and other students—on this subject. Of the printed sources below, the best ones for this purpose will be: the *Almanac of the Federal Judiciary, The American Bench,* the *Judicial Yellow Book,* and written evaluations from former law clerks, if your school assembles them.

As we discussed previously, you will also need to learn about the judge's application requirements and procedures, using: the Federal Law Clerk Information System, *NALP State Judicial Clerkship Directory,* Vermont Law School's *Guide to State Judicial Clerkship Procedures,* any collections of letters from judges or other job postings available at your school, and phone calls to chambers. A great deal of this information is available on-line through a central resource on judicial clerkships: www.judicialclerkships.com, which includes key links to court sites and judicial clerkship listings (and yes, this is my website, so I will make sure to keep you posted there with updated information and advice!). To the extent possible, your goal at this stage will be to decide for whom you would like to clerk (and conversely, eliminating from your list those courts and judges for whom you would not like to clerk), using the criteria and factors discussed in the previous chapters.

A second round of research will follow in preparation for the interview, when you will need to ascertain further information about the judge, by reading his or her recent opinions, investigating and reading the prominent cases, and seeing if anything interesting has surfaced about this judge and his or her cases in the media. For this purpose, you can consult these resources, among others: the *Almanac of the Federal Judiciary,* WESTLAW®/LEXIS®, and web search engines. For example, using www.google.com, you can always try a general search on judicial clerkships or a specific news search with the name of the judge. Before the interview, it is also a good idea to read through the *Chambers Handbook,* to get a flavor of the atmosphere, ethics and protocol in a judge's chambers, as well as some of the general tasks of a law clerk. (*See* Chapter 8 for more on the Interview.)

With these different kinds and times of research in mind, more information on a comprehensive list of resources for research on judicial clerkships is set forth below.

THE BEST RESOURCES

First, I want to highlight what I believe are the top 10 resources (if you are overwhelmed, this will help you use your time most efficiently), and explain why (that is, for what purposes). By the way, you don't just have to take my word on this; the career development professionals and law students in the National Judicial Clerkship Study also appraised several of these resources as the most useful.[1] Then, I will list *everything* for you, by printed directories and sources, on-line resources, computer databases and people to consult.

1. Federal Law Clerk Information System

In October 2000, a new concept was launched on-line for federal courts—the Federal Law Clerk Information System. This is a database of information developed by the Administrative Office of the United States Courts under a directive from the Judicial Conference Executive Committee, with information posted directly by the judges. For applicants, the system provides a searchable database of judicial clerkship postings, which enables a student to generate a list of judges and for each, whether a clerkship position is open, the hiring schedule and application requirements. Still in its infancy, it is much anticipated that this on-line system will continue to grow and expand, as the judges increasingly submit their postings for law clerk positions and possible additional features are developed. According to Michele Reed, Attorney Advisor of the Article III Judges' Division, this system is "a way to even the playing field, because it makes information available to everyone." Rather than being limited by what staff and resources your law school has devoted to clerkships, you can now pull that information out for yourself. Beware, though, of outdated postings that have not been pulled by the judges as the positions were filled (on older listings you may still need to call chambers). At least for federal clerkships, this system should ultimately make searching and applying for these positions much easier.

2. The Web Site: *Welcome to the World of Judicial Clerkships*— www.judicialclerkships.com—"Your clerkship source."™

If you are looking for a central on-line source, this is it, if I do say so myself. Designed to save you from hours of bewildering meandering on the web, this website provides my information and advice on judicial clerkships, as well as a forum for law clerks, key links to the best federal and state court sites, and judicial clerkship listings (including the Federal Law Clerk Information System). More services for law students and judges are soon to follow on this site.

3. Almanac of the Federal Judiciary

This two-volume set is a very good resource because the *Almanac* goes further than simple listings and biographies. This publication contains relevant background information on the judges, providing information as to their affiliations, associations and activities, as well as their most prominent cases. In addition, it gives lawyers' opinions regarding most of the judges, which is something extra that is very useful. Keep in mind as a limitation, however, that the view of this judge might be different on the other side of the bench to a law clerk. Indeed, a judge who is perceived as "tough" and "a bear" to a lawyer who appears before him in court may be to his law clerks in actuality a "teddy bear" in chambers who has a good control of his courtroom, running it in a highly efficient and well-organized manner (which is generally beneficial for a law clerk). Still, this is an important perspective to consider, offering clues as to the judge's personality, reputation as a judge and degree of respect in the legal community—just be sure also to get the other side from present and former law clerks.

4. NALP State Judicial Clerkship Directory

A hard copy of this publication should be on the shelves at your law school, and also available on-line through LEXIS®. Compiled annually by the National Association for Law Placement, this has been useful as a directory of clerkships rather than simply of judges. Each listed judge provides information on his or her clerkship application procedures and preferences as to the elements such as the number of required letters of recommendation, as well as the names of past law clerks. Judges have the option also to indicate on their form that they are not hiring law clerks. While helpful, this directory is limited because not all judges send back the completed form to NALP in any given year. In past years, the directory included federal judges, but due to its ongoing support of the Federal Law Clerk Information System, NALP has decided to focus exclusively on state court judges beginning in the fall of 2001. For those judges and staff who do take the time to submit their information, this is one of the most direct and reliable sources; and you should consider yourself on notice of its contents. Accordingly, you should follow the practice of checking the NALP Directory—for any state judge to whom you plan to apply—to see whether that judge has posted vital clerkship information. (To access the on-line version, which should be updated more often than the annual printed directory, go to www.lexis.com/lawschool; click "Career Center," then "NALP Resources" and "NALP Judicial Clerkship Directory.")

5. WESTLAW® and LEXIS®

These computer databases are also important resources, particularly in terms of finding judicial opinions with relative ease and speed, as they are searchable by judge. You should be aware, though, that the number of opinions listed from a judge is not reflective of how much the judge has written during that time period. The behind-the-scenes procedure and protocol in the publication of an opinion is as follows: each judge (or court) decides how many and which decisions to send in to WESTLAW® and LEXIS® to put on-line or even into the printed reporters. Some judges like to send in everything or nearly so (perhaps they like to see their name in print!), while others prefer to restrict the amount of paper/trees or kilobytes they are responsible for, limiting their reporting of decisions to ones they believe to be of particular importance to the body of law. (Note that the unpublished opinions still have the same impact on the parties but, depending on the circuit, their precedential value might be limited.) Thus, if the opinion is published, it is usually because the judge chooses to send it in, unless the opinion was somehow picked up by the press or another source. For the purpose of locating and reading the judge's prominent or most recent cases, this efficient source will serve you well.

In addition, WESTLAW® and LEXIS® are the most direct source for nominations and confirmations in the judiciary. I have included below an automatic search you can run on a regular basis to find these names immediately as they appear in the *Congressional Record*; so you can really get a good feel for judges coming up to be confirmed on the spot—rather a relying on this information to be input by someone else on a website or printed source, which entails further delay (*see* section below on judicial nominations and confirmations). These computer sources also have directories of judges with contact, biographical and application information, such as: *NALP Judicial Clerkship Directory* (LEXIS®) (*e.g.*, use to find the names of current or former judicial clerks from your law school), *Judicial Staff Directory* (LEXIS®), *Judicial Clerk Directory* (WLD-CLERK on WESTLAW®), and *Almanac of the Federal Judiciary* (WESTLAW®). Before an interview, you can also search for articles in the news about the judge and any law review articles, in addition to opinions, written by the judge (*see* specific searches included below). The key is that these directories, some of which are also available in printed form, in the on-line version are more convenient, searchable and (potentially) current.

6. *Judicial Yellow Book*

As directories go, this one is a very highly regarded and thorough source of contact and biographical information on a huge number of federal and state judges, all in one volume. At last count, the most recent edition (2001) featured listings for more than 2,000 judges in the federal court system, including the U.S. Supreme Court, U.S. Courts of Appeals, U.S. District Courts, U.S. Bankruptcy Courts, U.S. Tax Court, and bankruptcy appellate panels for U.S. Circuit Courts; and more than 1,250 state judges at the highest appellate courts in the

50 states and the District of Columbia, including state supreme courts and state courts of appeals. In addition, the *Judicial Yellow Book* provides listings of chambers staff, including the educational background of the current law clerks for each judge. All information in all listings is verified directly with each organization listed, making the *Judicial Yellow Book* an accurate and reliable source of contact information for judges, judges' staff and court staff in federal and state courts. Despite its popularity, here is a tip that is not widely known: daily updates of this printed directory (which is updated semiannually) are available on-line at www.leadershipdirectories.com in its *The Leadership Library*® on Internet and CD-ROM.

7. *BNA's Directory of State and Federal Courts, Judges and Clerks*

This is another comprehensive directory of both federal and state judges, almost as highly rated by career development professionals and law students according to the National Clerkship Study.[2] The publication boasts that its facts have been updated and verified for accuracy by the court officials themselves, providing key contact and resource information on 14,087 judges, and 5,120 clerks. Included as well are organizational charts and Internet sites for federal and state courts. A quick reference guide as to the names and addresses of judges and clerks in a given court, it does not serve the function of providing the biographical or background data on these judges or clerkships.

8. *Guide to State Judicial Clerkship Procedures* (Vermont Law School)

If you are interested in state court clerkships, this relatively brief volume is the only printed source that contains an overview of all state court clerkships. For each state, there is a quick paragraph or two identifying for each level of court the name, application summary (how, when and where to apply), and salary. This is an excellent place to start if you seek a range of the state clerkship opportunities or wish to consider several states at the outset, for example, based on timing of the application. In addition, remember to check with each state court directly, verifying the information with the court administrator as listed, and researching on the court's website for more detailed information on the court. (Unfortunately, the Vermont Guide does not include websites—this is my suggestion for the future—but see my listings and links below.)

9. The Best People Sources

The comments from present and former law clerks, faculty, and attorneys in practice—anyone reliable you can really talk to to get information about this judge—are very helpful to have, but particularly former law clerks. The career services office of your school may have some written sources on that as well, such as contact lists of faculty, alumni and the judges for whom they have clerked. Many law schools collect some of that information from graduates who have gone on to clerk, in the form of clerkship evaluations or written feedback from alumni law clerks about their clerkship experiences—and that is one of the most valuable sources of inside information on the judges.

10. Your Law School

Don't forget to look in your own backyard! Always investigate all resources and sources of information that are offered to you! Check with your law school to see the career services office publications that are available. Many schools put together a judicial clerkship handbook containing the specific policies and procedures of the law school.[3] In addition, the career development office typically collects postings from judges in some form of binders; these letters from individual judges seeking law clerks and setting forth their application requirements for students are among the most valued resources of your school.[4] Your law school may also have a section on its website for more timely announcements regarding judicial clerkships. A judges' database, if your school maintains one,[5] further provides contact and other information to help with the mechanics of processing your letters.

PRINTED SOURCES

The following is the full list of publications and directories that contain specific information about federal and state judges, courts and clerkship opportunities. Some of these are also available on the Internet, as noted. For your convenience, I have broken the printed sources down further into these broad categories: directories that list contact and/or background information on the judges; resources which provide information as to clerkship availability and application requirements or procedures; judicial nominations and confirmations; and publications offering further insight into courts and clerkships.

Directories of Contact and/or Background Information on the Judges:

- *Almanac of the Federal Judiciary.* Englewood Cliffs, N.J.: Aspen Law and Business: Volumes 1 and 2. Updated semi-annually, Volume 1 includes information on district, bankruptcy and magistrate judges; and Volume 2 includes information on U.S. Supreme Court Justices and appellate judges. This publication provides extensive background information on the federal judiciary, including attorneys' comments, case management statistics, American Bar Association evaluations, lists of judges' publications and summaries of each judge's significant rulings. It is available in print and on-line through WESTLAW®.

- *The American Bench: Judges of the Nation 2000/2001.* Ruth A. Kennedy (Editor), Sacramento: Forster-Long, Inc., October 2000. Provides biographical information on approximately 18,000 judges from all levels of federal and state courts. The information is gathered annually from a questionnaire sent to judges and court personnel. The first section covers U.S. courts; remaining sections cover the 50 states and the District of Columbia. Includes jurisdictional maps by state.

- *BNA's Directory of State and Federal Courts, Judges and Clerks.* Kitchell, Catherine A. with Staff of the BNA Library (2002 edition), Washington, D.C.: The Bureau of National Affairs. Annual

publication with listings for 2,139 state courts, 220 federal
courts, 14,087 judges, and 5,120 clerks in the federal court system, the 50 states, the District of Columbia, and U.S. territories.
It also includes charts on state court structure, list of nominations for federal judgeships, and Internet sites for federal and
state courts.

· *Directory of Minority Judges of the United States.* Chicago: American Bar Association, Judicial Division, Task Force on Minorities
in the Judiciary (3rd edition 2001). Provides names and
addresses of more than 2,000 minority judges, divided into four
sections: African-American, Asian/Pacific, Hispanic, and Native
American.

· *Judicial Staff Directory.* Mt. Vernon, Va: Congressional Quarterly,
Inc. Annual directory that includes biographies, addresses and
phone numbers of federal judges and staff. Indexes of judges by
appointing President and year of appointment. Profiles more
than 15,000 federal court personnel, U.S. Attorneys and U.S.
marshals, 1,900 biographies of judges and staff, 14,000 counties
and cities with their judicial circuits and districts, maps of juris-
dictions, Judicial Conference, Administrative Office of U.S.
Courts. Also available on-line through LEXIS®.

· *Judicial Yellow Book: Who's Who in Federal and State Courts.* Washington, D.C.: Leadership Directories, Inc. Updated semi-annually.
This popular directory contains biographical and directory information on judges in all federal circuit, district, bankruptcy and
courts of limited jurisdiction, plus all appellate courts for the 50
states and the District of Columbia. Includes nominating President for federal judges and information on the education of their
law clerks. Updated daily through *The Leadership Library*® on
Internet and CD-ROM at www.leadershipdirectories.com.

· *State and regional reports.* Available in most states, provide directory listings of state judges.

· *United States Court Directory.* United States Government Printing Office (annually). An official list for the federal judiciary of
all federal judges, court clerks, and other key personnel in the

federal trial and appellate courts, including addresses and phone numbers.

· *Want's Directory of State Court Clerks and County Courthouses.* WANT Publishing Co. Published annually. Geographical listing of names, addresses, and telephone numbers of all court clerks and courthouses on the state and local court level, including state attorneys general, for all 50 states. Offers a variety of other information, including court decisions, real estate records, UCC and tax liens, criminal convictions, and other important records maintained by state appellate and trial courts and county courthouses nationwide. State-by-state guide to corporate and UCC filings, state offices of vital statistics and how to order records, trends in state court litigation, and a listing of state court websites.

· *Want's Federal-State Court Directory.* WANT Publishing Co. Available on-line through www.courts.com (website also lists corrections to the printed versions). This annual directory includes: the names, addresses, and phone numbers of all U.S. appellate and district judges and clerks of court; U.S. magistrate judges and bankruptcy judges; places of holding court and counties in federal districts; U.S. Attorneys; federal and state court organization charts; alternative dispute resolution sources; agencies and Administrative Law Judges; State Bar Associations; a guide to on-line access to federal court and bankruptcy records; a glossary of terms and a guide to how a case is litigated.

Clerkship Availability and Application Information:

· *NALP State Judicial Clerkship Directory.* Annual compilation of state clerkship opportunities across the country, with detailed information on listing judges' hiring criteria and practices including the timing and contents of the clerkship application. In addition, each judge is asked to list names of current clerks, and whether they will in fact be hiring any new clerks. Note that this directory replaces the *NALP Federal and State Judicial Clerkship Directory.*

- *Guide to State Judicial Clerkship Procedures.* Vermont Law School publishes annually. Gives a concise description of law clerk hiring procedures for each state by level of court, including when and where to apply and salary ranges.

- *Your School's Judicial Clerkship Handbook* (if any). More advice is wise to collect, and especially information as to the particular practices and policies of your school. By the way, I include in this category any collections of letters from judges or other job postings available at your school. So, check with your career services office on this.

- *More is available on-line!* (*See* section below for web listings of clerkship opportunities and application information through the Federal Law Clerk Information System and individual federal and state court sites.)

Judicial Nominations and Confirmations:

In addition to printed resources, this section includes the on-line sources of judicial nominations and confirmations.

- *Federal Court Appointments Report.* WANT Publishing Co. Bi-monthly listing of vacancies, new appointments, retirements, resignations, nominations and biographies of recent appointees, all in the federal judiciary. Much of this information is also available on-line at www.courts.com. *See, e.g.,* "Recent Appointments and Transitions" at http://www.courts com/appoint.htm.

- *Federal Judges and Justices: A Current Listing of Nominations, Confirmations, Elevations, Resignations, Retirements.* Littleton, Colo.: Fred B. Rothman & Co. Supplemented quarterly. This loose-leaf collection gathers information on judicial appointments and changes in status from such sources as the *Congressional Record, Weekly Compilation of Presidential Documents,* and news services.

- *The Third Branch: Bulletin of the Federal Courts.* Official monthly newsletter of the federal judiciary from the Administrative Office of United States Courts. Contains information on federal judicial appointments, confirmations, deaths, and resignations in its

"Milestones" section, as well as other topics of general interest. This is a good resource for use in supplementing the information provided by the various directories that are produced once a year. Also available on-line at http://www.uscourts.gov/ttb/index.html.

- *United States Law Week.* Washington, D.C.: The Bureau of National Affairs. Weekly publication lists judicial nominations by the President and confirmations by the U.S. Senate, as well as coverage of other judicial personnel changes. Also available on WESTLAW® and LEXIS®.

- *Vacancies in the Federal Judiciary.* Official list of judicial vacancies on the site of the Administrative Office of the United States Courts, along with corresponding nominations. http://www.uscourts.gov/vacancies/judgevacancy.htm.

- *Senate Judiciary Committee.* Direct from the source listings of recent nominations and confirmations, judicial and others, submitted by the President and under consideration by the committees. http://www.senate.gov/legislative/legis_act_nominations_civilian.html; http://www.senate.gov/~judiciary/.

- *Weekly Compilation of Presidential Documents.* Washington, D.C.: Government Printing Office. Names of people nominated to the federal bench.

- *WESTLAW® and LEXIS-NEXIS®.* Searchable for nominations and confirmations in the federal judiciary directly as they appear from the databases of the *Congressional Record.*

To search for newly nominated or confirmed judges—

On LEXIS® (software): library: GENFED; File: RECORD.

On LEXIS® (http://lawschool.lexis.com/): Federal Legal-U.S.; Individual Congressional Record Material; Congressional Record Current Congress; Search: nomination w/3 received or confirmed and judge w/3 circuit or district.

On WESTLAW® (http://lawschool.westlaw.com/): Database: CR; Search: nomination /s received confirmed & judge /s circuit district.

ADDITIONAL READING ON COURTS AND CLERKSHIPS:

· *Chambers Handbook for Judges' Law Clerks and Secretaries.* 1994 Federal Judicial Center, with reprinted version by West Publishing. Useful guide to read before your clerkship, and even before an interview to gather a flavor of the atmosphere and protocol in chambers. Condensed information covering the role of a law clerk, the judicial code of conduct, civil and criminal procedure, federal court structure, chambers and case management. Includes a helpful section on research and writing particular for judicial clerkships.

· *Courting the Clerkship: Perspectives on the Opportunities and Obstacles for Judicial Clerkships,* Report on the 2000 National Judicial Clerkship Study (National Association for Law Placement 2000). All the empirical data you ever need to know about judicial clerkships and the application process from this first-ever national comprehensive study. Also available on-line at http://www.nalp.org/nalp-research/clrksumm.htm.

· *The Courts: An Excellent Place for Attorneys of Color to Launch Their Careers.* 1998. Overview brochure published by the National Association for Law Placement with the assistance of the American Bar Association Judicial Administration Division Task Force on Opportunities for Minorities, also available on-line at www.abanet.org/minorities/judiciary/courts.html. (For more specialized resources regarding women and minorities, *see* Chapter 14 on Minorities, Women, and Clerkships.)

· *Federal Law Clerk.* Administrative Office of United States Courts. This brochure provides a brief overview of the role of law clerks and general information regarding the application and appointment process for the federal judiciary.

· *Judicial Externships: The Clinic Inside the Courthouse.* Cochran, Rebecca A., Cincinnati: Anderson Publishing Co. (Second edition 1999). Instructional text for classroom component of a judicial externship, which includes materials on the role of the law clerk, judicial ethics, and opinion writing.

- *Judicial Process in America.* Carp, Robert A. and Stidham, Ronald. Congressional Quarterly, Inc. / January 2001. Discussion of the work of lawyers and judges in civil and criminal courts at the state and federal levels.

- *Judicial Writing Manual.* Federal Judicial Center 1991. Manual to help judges organize opinions and improve their opinion writing (including the use of law clerks). Drawing on interviews with 24 experienced judges and guided by a board of editors comprising judges, law professors and writers, the manual offers advice on writing tailored to the needs of the federal judiciary.

- **The Roles of Magistrates in Federal District Courts.** Seron, Carroll. Federal Judicial Center 1983. A description of the scope of responsibilities and experiences from a survey of 191 full-time magistrate judges in 82 district courts. The report also describes the processes by which magistrate judges are assigned those responsibilities and the frequency with which they are assigned various tasks. Note, however, the date of publication; this interesting report is helpful mainly to show you some of the functions of a magistrate judge, the scope of which has expanded even further since then.

On-line Sources

Here are some selected on-line resources. Since information on the Internet is continually growing and changing, this is just a starting point for your exploration of the web. In addition, many law school websites with judicial clerkship resources are also available and may be found through a browser search for information on judicial clerkships. (For Internet resources regarding judicial nominations and confirmations, *see* section above.)

- *Welcome to the World of Judicial Clerkships—www.judicialclerkships.com— "Your clerkship source."*™ As discussed above, my website will serve as the starting point to help you navigate the maze of courts and clerkship opportunities on the web. In addition to my most current information and advice, this central site includes key links to the best court sites and judicial clerkship listings (some of which are listed here below), along with other services for students and judges.

- *Federal Law Clerk Information System*—https://lawclerks.ao.uscourts.gov. The Administrative Office of the United States Courts has developed an on-line database containing general law clerk employment information and details supplied by judges regarding their own particular hiring schedules and application criteria. This searchable database includes postings of clerkship positions from the following types of courts: all 13 Circuit Courts, including Federal Circuit, Claims Court, International Trade; types of judges: Appellate, District, Magistrate, Bankruptcy, Claims, International Trade; types of clerkships: term, career, and temporary. Note that staff attorney positions are not included in this database. For postings of staff attorney positions, you should first check the general employment opportunities on the Federal Judiciary website, at http://www.uscourts.gov/employment/opportunity.html (listed under the position title "Staff Attorney"), and then the other job listings for the United States Office of Personnel Management at http://www.usajobs.opm.gov. In addition, staff attorney openings are often posted directly on the individual court websites (listed below).

- *The Federal Judiciary Homepage*—http://www.uscourts.gov/links.html. Maintained by the Administrative Office of United States Courts, provides information about the federal court system, news and publications, including extensive links to other federal court sites.

- *Federal Judges Biographical Information*—http://air.fjc.gov/history/judges_frm.html. Profiles of all federal judges who have served on the U.S. District Courts, U.S. Courts of Appeal and U.S. Supreme Court since 1789, provided by the Federal Judicial Center.

- *The Nation's Court Directory*—http://www.courts.net/. Links to state and federal courts and other sites of interest.

- *National Center for State Courts*—http://www.ncsconline.org/. Contains links to state, federal and international courts, plus various job announcements for state and federal court positions (not necessarily law clerks, but court clerks, deputy clerks, court administrators and so forth).

- *The Federal Court Locator*—Villanova University School of Law http://vls.law.vill.edu/Locator/fedcourt.html. Includes links to U.S. Courts of Appeal, U.S. District Courts, other federal courts and related federal agencies.

- *The State Court Locator*—Villanova University School of Law http://vls.law.vill.edu/Locator/fedcourt.html. Provides links to home pages and opinions by numerous state judiciaries.

- *U.S. Supreme Court*—http://www.supremecourtus.gov. Official website of the United States Supreme Court, with information about cases and the Court. (For more specialized resources regarding the U.S. Supreme Court, *see* Chapter 11 on Clerking for the Supreme Court.)

- U.S. Courts of Appeals by Circuit—case law and the courts (sample these, or use links from other sites, above):

First	http://www.ca1.uscourts.gov/ or www.law.emory.edu/1circuit
Second	www.tourolaw.edu/2ndCircuit/indexf.html or http://csmail.law.pace.edu/lawlib/legal/us-legal/judiciary/second-circuit.html
Third	http://www.ca3.uscourts.gov/
Fourth	www.ca4.uscourts.gov or www.law.emory.edu/4circuit
Fifth	www.ca5.uscourts.gov
Sixth	www.ca6.uscourts.gov or www.law.emory.edu/6circuit
Seventh	www.ca7.uscourts.gov or www.kentlaw.edu/7circuit/
Eighth	www.ca8.uscourts.gov/index.html
Ninth	www.ca9.uscourts.gov
Tenth	www.ck10.uscourts.gov
Eleventh	www.ca11.uscourts.gov
District of Columbia	www.cadc.uscourts.gov
Federal Circuit	www.fedcir.gov

- *Other Federal Courts:*

U.S. Court of Federal Claims	http://www.law.gwu.edu/fedcl/
U.S. Court of International Trade	http://www.uscit.gov/
U.S. Tax Court	http://www.ustaxcourt.gov/ustcweb.htm

- *U.S. Judicial Branch Resources*—http://lcweb.loc.gov/global/judiciary.html. Source of information from the Library of Congress with access to judicial opinions, court rules, statutes, regulations and other links.

- *U.S. Department of Justice*—http://www.usdoj.gov/02organizations/02_6.html. Offers legal documents, organization chart, employment opportunities and links to websites of other federal government sites, including federal agencies.

- *WashLaw WEB*—http://www.washlaw.edu. Comprehensive set of links to legal websites and federal and state courts, plus state and local government resources.

- *Findlaw*—http://www.findlaw.com. Legal search engine to on-line legal resources with links to government and court websites. You can also use this resource to find judicial opinions or case law of the judge to aid in preparation for the interview.

- *Legal Information Institute*—http://www.law.cornell.edu/. Provides information on a variety of legal issues, court opinions, laws and news, plus a directory of the highest federal and state courts with links to background, composition and decisions of each court.

- *American Judicature Society*—http://www.ajs.org/. This is a nonpartisan organization with a national membership of judges, lawyers and non-legally trained citizens interested in the administration of justice. Site includes publications and links to websites of court- and law-related organizations and information resources.

OTHER COMPUTER RESOURCES FOR DIRECTORIES, JUDICIAL OPINIONS, AND NEWS

You can conduct searches on LEXIS® and WESTLAW® to gather information about judges, clerkship openings, current and former judicial clerks, and hiring criteria. Judicial opinions, which may be easily obtained on either of these databases, offer insight into a particular judge's cases, writing style, and philosophy; as I said earlier, this is an important part of your interview preparation. Moreover, LEXIS-NEXIS® and WESTLAW®, as well as Internet searches, can locate relevant articles about these judges. (Remember too that you can also use LEXIS® and WESTLAW® to search for judicial nominations and confirmations, using the search listed in that section above.) So, what follows here is the nitty-gritty on how to access this information efficiently using these resources.

As a caveat, it should be noted that the directories and resources available on LEXIS® and WESTLAW® are continually changing and expanding, along with the applicable search language and techniques. Be sure to look for whatever updated instructional materials on these computer resources may be periodically distributed at your school. Note that LEXIS® and WESTLAW® are available both as a computer software package and, more recently, on-line as a web-based searchable application.

· **LEXIS-NEXIS® (www.lawschool.lexis.com)[6]**

The current issue of *The Judicial Staff Directory* (JUDDIR) is available on LEXIS®, as well as the on-line version of the *NALP Judicial Clerkship Directory* and many other useful sources. I have categorized the types of sample searches below depending on your preferred method of using this service, whether on-line or as a software database.

ON-LINE SEARCHES:

To find all sources that list information about a particular judge or court—
    SOURCE: Judicial Job Sources—All
    TERMS: court(seventh circuit)
To find biographical information on a particular judge
    SOURCE: Judicial Staff Directory
    TERMS: name(guido w/3 calabresi)

To find a judge's listing for more background information
SOURCE: Martindale-Hubbell
TERMS: name(guido w/3 calabresi)

To find the names of judicial clerks from your law school
SOURCE: NALP Judicial Clerkship Directory
TERMS: clerk–98/99(Cornell)

To find recent news articles that discuss judicial clerkship positions
SOURCE: News Sources—Last 90 Days
TERMS: judicial or law w/3 clerk! w/10 judge w/10 interview or application

To investigate any current events involving a particular judge
SOURCE: News Sources—Last 90 Days
TERMS: name(guido w/3 calabresi)

To read opinions written by a particular judge
SOURCE: Explore in Federal Legal US for the jurisdiction
TERMS: opinionby(guido w/3 calabresi); Dates: Previous Year

To view the listing for a particular bankruptcy court
SOURCE: Directory of Bankruptcy Attorneys
TERMS: district (Ohio and Southern)

To find the information about federal jobs in a particular agency
SOURCE: Federal Careers for Attorneys
TERMS: agency (Treasury)

SOFTWARE SEARCHES:

Library: CAREER; File: JCLERK

Contains the *Judicial Clerkship Directory,* which is a database compiled from judges' responses to a questionnaire. It covers judges at the federal courts, including appellate, district, bankruptcy and magistrate, and at the highest state courts. For those judges who respond, the database provides information on law clerk openings, salary, application and interview dates, clerkship length, hiring criteria and procedures, and the names of past and present clerks along with their law schools.

Library: CAREER; File: ARCHV

Includes the *Judicial Clerkship Directory* from 1992 to the current year. Information may not be complete if a judge did not respond to the questionnaire in some years. This is a handy technique to ascertain a wider perspective on identifying past clerks and the law schools from which they graduated.

Library: CAREER; File: JUDDIR

Provides the *Judicial Staff Directory,* which includes lists of all circuit judges, their secretaries and their law clerks, as well as some limited judicial biographies with notable opinions. However, this information may not be as up-to-date as other files, so you should consult JCLERK for current staff and law clerk information.

Library: CAREER; File: FCA

Features the publication *Federal Careers for Attorneys,* which gives detailed descriptions of the application requirements for jobs in all three branches of the government, including employment in federal agencies.

Library: GENFED; File: USLW

Contains the *United States Law Week,* which you can search to find names of recent judicial appointments. In the GENFED library, you can also find topical opinions written by a particular judge.

Library: LEGNEW; File: ALLNWS

Search to find recent stories discussing judicial clerkships. For example, judicial or law w/3 clerk! w/10 judge w/10 interview or application.

Library: NEWS; File: CURNWS

Search CURNWS to find recent stories about significant cases in which a particular judge has been involved. For example, judge w/s barrington w/s parker.

Segment Search

To find opinions the judge has written, run a segment search in the library and file of the court in which the judge is located. For example, writtenby(parker).

· WESTLAW® (www.lawschool.westlaw.com)

Featured on WESTLAW® are the West's *Legal Directory of Judicial Clerkships* (WLD-CLERK), and the *Almanac of the Federal Judiciary* (AFJ). The following overview demonstrates the databases and searches most useful for discovering information about judges and judicial clerkships on WESTLAW®:

Database: WLD-CLERK

Contains West's *Legal Directory of Judicial Clerkships*, which is a database derived from judges' responses to questionnaires. For those federal appellate, district, bankruptcy, magistrate and state court (including trial court) judges who respond, the database provides information on clerk openings, salary, interview dates, clerkship length, application procedures, and previous clerks and their law schools. For example, for a description of clerkships in a court, simply fill in the *Court* and *State* blanks. To find a listing for a particular judge, type his or her name in the *Hiring Judge* text box. You can also utilize as searchable the text boxes for *Selection Criteria* (*e.g.*, type in "law review") or *Past and Present Clerks* (*e.g.*, type in "georgetown").

Database: WLD-JUDGE

Houses the West's *Legal Directory of Judges*. In addition to contact information, it displays information on the judge's education, work history, teaching experience, published works, affiliations and significant decisions. Enter the particular judge's name in the *Judge's Name* blank. If you wish to view a list of judges who attended your law school, enter its name in the *Law School* text box. You may also use the *State* text box to limit your list further by this factor.

Database: WLD-COURT

Contains the West's *Legal Directory of Courts*, which provides a convenient way to obtain information about state courts as well, simply by entering the word "state" in the *Court* blank, and the abbreviation for that state in the *State* blank.

Database: AFJ

Carries the *Almanac of the Federal Judiciary*. In addition to contact information, it includes information on the judge's nominating President, family, education, work history, previous judicial positions, associations, publications, and noteworthy decisions (the decisions section may be more comprehensive in the AFJ database than in the WLD-JUDGE database). It is important to note that the *Almanac of the Federal Judiciary* is available in print as well (*see* above). The printed version contains two important sections not available on-line: Lawyers' Evaluations and Media Coverage. Here is a sample search for biographical information on a judge: ju(guido /3 calabresi).

Database: WLD

To find the names of attorneys who have clerked for a particular judge, click "Terms & Connectors" in the *Search type* box, and enter the search, *e.g.*: stephen /3 breyer /s clerk.

Database: WLD-GOVMAN

To retrieve information on the agencies of the judicial branch of the United States government, use this database, which contains the *United States Government Manual*. Restrict your search to the prelim field as follows: pr(judicial).

Database: ALLNEWS

Search ALLNEWS to find recent stories about noteworthy cases in which a particular judge has been involved. For example, judge /s barrington /s parker.

Database Search

To find opinions the judge has written, run a segment search in the database of the court in which the judge is located. For example, ju(parker). You may also add a date restriction such as—& da(aft 6/2000).

A variety of people can give you valuable input as you research different judges and clerkship opportunities. People to contact include:

- *Current clerks:* The most accurate information will come from the judge's current clerks (but remember that they are "interviewing" you and be careful not to alienate them). When in doubt, a polite phone call to chambers to inquire about the judge's application procedures or the status of your application is always acceptable. This recommendation and caveat applies as well to the other staff in the judges' chambers and court personnel offices.

- *Former clerks:* Former clerks are a good (and safe) source of information, particularly the graduates of your school. Recent graduates are best for this purpose, as they can give you the most current information. As a rule, they are generally very willing to help out and speak enthusiastically about their clerkship experiences. You can either contact them directly through lists maintained in your school, or consult any written letters or evaluations your school collects. By the way, you can consult former clerks not only about their own judges, but about all of the judges in the jurisdiction in which they clerked and in which they currently practice. Note, however, that the best source of information about a judge comes from someone who actually clerked for that judge; thus, you may need to discount the more indirect information accordingly.

- *Local attorneys:* Attorneys from the city in which the judge sits generally will have valuable information to share. Often they will have practiced before the judge, or know someone who has. Attorneys in practice can give you a sense of the reputation of a judge and degree of respect in the legal community. Although attorneys almost always have opinions about judges based largely on their own personal encounters, you should consider the perspective of the source and weigh this information accordingly.

- *Third year students:* Many third year students will have gathered information from these sources in their second year, and should be willing to pass it along. Since they have finished the process you are entering, they are often a key source of advice for successful strategies and planning. Beware, though, of the rumor mill, which is rampant with false information and exaggeration. Oftentimes a student would call me in a panic with a far-fetched story (*e.g.*, calling from the airport: "I hear that a student has turned down an offer from a certain judge and now all of the judges in the Ninth Circuit are refusing to hire anyone from our school—should I cancel my interview?"). Sometimes I was able to recognize the original source of the wild rumor before it went astray, and sometimes not—but it was invariably false! Also be sure not to limit yourself to the judges and courts talked of so much by your fellow students. Forge your own pathways!

· *Faculty:* Many faculty members will be able to convey information about some judges and direct you to other faculty members with knowledge of particular courts or judges. Knowing whom they have connections with may influence the direction of your applications as well. The earlier you enlist their help the better, both for your initial information-gathering efforts and for your eventual letters of recommendation as part of your clerkship applications.

· *Career Counselors:* They know a lot, if I do say so myself (having been one at Yale), and can give you a broader perspective from years of working with students and judges. Share with them your career plans and goals, and let them advise you in your personal decision whether to clerk and in your clerkship application process.

CONCLUSION

Of course, your best resource is in your hands right now—this book! As you can see, there is a great deal out there to explore about particular judges, courts, and clerkship opportunities. In order to do so efficiently and wisely, you are now favorably equipped with this book as your handy guide. The need for such a master handbook has been clearly documented by the National Judicial Clerkship Study through the requests of career services professionals and law students for more centralized resources—hence this book! Hopefully, it will serve you well in your quest for the ideal judicial clerkship for you. Bon voyage!

Notes

1. Among the resources most valued were the *Almanac of the Federal Judiciary*, the *NALP Federal and State Judicial Clerkship Directory*, and the WESTLAW® and LEXIS® resources. *See* NALP Report at 34–35, 56–57; Tables 14 and 41. Note that the surveys from this study did not include for evaluation the Federal Law Clerk Information System or the Judicial Clerkship Website, as they had not at that time been developed, but many respondents did ask for such centralized resources.
2. NALP Report at 34–35, 56–57; Tables 14 and 41.
3. According to the National Judicial Clerkship Study, law school students as well as career professionals highly value the clerkship handbooks published by their career services offices; however, 23% of schools, mostly the smaller schools, do not publish a clerkship handbook. *See* NALP Report at 34 and 56.
4. Postings of letters from judges seeking clerks proved to be the most highly valued resource in the eyes of career services professionals. However, more than half of the students noted that they did not use this resource.
5. More than half of the law schools have a judges' database, to which they devote considerable time and resources in keeping it updated. (*See* NALP Report at 34–35, and Table 15.) Most students find the databases of their schools to be very or moderately useful in the clerkship application process. (*See* NALP Report at 56–57, Table 41.)
6. LEXIS is a registered trademark of Reed Elsevier Properties Inc., used with the permission of LexisNexis.

CHAPTER fourteen

Minorities, Women, and Clerkships

This chapter is directed more broadly to reach not only students but their law schools and other organizations—with the key information and strategies here, you will be well equipped to use this as your handbook to further the goals of minorities and women in the clerkship arena. As recent efforts from several fronts have been directed towards increasing racial and ethnic diversity in the legal profession, this is indeed a good time for women and minorities to pursue a judicial clerkship. The American Bar Association ("ABA") set forth as Goal IX: "to create full and equal participation in the profession by minorities and women." Attention is now being focused in particular on the representation of minorities in judicial clerkships. During his term as President of the ABA, William G. Paul asserted:

Judicial law clerks become leaders in the profession, become
judges and partners in law firms. They are very visible in the
justice system and are role models for law students. Having
minority clerks provides judges with more diverse views
about the law and about the effects of judicial decisions.[1]

With this charge, the ABA has led the initiative to expand the
opportunities for minorities and women to serve as judicial clerks,
launching innovative programs described below, as well as co-spon-
soring the National Judicial Clerkship Study conducted by the
National Association for Law Placement.

THE DEMOGRAPHIC REALITY

The National Judicial Clerkship Study included among its most significant findings the discovery that minority representation in clerkships is generally lower than in law school populations, although this
does vary somewhat by ethnic group. Overall, only 15% of all judicial
clerkships are held by minorities, despite the fact that minorities
make up 30% of the general population and 20% of the law students.
However, this discrepancy did not result from a difference in the success of their applications, but rather a lower application rate of the
minority students.

For four of the last five years included in the study (1994–1998),
women comprised a majority of the law clerk population. Yet a disproportionately high percentage of women serve in local and state courts
rather than the more competitive and prestigious federal courts. This
gap has decreased slightly through the years and varied greatly by the
courts of each circuit, but the study also revealed that success rates of
women applicants as a whole were lower than those of males.

Taken together, the findings indicate that both women and minorities have not yet achieved parity in all levels of judicial clerkships. (See
the Appendix of this book for more of the statistics and reprints of
the accompanying tables).[2] It should be noted that as the number of
women in the law school class has recently increased to surpass the

number of men, one would expect the number of women in clerkships to rise accordingly. Consider also an interesting statistic regarding the number of women judges; of 655 federal district court judgeships, only 136 are women.[3] It is anticipated that, with the increasing numbers in the law school class, this figure should advance as well.

TOWARD THE GOAL

Since the under-representation of minority law clerks resulted from a smaller number of applicants rather than from a rejection of their applications by judges, the National Clerkship Study identified the need for the applicant pool to become more diverse: "Law schools should adopt as a priority encouraging more minority students to apply for judicial clerkships by offering more programs, resources, and counseling for these students." As part of its Action Plan, the study also calls for the judiciary to "join many other organizations who have embraced the goal of diversity in background, experience, race, ethnicity, gender, sexual orientation, and age for the legal profession by setting a similar goal for their clerkship ranks."[4]

In the spirit of the goal of diversity, this chapter will present some special strategies, programs, and resources available to women and minorities in order to encourage your successful application for a judicial clerkship. A clerkship is, after all, a key to advancement in all areas of the legal profession.

INNOVATIVE PROGRAMS

· Law Schools

Law schools can enhance the application efforts of their students in several ways. Faculty should direct support to women and students of color, as both mentors in the process and providers of weighty letters of recommendation for clerkship applications. Faculty mentoring can take the form of individual one-on-one counseling and through programs such as panels of faculty members giving information and advice. Also helpful are programs run by student organizations, possibly in conjunction with career services offices, that utilize peer advice. General sessions on judicial clerkships can be co-sponsored by minority organizations to encourage attendance by their members. In addition, law schools should offer other forms of institutional support such as financial assistance for the costs of the application and interviewing, and especially for the clerkship term.

At the outset, you should consider your options and take advantage of any assistance offered by the career office of your school, particularly services directed to women and minorities. Pursue every avenue in your quest to find mentors, develop a network, explore various career opportunities and facilitate your application process. Consult with the financial aid office of your law school to investigate any further support that may be available (*e.g.,* low-cost loans or grants).

· **Bar Associations**

Programs mixing judges and current or former law clerks are particularly beneficial whether initiated by the law schools, the judiciary, bar associations or other organizations. The substantive networking can result in a valuable exchange of knowledge and understanding.

The American Bar Association recently launched one such program, a joint effort by the Judicial Division and the Commission on Racial and Ethnic Diversity in the Profession. The ABA Judicial Clerkship Program provides structured networking activities in which students can demonstrate knowledge and research skills in a small-group setting while interacting with the judges in a team-building project. The participating judges are asked to make a commitment to hire at least two minority judicial law clerks over the next five years. When it debuted in February 2001 at the ABA midyear meeting, the program included nearly 30 minority students from five law schools as participants, providing the opportunity to network with over 20 judges from around the country. Having garnered initial positive feedback, the program will be expanded to include additional law schools and judges in future years.

One of the student participants in the debut of the ABA Judicial Clerkship Program commented: "As a first year law student, this was definitely exciting; I had the opportunity to work with judges on an assignment. I was not sure what to expect. The judges were very enthusiastic and welcoming. I had never worked with a judge and was surprised by their demeanor. We were able to ask questions about what law clerks actually do, what qualifications the judges sought when screening clerkship applicants, and what we could do to better prepare ourselves to work with judges." Based on her positive interaction with the judges and her realization of the need for minority law clerks, she has decided to pursue the goal of obtaining a clerkship. In sum, a presenter commented: "I felt the program was a success. The students left motivated to pursue clerkships, reassured that they were viable candidates, and with a few more contacts. Also, the comfort of having spoken with judges, our own legal royalty, will serve them well as they pursue clerkships and other aspects of their professional careers."[5]

The ABA Section of Antitrust Law has sponsored a second initiative in this area. The Racial and Ethnic Minority Judicial Externship program is a full-time, eight-week minimum, summer externship program open to all first or second year minority law students who want to do legal research and writing for state or federal trial and appellate judges in Illinois, Southern Texas, San Francisco, Seattle or Los Angeles, with expansion to judges from other cities and regions likely in the future. Each of the externs receives a stipend of $1500 for the summer, as well as invaluable exposure to the judicial system. Applications are due at the beginning of each year for the limited number of spaces in the program.[6] Ky P. Ewing, Jr., chair of the section, underscored the importance of this program: "The efforts of the ABA will ensure that minority students have access to opportunity in the profession, including clerkships in the courts after graduation. The summer extern program provides these students with direction and provides a model for skill building in legal research and writing. Their work for state and federal judges will be invaluable to them in their careers and ensure they have the door of equal opportunity open to them."[7]

You might consider participating in one of these exciting programs, and investigating any others that come along. Moreover, you can actively encourage the organizations in which you participate to address these specialized issues and set up further informational and networking programs.

· The Judiciary

The judiciary also has been assuming a greater role in developing more judicial outreach programs.[8] For instance, in 1999 then-Florida Supreme Court Chief Justice Major B. Harding formed a 13-member equal opportunity committee of judges, court administrators, and attorneys with the goal of developing strategies to increase minority representation among all court staff members, including law clerks. As a consequence, minority representation rose to about 18%of the state's 27 Supreme Court's clerks. "He made a concerted effort to get more diversity among law clerks, so he reached out to us," observed Stephanie Redfearn, Assistant Dean for Academic Affairs at Florida State University.[9] Justices also participate in panels the school sponsors. In New Jersey, the Administrative Office of the Courts has spearheaded an annual program designed to encourage minorities to apply for clerkships in the state courts, including holding seminars with judges and clerks at the state's three law schools in cooperation with minority student groups, and sending out recruiting materials to organizations to help recruit minorities for state court jobs. The results thus far in the diversity of law clerks have been strikingly positive.[10] For more such initiatives, be sure to check with the courts and schools in your area to see what programs they may be planning to increase contacts with the judges and to encourage diversity in the judiciary.

SPECIALIZED RESOURCES

In addition to the general resources on judges and clerkships, you can gather some valuable information through these specialized publications, many of which are available at the career services office of your school.

- *Directory of Minority Judges of the United States.* Chicago: American Bar Association, Judicial Division, Task Force on Minorities in the Judiciary (3d ed. 2001). This book provides names, courts and addresses of more than 2,000 minority judges, divided into four sections: African-American, Asian/Pacific, Hispanic, and Native American.

- *The Courts: An Excellent Place for Attorneys of Color to Launch Their Careers.* 2002 (brochure published by the National Association for Law Placement with the assistance of the American Bar Association Judicial Administration Division Task Force on Opportunities for Minorities), also available on-line at www.abanet.org/minorities/judiciary/courts.html.

- Alliance for Justice is a national association of environmental, civil rights, mental health, women's, children's and consumer advocacy organizations. Their website, http://www.afj.org/jsp/home.html, contains valuable information on these issues, including the *Annual Report on the Judiciary* (with statistics about the diversity of judicial nominations and confirmations) and a map delineating the racial demographics of the federal courts of appeals.

- Court websites, *e.g.,* http://www.uscourts.gov/links.html (*see also* Resources Chapter).

Organizations to Consult

National, local, and regional organizations for women and minorities in the legal profession also can provide significant information and career connections. As a start, you can consult their websites for resources and programs. The following organizations, many of which also include law student divisions, might be helpful in your networking and information-gathering efforts:

Student Organizations:

- Specific law school student organizations for women and minorities-check with your own school.

- National Black Law Students Association (BLSA), http://www.nblsa.org/.

- National Native American Law Student Association (NNALSA), http://www.utulsa.edu/law/indianlaw/nalsa/.

- National Women Law Students' Association, http://www.nwlsa.org/.

American Bar Association Activities:

- Commission on Racial and Ethnic Diversity in the Profession, http://www.abanet.org/minorities. Includes information on careers, networking opportunities, the judicial clerkship program and other resources.

- Section of Antitrust Law, http://www.abanet.org/antitrust/program2002.html. Information on the Racial and Ethnic Minority Judicial Externship program.

- Young Lawyers Division Minorities in the Profession Committee, http://www.abanet.org/yld/minorities/home.html.

- Judicial Division, http://www.abanet.org/jd.

- The Multicultural Women Attorneys Network (MWAN), http://www.abanet.org/minorities/mwan. A joint project of the ABA Commission on Women in the Profession and the ABA Commission on Racial and Ethnic Diversity in the Profession; addresses issues of special concern to women lawyers who are members of minority groups.

- Commission on Women in the Profession, http://www.abanet.org/women/home.html.

Other Organizations:

· National Association of Women Lawyers,
  http://www.abanet.org/nawl/. Offers law student memberships
  that include a free copy of the *National Directory of Women-Owned
  Law Firms and Women Lawyers*, a networking resource.

· Regional and local bar associations and organizations. *See Directory of Women and Minority Bar Associations* (provided by the
  Women and Minorities Involvement Committee of the Tort and
  Insurance Practice Section of the ABA), available on-line at
  http://www.abanet.org/tips/wami/barassociations.html.

· National Association for Law Placement, http://www.nalp.org/.

· National Bar Association, http://www.nationalbar.org, an organization for African-American lawyers and judges, with free membership to law students.

· Hispanic National Bar Council, http://www.hnba.com/ (has a
  student division).

· National Asian Pacific American Bar Association,
  http://www.napaba.org/.

· Native American Bar Association, http://www.nativeamerican-
  bar.org/.

· National Association of Women's Bar Associations,
  http://www.ncwba.org/.

· National Association of Women Judges,
  http://www.nawj.org/default.htm.

· National Women's Law Center, http://www.nwlc.org/.

STRIVE FOR DIVERSITY

The efforts to encourage students to apply are starting to show results
in the growing number of minority and women law clerks—and so, if
you apply, you will be contributing towards diversity and helping this

trend to continue! As you have discovered throughout this book, there are a multitude of reasons why doing so will advance your future career as well. The atmosphere is primed for you to achieve your personal goals, so take advantage of this great opportunity, and together we can strive for further progress in this area.

Notes

1. News release, "ABA Launches Two Programs to Boost Number of Minorities Serving in Judicial Clerkships," Chicago, Ill. (Internet Wire), 2/15/2000, (http://www.abanet.org/media/feb00/dallasrelease.html). Mr. Paul served as President of the ABA from August 1999 to July 2000. The initiatives he inspired in this area continue to grow.
2. NALP Report at 9–17, 26, 31, 34, and 44; *see* Tables 2–6 and 28, reproduced here in the Appendix.
3. Glater, Jonathan D., "Women are Close to Being Majority of Law Students," *New York Times*, March 26, 2001, A1, A16 (*citing* the Alliance for Justice, a Washington-based organization for nonprofit advocacy groups).
4. NALP Report at 16 and 17.
5. For more information about this program, *see* http://www.abanet.org/minorities/jcp/home.html.
6. For application information, *see* http://www.abanet.org/antitrust/program2002.html.
7. News release, "More than 30 Judges to Participate in 2001 Minority Judicial Clerkship Program, Minority Law Students to Serve as Externs for Federal and Local Judges," Chicago, Ill. (Internet Wire), 1/31/01 (http://www.abanet.org/media/jan01/clerkship.html).
8. *See, e.g.*, Fruin, Judge Richard, *Judicial Outreach on a Shoestring: A Working Manual* (American Bar Association Judicial Division, 1999) (a workbook for courts and schools in implementing community outreach efforts); and *Roadmap*, "Racial and Ethnic Bias in the Courts" (ABA Office of Justice Initiatives, 2000) (provides valuable information and specific examples of projects and programs focused on bias issues).
9. Nealy, Jounice, "Minorities Finding Clerkships Key to Law Careers," *St Petersburg Times*, Dec. 25, 2000, on-line at http://www.sptimes.com/News/122500/State/Minorities_finding_cl.shtml.
10. Of the 461 total law clerks in the New Jersey state courts for the 2001–2002 term, 22% were minorities, surpassing the diversity of the graduating classes of its three law schools, in which minorities made up 19%. *See* Toutant, Charles, "Minority Clerkships Holding Steady: New Jersey judiciary boasts hiring rate upward of 22 percent," *New Jersey Law Journal*, Feb. 22, 2002.

APPENDIX

A

Proper Forms of Address

Addressee	Address on cover letter and envelope	Salutation
U.S. Supreme Court		
The Chief Justice	The Honorable (full name) Chief Justice of the United States The Supreme Court 1 First Street, N.E. Washington, D.C. 20543	Dear Chief Justice (last name):
Associate Justice	The Honorable (full name) Associate Justice The Supreme Court 1 First Street, N.E. Washington, D.C. 20543	Dear Justice (last name):
U.S. Court of Appeals		
Chief Judge Senior Judge	Honorable (full name) Chief Judge (Senior Judge) United States Court of Appeals for the (Number-th) Circuit Address	Dear Judge (last name):

| Judge | Honorable (full name)
United States Court of Appeals
for the (Number-th) Circuit
Address | Dear Judge (last name): |

U.S. District Court

| Chief Judge
Senior Judge | Honorable (full name)
Chief Judge (Senior Judge)
United States District Court
for the (District Name)
Address | Dear Judge (last name): |
| Judge | Honorable (full name)
United States District Court
for the (District Name)
Address | Dear Judge (last name): |

U.S. Magistrate:

| Judge | Honorable (full name)
United States Magistrate Judge
United States District
Court for the (District Name)
Address | Dear Judge (last name): |

U.S. Bankruptcy:

| Chief Judge | Honorable Judge (full name)
Chief Judge
United States Bankruptcy
Court for the (District Name)
Address | Dear Judge (last name): |

U.S. Bankruptcy:

| Judge | Honorable Judge (full name)
United States Bankruptcy Court
for the (District Name)
Address | Dear Judge (last name): |

Other Federal Courts

| Chief Judge
Judge | Honorable (full name)
(Title of Judge)
Name of Court
Address | Dear Judge (last name): |

State Courts

State Supreme Court:

Chief Justice	Honorable (full name)	Dear Justice (last name):
	Chief Justice	
	Supreme Court for the State	
	(Commonwealth) of (State)	
	Address	
Justice	Honorable (full name)	Dear Justice (last name):
	Supreme Court for the State	
	(Commonwealth) of (State)	
	Address	

Other State Courts:

Chief Judge	Honorable (full name)	Dear Judge (last name):
Judge	(Title of Judge)	
	Name of Court	
	Address	

The Federal Courts by Circuit, District, and Location[1]

United States Courts of Appeals

Court of Appeals	Districts Included in Circuit	Number of Authorized Judgeships	Location/Postal Address
Federal Circuit	United States	12	Washington, DC 20439
District of Columbia Circuit	District of Columbia	12	Washington, DC 20001
First Circuit	Maine Massachusetts New Hampshire Rhode Island Puerto Rico	6	Boston, MA 02109
Second Circuit	Connecticut New York Vermont	13	New York, NY 10007
Third Circuit	Delaware New Jersey Pennsylvania Virgin Islands	14	Philadelphia, PA 19106

Fourth Circuit	Maryland North Carolina South Carolina Virginia West Virginia	15	Richmond, VA 23219
Fifth Circuit	Louisiana Mississippi Texas	17	New Orleans, LA 70130
Sixth Circuit	Ohio Kentucky Michigan Tennessee	16	Cincinnati, OH 45202
Seventh Circuit	Illinois Indiana Wisconsin	11	Chicago, IL 60604
Eighth Circuit	Arkansas Iowa Minnesota Missouri Nebraska North Dakota South Dakota	11	St. Louis, MO 63101
Ninth Circuit	Alaska Arizona California Hawaii Idaho Montana Nevada Oregon Washington Guam N. Mariana Islands	28	San Francisco, CA 94101
Tenth Circuit	Colorado Kansas New Mexico Oklahoma Utah Wyoming	12	Denver, CO 80294
Eleventh Circuit	Alabama Florida Georgia	12	Atlanta, GA 30303

United States District Courts

STATE	District	Number of Authorized Judgeships	Location
Alabama	Northern district	7	Birmingham, AL 35203
	Middle district	3	Montgomery, AL 36101
	Southern district	3	Mobile, AL 36602
Alaska		3	Anchorage, AK 99513
Arizona		9	Phoenix, AZ 85025
Arkansas	Eastern district	5	Little Rock, AR 72203
	Western district	3	Fort Smith, AR 72902
California	Northern district	14	San Francisco, CA 94102
	Eastern district	6	Sacramento, CA 95814
	Central district	27	Los Angeles, CA 90012
	Southern district	8	San Diego, CA 92189
Colorado		7	Denver, CO 80294
Connecticut		8	New Haven, CT 06510
Delaware		4	Wilmington, DE 19801
District of Columbia		15	Washington, DC 20001
Florida	Northern district	4	Tallahassee, FL 32301
	Middle district	11	Jacksonville, FL 32201
	Southern district	17	Miami, FL 33128
Georgia	Northern district	11	Atlanta, GA 30335
	Middle district	4	Macon, GA 31202
	Southern district	3	Savannah, GA 31412
Guam		1	Agana, GU 96910
Hawaii		3	Honolulu, HI 96850
Idaho		2	Boise, ID 83724
Illinois	Northern district	22	Chicago, IL 60604
	Southern district	3	East St. Louis, IL 62202
	Central district	3	Springfield, IL 62705
Indiana	Northern district	5	South Bend, IN 46601
	Southern district	5	Indianapolis, IN 46204
Iowa	Northern district	2	Cedar Rapids, IA 52401
	Southern district	3	Des Moines, IA 50309
Kansas		5	Wichita, KS 67202
Kentucky	Eastern district	5	Lexington, KY 40596
	Western district	4	Louisville, KY 40202
	Eastern and Western	1	
Louisiana	Eastern district	13	New Orleans, LA 70130
	Middle district	2	Baton Rouge, LA 70821
	Western district	7	Shreveport, LA 71101

Maine		3	Portland, ME 04101
Maryland		10	Baltimore, MD 21201
Massachusetts		13	Boston, MA 02109
Michigan	Eastern district	15	Detroit, MI 48226
	Western district	4	Grand Rapids, MI 49503
Minnesota		7	St. Paul, MN 55101
Mississippi	Northern district	3	Oxford, MS 38655
	Southern district	6	Jackson, MS 39201
Missouri	Eastern district	6	St. Louis, MO 63101
	Western district	5	Kansas City, MO 64106
	Eastern and Western	2	
Montana		3	Billings, MT 59101
Nebraska		3	Omaha, NE 68101
Nevada		5	Las Vegas, NV 89101
New Hampshire		3	Concord, NH 03301
New Jersey		17	Newark, NJ 07102
New Mexico		6	Albuquerque, NM 87103
New York	Northern district	4	Syracuse, NY 13261
	Eastern district	15	Brooklyn, NY 11201
	Southern district	28	New York, NY 10007
	Western district	4	Buffalo, NY 14202
North Carolina	Eastern district	4	Raleigh, NC 27611
	Middle district	4	Greensboro, NC 27402
	Western district	3	Asheville, NC 28801
North Dakota		2	Bismarck, ND 58502
N. Mariana Islands		1	Saipan, N. Mar. I. 96950
Ohio	Northern district	11	Cleveland, OH 44114
	Southern district	8	Columbus, OH 43215
Oklahoma	Northern district	3	Tulsa, OK 74103
	Eastern district	1	Muskogee, OK 74401
	Western district	6	Oklahoma City, OK 73102
	Northern, Eastern, and Western	1	
Oregon		6	Portland, OR 97205
Pennsylvania	Eastern district	22	Philadelphia, PA 19106
	Middle district	6	Scranton, PA 18501
	Western district	10	Pittsburgh, PA 15230
Puerto Rico		7	Hato Rey, PR 00918
Rhode Island		3	Providence, RI 02903
South Carolina		10	Columbia, SC 29201
South Dakota		3	Sioux Falls, SD 57102

Tennessee	Eastern district	5	Knoxville, TN 37901
	Middle district	4	Nashville, TN 37203
	Western district	5	Memphis, TN 38103
Texas	Northern district	12	Dallas, TX 75242
	Southern district	19	Houston, TX 77208
	Eastern district	7	Tyler, TX 75702
	Western district	11	San Antonio, TX 78206
Utah		5	Salt Lake City, UT 84101
Vermont		2	Burlington, VT 05402
Virgin Islands		2	St. Thomas, V.I. 00801
Virginia	Eastern district	10	Alexandria, VA 22320
	Western district	4	Roanoke, VA 24006
Washington	Eastern district	4	Spokane, WA 99210
	Western district	7	Seattle, WA 98104
West Virginia	Northern district	3	Elkins, WV 26241
	Southern district	5	Charleston, WV 25329
Wisconsin	Eastern district	5	Milwaukee, WI 53202
	Western district	2	Madison, WI 53701
Wyoming		3	Cheyenne, WY 82001

Notes

1. Reprinted from the Administrative Office of U.S. Courts, *Understanding the Federal Courts* (1999), http://www.uscourts.gov/UFC99.pdf, pp. 43–45.

APPENDIX

C

Code of Conduct for Judicial Employees

This Code of Conduct applies to all employees of the Judicial Branch except Justices; judges; and employees of the United States Supreme Court, the Administrative Office of the United States Courts, the Federal Judicial Center, the Sentencing Commission, and Federal Public Defender offices.[1] As used in this code in canons 3F(2)(b), 3F(5), 4B(2), 4C(1), and 5A, a member of a judge's personal staff means a judge's secretary, a judge's law clerk, and a courtroom deputy clerk or court reporter whose assignment with a particular judge is reasonably perceived as being comparable to a member of the judge's personal staff.[2]

Contractors and other nonemployees who serve the Judiciary are not covered by this code, but appointing authorities may impose these or similar ethical standards on such nonemployees, as appropriate.

The Judicial Conference has authorized its Committee on Codes of Conduct to render advisory opinions concerning the application and interpretation of this code. Employees should consult with their supervisor and/or appointing authority for guidance on questions concerning this code and its applicability before a request for an advisory opinion is made to the Committee on Codes of Conduct. In assessing the propriety of one's proposed conduct, a judicial employee should take care to consider all relevant canons in this code, the Ethics Reform Act, and other applicable statutes and regulations[3] (e.g., receipt of a gift may implicate canon 2 as well as canon 4C(2) and the Ethics Reform Act gift regulations). Should a question remain after this consultation, the affected judicial employee, or the chief judge, supervisor, or appointing authority of such employee, may request an advisory opinion from the Committee. Requests for advisory opinions may be addressed to the Chairman of the Committee on Codes of Conduct in care of the General Counsel, Administrative Office of the United States Courts, One Columbus Circle, N.E., Washington, D.C. 20544

Adopted September 19, 1995 by the
Judicial Conference of the United States
Effective January 1, 1996

CANON 1:   A JUDICIAL EMPLOYEE SHOULD UPHOLD THE INTEGRITY AND INDEPENDENCE OF THE JUDICIARY AND OF THE JUDICIAL EMPLOYEE'S OFFICE

An independent and honorable Judiciary is indispensable to justice in our society. A judicial employee should personally observe high standards of conduct so that the integrity and independence of the Judiciary are preserved and the judicialorder, or by the appointing authority.

CANON 2:   A JUDICIAL EMPLOYEE SHOULD AVOID IMPROPRIETY AND THE APPEARANCE OF IMPROPRIETY IN ALL ACTIVITIES

A judicial employee should not engage in any activities that would put into question the propriety of the judicial employee's conduct in carrying out the duties of the office. A judicial employee should not allow family, social, or other relationships to influence official conduct or judgment. A judicial employee should not lend the prestige of the office to advance or to appear to advance the private interests of others. A judicial employee should not use public office for private gain.

CANON 3: A JUDICIAL EMPLOYEE SHOULD ADHERE TO APPROPRIATE STANDARDS IN PERFORMING THE DUTIES OF THE OFFICE

In performing the duties prescribed by law, by resolution of the Judicial Conference of the United States, by court order, or by the judicial employee's appointing authority, the following employee's office reflects a devotion to serving the public. Judicial employees should require adherence to such standards by personnel subject to their direction and control. The provisions of this code should be construed and applied to further these objectives. The standards of this code shall not affect or preclude other more stringent standards required by law, by court standards apply:

A. A judicial employee should respect and comply with the law and these canons. A judicial employee should report to the appropriate supervising authority any attempt to induce the judicial employee to violate these canons.

   Note: A number of criminal statutes of general applicability govern federal employees' performance of official duties. These include:

   18 U.S.C. § 201 (bribery of public officials and witnesses);

   18 U.S.C. § 211 (acceptance or solicitation to obtain appointive public office);

   18 U.S.C. § 285 (taking or using papers relating to government claims);

   18 U.S.C. § 287 (false, fictitious, or fraudulent claims against the government);

18 U.S.C. § 508 (counterfeiting or forging transportation requests);

18 U.S.C. § 641 (embezzlement or conversion of government money, property, or records);

18 U.S.C. § 643 (failing to account for public money);

18 U.S.C. § 798 and 50 U.S.C. § 783 (disclosure of classified information);

18 U.S.C. § 1001 (fraud or false statements in a government matter);

18 U.S.C. § 1719 (misuse of franking privilege);

18 U.S.C. § 2071 (concealing, removing, or mutilating a public record);

31 U.S.C. § 1344 (misuse of government vehicle);

31 U.S.C. § 3729 (false claims against the government).

In addition, provisions of specific applicability to court officers include:

18 U.S.C. § 153, 154 (court officers embezzling or purchasing property from bankruptcy estate);

18 U.S.C. § 645 (embezzlement and theft by court officers);

18 U.S.C. § 646 (court officers failing to deposit registry moneys);

18 U.S.C. § 647 (receiving loans from registry moneys from court officer).

This is not a comprehensive listing but sets forth some of the more significant provisions with which judicial employees should be familiar.

B. A judicial employee should be faithful to professional standards and maintain competence in the judicial employee's profession.

C. A judicial employee should be patient, dignified, respectful, and courteous to all persons with whom the judicial employee deals in an official capacity, including the general public, and should require similar conduct of personnel subject to the judicial employee's direction and control. A judicial employee should diligently discharge the responsibilities of the office in a prompt, efficient, nondiscriminatory, fair, and professional manner. A judicial employee should never influence or attempt to influence the assignment of cases, or perform any discretionary or ministerial function of the court in a manner that improperly favors any litigant or attorney, nor should a judicial employee imply that he or she is in a position to do so.

D. A judicial employee should avoid making public comment on the merits of a pending or impending action and should require similar restraint by personnel subject to the judicial employee's direction and control. This proscription does not extend to public statements made in the course of official duties or to the explanation of court procedures. A judicial employee should never disclose any confidential information received in the course of official duties except as required in the performance of such duties, nor should a judicial employee employ such information for personal gain. A former judicial employee should observe the same restrictions on disclosure of confidential information that apply to a current judicial employee, except as modified by the appointing authority.

E. A judicial employee should not engage in nepotism prohibited by law.

> *Note: See also* 5 U.S.C. § 3110 (employment of relatives); 28 U.S.C. § 458 (employment of judges' relatives).

F. *Conflicts of Interest.*

(1) A judicial employee should avoid conflicts of interest in the performance of official duties. A conflict of interest arises when a judicial employee knows that he or she (or the spouse, minor child residing in the judicial employee's household, or other close relative of the judicial employee) might be so personally or financially affected by a matter that a reasonable person with knowledge of the relevant facts would question the judicial employee's ability properly to perform official duties in an impartial manner.

(2) Certain judicial employees, because of their relationship to a judge or the nature of their duties, are subject to the following additional restrictions:

   (a) A staff attorney or law clerk should not perform any official duties in any matter with respect to which such staff attorney or law clerk knows that:

     (i) he or she has a personal bias or prejudice concerning a party, or personal knowledge of disputed evidentiary facts concerning the proceeding;

     (ii) he or she served as lawyer in the matter in controversy, or a lawyer with whom he or she previously practiced law had served (during such association) as a lawyer concerning the matter, or he, she, or such lawyer has been a material witness;

     (iii) he or she, individually or as a fiduciary, or the spouse or minor child residing in his or her household, has a financial interest in the subject matter in controversy or in a party to the proceeding;

     (iv) he or she, a spouse, or a person related to either within the third degree of relationship,[4] or the spouse of such person (A) is a party to the proceeding, or an officer, director, or trustee of a party; (B) is acting as a lawyer in the proceeding; (C) has an interest that could be substantially affected by the outcome of the proceeding; or (D) is likely to be a material witness in the proceeding;

     (v) he or she has served in governmental employment and in such capacity participated as counsel, advisor, or material witness concerning the proceeding or has expressed an opinion concerning the merits of the particular case in controversy.

   (b) A secretary to a judge, or a courtroom deputy or court reporter whose assignment with a particular judge is reasonably perceived as being comparable to a member of the judge's personal staff, should not perform any official duties in any matter with respect to which such secretary, courtroom deputy, or court reporter knows that he or she, a spouse, or a person related to either within the third degree of relationship, or the spouse of such person (i) is a party to the proceeding, or an officer, director, or trustee of a party; (ii) is acting as a lawyer in the proceeding; (iii) has an interest that could be substantially affected by the outcome of the proceeding; or (iv) is likely to be a material witness in the proceeding; provided, however, that when the foregoing restriction presents undue hardship, the judge may authorize the secretary, courtroom deputy, or court reporter to participate in the matter if no reasonable alternative exists and adequate safeguards are in place to ensure that official duties are properly performed. In the event the secretary, courtroom deputy, or court reporter possesses any of the foregoing characteristics and so advises the judge, the judge should also consider whether the Code of Conduct for United States Judges may require the judge to recuse.

(c) A probation or pretrial services officer should not perform any official duties in any matter with respect to which the probation or pretrial services officer knows that:

(i) he or she has a personal bias or prejudice concerning a party;

(ii) he or she is related within the third degree of relationship to a party to the proceeding, or to an officer, director, or trustee of a party, or to a lawyer in the proceeding;

(iii) he or she, or a relative within the third degree of relationship, has an interest that could be substantially affected by the outcome of the proceeding.

(3) When a judicial employee knows that a conflict of interest may be presented, the judicial employee should promptly

inform his or her appointing authority. The appointing authority, after determining that a conflict or the appearance of a conflict of interest exists, should take appropriate steps to restrict the judicial employee's performance of official duties in such matter so as to avoid a conflict or the appearance of a conflict of interest. A judicial employee should observe any restrictions imposed by his or her appointing authority in this regard.

(4) A judicial employee who is subject to canon 3F(2) should keep informed about his or her personal, financial and fiduciary interests and make a reasonable effort to keep informed about such interests of a spouse or minor child residing in the judicial employee's household.

(5) A member of a judge's personal staff should inform the appointing judge of any circumstance or activity of the staff member that might serve as a basis for disqualification of either the staff member or the judge, in a matter pending before the judge.

CANON 4:   IN ENGAGING IN OUTSIDE ACTIVITIES, A JUDICIAL EMPLOYEE SHOULD AVOID THE RISK OF CONFLICT WITH OFFICIAL DUTIES, SHOULD AVOID THE APPEARANCE OF IMPROPRIETY, AND SHOULD COMPLY WITH DISCLOSURE REQUIREMENTS

A. *Outside Activities.* A judicial employee's activities outside of official duties should not detract from the dignity of the court, interfere with the performance of official duties, or adversely reflect on the operation and dignity of the court or office the judicial employee serves. Subject to the foregoing standards and the other provisions of this code, a judicial employee may engage in such activities as civic, charitable, religious, professional, educational, cultural, avocational, social, fraternal, and recreational activities, and may speak, write, lecture, and teach. If such outside activities concern the law, the legal system, or the administration of justice, the judicial employee should first consult with the appointing authority to determine whether the proposed activities are consistent with the foregoing standards and the other provisions of this code.

B. *Solicitation of Funds.* A judicial employee may solicit funds in connection with outside activities, subject to the following limitations:

    (1) A judicial employee should not use or permit the use of the prestige of the office in the solicitation of funds.

    (2) A judicial employee should not solicit subordinates to contribute funds to any such activity but may provide information to them about a general fund-raising campaign. A member of a judge's personal staff should not solicit any court personnel to contribute funds to any such activity under circumstances where the staff member's close relationship to the judge could reasonably be construed to give undue weight to the solicitation.

    (3) A judicial employee should not solicit or accept funds from lawyers or other persons likely to come before the judicial employee or the court or office the judicial employee serves, except as an incident to a general fund-raising activity.

C. *Financial Activities.*

    (1) A judicial employee should refrain from outside financial and business dealings that tend to detract from the dignity of the court, interfere with the proper performance of official duties, exploit the position, or associate the judicial employee in a substantial financial manner with lawyers or other persons likely to come before the judicial employee or the court or office the judicial employee serves, provided, however, that court reporters are not prohibited from providing reporting services for compensation to the extent permitted by statute and by the court. A member of a judge's personal staff should consult with the appointing judge concerning any financial and business activities that might reasonably be interpreted as violating this code and should refrain from any activities that fail to conform to the

foregoing standards or that the judge concludes may otherwise give rise to an appearance of impropriety.

(2) A judicial employee should not solicit or accept a gift from anyone seeking official action from or doing business with the court or other entity served by the judicial employee, or from anyone whose interests may be substantially affected by the performance or nonperformance of official duties; except that a judicial employee may accept a gift as permitted by the Ethics Reform Act of 1989 and the Judicial Conference regulations thereunder. A judicial employee should endeavor to prevent a member of a judicial employee's family residing in the household from soliciting or accepting any such gift except to the extent that a judicial employee would be permitted to do so by the Ethics Reform Act of 1989 and the Judicial Conference regulations thereunder.

Note: See 5 U.S.C. § 7353 (gifts to federal employees). *See also* 5 U.S.C. § 7342 (foreign gifts); 5 U.S.C. § 7351 (gifts to superiors).

(3) A judicial employee should report the value of gifts to the extent a report is required by the Ethics Reform Act, other applicable law, or the Judicial Conference of the United States.

Note: See 5 U.S.C. app. 6, § 101 to 111 (Ethics Reform Act financial disclosure provisions).

(4) During judicial employment, a law clerk or staff attorney may seek and obtain employment to commence after the completion of the judicial employment. However, the law clerk or staff attorney should first consult with the appointing authority and observe any restrictions imposed by the appointing authority. If any law firm, lawyer, or entity with whom a law clerk or staff attorney has been employed or is seeking or has obtained future employment appears in any matter pending before the appointing authority, the law clerk or staff attorney should promptly bring this fact to the attention of the appointing authority.

D. *Practice of Law.* A judicial employee should not engage in the practice of law except that a judicial employee may act pro se, may perform routine legal work incident to the management of the personal affairs of the judicial employee or a member of the judicial employee's family, and may provide pro bono legal services in civil matters, so long as such pro se, family, or pro bono legal work does not present an appearance of impropriety, does not take place while on duty or in the judicial employee's workplace, and does not interfere with the judicial employee's primary responsibility to the office in which the judicial employee serves, and further provided that:

(1) in the case of pro se legal work, such work is done without compensation (other than such compensation as may be allowed by statute or court rule in probate proceedings);

(2) in the case of family legal work, such work is done without compensation (other than such compensation as may be allowed by statute or court rule in probate proceedings) and does not involve the entry of an appearance in a federal court;

(3) in the case of pro bono legal services, such work (a) is done without compensation; (b) does not involve the entry of an appearance in any federal, state, or local court or administrative agency; (c) does not involve a matter of public controversy, an issue likely to come before the judicial employee's court, or litigation against federal, state or local government; and (d) is reviewed in advance with the appointing authority to determine whether the proposed services are consistent with the foregoing standards and the other provisions of this code.

Judicial employees may also serve as uncompensated mediators or arbitrators for nonprofit organizations, subject to the standards applicable to pro bono practice of law, as set forth above, and the other provisions of this code.

A judicial employee should ascertain any limitations imposed by the appointing judge or the court on which the appointing judge serves concerning the practice of law by a former judicial employee before the judge or the court and should observe such limitations after leaving such employment.

Note: See also 18 U.S.C. § 203 (representation in matters involving the United States); 18 U.S.C. § 205 (claims against the United States); 28 U.S.C. § 955 (restriction on clerks of court practicing law).

E.   *Compensation and Reimbursement.* A judicial employee may receive compensation and reimbursement of expenses for outside activities provided that receipt of such compensation and reimbursement is not prohibited or restricted by this code, the Ethics Reform Act, and other applicable law, and provided that the source or amount of such payments does not influence or give the appearance of influencing the judicial employee in the performance of official duties or otherwise give the appearance of impropriety. Expense reimbursement should be limited to the actual cost of travel, food, and lodging reasonably incurred by a judicial employee and, where appropriate to the occasion, by the judicial employee's spouse or relative. Any payment in excess of such an amount is compensation.

A judicial employee should make and file reports of compensation and reimbursement for outside activities to the extent prescribed by the Ethics Reform Act, other applicable law, or the Judicial Conference of the United States.

Notwithstanding the above, a judicial employee should not receive any salary, or any supplementation of salary, as compensation for official government services from any source other than the United States, provided, however, that court reporters are not prohibited from receiving compensation for reporting services to the extent permitted by statute and by the court.

Note: See 5 U.S.C. app. 6, §§ 101 to 111 (Ethics Reform Act financial disclosure provisions); 28 U.S.C. § 753 (court reporter compensation). *See also* 5 U.S.C. App., §§ 501 to 505 (outside earned income and employment).

CANON 5: A JUDICIAL EMPLOYEE SHOULD REFRAIN FROM INAPPROPRIATE POLITICAL ACTIVITY

A. *Partisan Political Activity.* A judicial employee should refrain from partisan political activity; should not act as a leader or hold any office in a partisan political organization; should not make speeches for or publicly endorse or oppose a partisan political organization or candidate; should not solicit funds for or contribute to a partisan political organization, candidate, or event; should not become a candidate for partisan political office; and should not otherwise actively engage in partisan political activities.

B. *Nonpartisan Political Activity.* A member of a judge's personal staff, clerk of court, chief probation officer, chief pretrial services officer, circuit executive, and district court executive should refrain from nonpartisan political activity such as campaigning for or publicly endorsing or opposing a nonpartisan political candidate; soliciting funds for or contributing to a nonpartisan political candidate or event; and becoming a candidate for nonpartisan political office. Other judicial employees may engage in nonpartisan political activity only if such activity does not tend to reflect adversely on the dignity or impartiality of the court or office and does not interfere with the proper performance of official duties. A judicial employee may not engage in such activity while on duty or in the judicial employee's workplace and may not utilize any federal resources in connection with any such activity.

Note: *See also* 18 U.S.C. chapter 29 (elections and political activities).

Notes

1. Justices and employees of the Supreme Court are subject to standards established by the Justices of that Court. Judges are subject to the Code of Conduct for United States Judges. Employees of the AO and the FJC are subject to their respective agency

codes. Employees of the Sentencing Commission are subject to standards established by the Commission. Federal public defender employees are subject to the Code of Conduct for Federal Public Defender Employees. When Actually Employed (WAE) employees are subject to canons 1, 2, and 3 and such other provisions of this code as may be determined by the appointing authority.

2. Employees who occupy positions with functions and responsibilities similar to those for a particular position identified in this code should be guided by the standards applicable to that position, even if the position title differs. When in doubt, employees may seek an advisory opinion as to the applicability of specific code provisions.

3. *See Guide to Judiciary Policies and Procedures*, Volume II, Chapter VI, Statutory and Regulatory Provisions Relating to the Conduct of Judges and Judicial Employees.

4. As used in this code, the third degree of relationship is calculated according to the civil law system to include the following relatives: parent, child, grandparent, grandchild, great grandparent, great grandchild, brother, sister, aunt, uncle, niece and nephew.

The National Judicial Clerkship Study: Executive Summary and Action Plan

The following Executive Summary and Action Plan, excerpted from the Report of the National Judicial Clerkship Study at pages 8 to 18, summarize the most significant findings and suggested proposals for the judiciary, law schools and students. The complete findings are published in *Courting the Clerkship: Perspectives on the Opportunities and Obstacles for Judicial Clerkships*, Report on the 2000 National Judicial Clerkship Study (National Association for Law Placement, October 2000) (the "NALP Report"), also available on the NALP website at http://www.nalp.org/nalpresearch/clrksumm.htm. *See also* my article, "Empowering the Participants: Initiatives from the National Judicial Clerkship Study," *NALP Bulletin*, Vol. 13, No. 12, December 2000.

Courting Clerkships: The NALP Judicial Clerkship Study
Executive Summary and Action Plan

INTRODUCTION AND RATIONALE FOR STUDY

Judicial clerkships open doors to satisfying legal careers—yet the profession's understanding of who is applying for clerkships, why they do so, and how the process can be managed effectively is little understood. Motivated by several critical concerns about clerkships and diversity in the legal profession, the National Association for Law Placement (NALP) and the American Bar Association (ABA) undertook a comprehensive study of judicial clerkships as employment opportunities for law graduates.

The study, conducted in several phases, sought input from three significant populations: law school administrations/career service professionals, third-year students, and alumni law clerks. It has captured information on student perceptions about the clerkship application and selection processes; the value students perceive in clerkships; data on the presence of women graduates and graduates of color in federal, state, and local clerkships; the influence of clerkships on attorney careers; and the roles that law school faculty and administration assume in the student clerkship application processes.

METHODOLOGY

This study compiled data from four sources. The first portion of the study analyzed retrospective empirical data compiled by NALP for five years (1994–1998) to refute or substantiate anecdotal evidence about differences in the frequency of judicial clerk positions among men, women and graduates of color. The data, collected by NALP annually on the employment experiences of new law graduates, produces information on 86–90% of all graduates from ABA-accredited law schools each year and thus offers the most comprehensive insights regarding graduate employment as judicial clerks through these detailed analyses.

For the subsequent phases of the study, NALP designed and implemented three comprehensive surveys to elicit critical information from each of the three target groups: law school administrations/ career service professionals, third-year students, and alumni law clerks. The collective goals of these questionnaires, respectively, were:

- To determine the roles that law school administration and faculty assume in the student clerkship application process;
- To identify law school student perceptions regarding judicial clerkships and the application process; and
- To evaluate former and present law clerk perceptions regarding the application process, the value of the clerkship experience, and its impact on their future careers.

A joint letter from William Paul, President of the ABA, and Patricia Bass, President of NALP, notified the deans of all ABA-accredited law schools of the purposes of this study and invited each to participate in the administrative law school survey. One hundred and forty-seven law school career services offices, or 81%, returned their completed surveys to NALP.

Using standard survey selection methods, 61 law schools were identified to form a pool of schools for the law student and alumni inquiries. This pool included a representative sample of law schools that have a high number of federal clerkships, those with a high number of non-federal (state and/or local) clerkships, and some randomly selected from the remainder. As a result, the schools in the sample pool represent a diverse cross-section nationally of school characteristics (public, private, size, geographic region and reputation), with varying levels of students and graduates pursuing federal, state and local clerkships. These schools were invited to participate in an effort to survey all current third-year students, regardless of whether they have applied for or accepted a judicial clerkship, and graduates from the classes of 1998 and 1999 who pursued a clerkship following graduation.

A letter notifying the law schools in the sample pool was sent out by NALP in early December 1999 asking the schools to indicate their agreement to participate in the next phase of the study and to provide information as to the number of surveys needed for their third-year students and alumni from the classes of 1998 and 1999 who are serving or had served as law clerks, as well as their preferred method of distribution to the students and alumni.

Survey questionnaires were subsequently distributed to approximately 14,000 third-year students and 4,000 alumni law clerks in January 2000. Of the roughly 14,000 law students to whom the law student surveys were distributed, 1660 students, or 11%, returned their completed surveys to NALP. The law clerk survey was distributed to approximately 4,000 alumni, and 931 alumni returned their completed surveys—an extraordinary return rate that approaches 24%.

OVERVIEW OF THE FINDINGS: ANALYSIS OF EMPLOYMENT STATISTICS

- **Minority representation among the clerkship population is generally lower than in the law school population.** Historically, the representation of Hispanic and Black/African American law clerks has been significantly lower than the representation of these groups in the general law school population, with some variation observed by court types. In contrast, Asian-Pacific Islanders in the federal clerk population, particularly in certain circuit courts, increasingly maintain a representation equivalent or even exceeding their numbers in the law school class. The data show a trend towards a slightly decreasing percentage of white law clerks, from 87.1% in the Class of 1994 to 85.1% in the Class of 1998.

- **For the last four of the five years included in the study, women comprised a majority of the law clerk population.** However, there is a disproportionately high percentage of women serving as local and state clerks and a greater percentage of men than women as federal clerks, although the gap has decreased slightly through the years. Vastly different patterns emerge within each federal circuit, both with the relative percentages of men in comparison to women and with the degree of variation in these distributions from year to year.

· **Different patterns of clerkship populations emerge based on law school characteristics.** Federal clerkships comprise a significant percentage of the judicial clerkships taken by graduates of private law schools. In contrast, for public schools the distribution is sharply skewed towards state clerkships. Both school types show a relatively small, constant proportion of local clerks. When the law schools are aggregated according to their total J.D. enrollment, other patterns can be observed. As a whole, the law schools in all of the size categories report a higher percentage of state clerks than federal clerks, with the smallest portion being local clerks. However, in the smallest school size (500 or fewer students), prevalence of state clerkships significantly outweighs the other levels; the percentage of federal clerks is highest in the intermediate school size (501–750 students), where it approaches most closely the state clerk population.

FINDINGS FROM THE ADMINISTRATIVE SURVEY OF LAW SCHOOLS

· **Nearly all law schools offer programs on judicial clerkships, but the number and range of subjects vary widely.** One of the most visible indicators of support for, or efforts devoted to, the judicial clerkship process is evident in the number and scope of programs on this subject. Almost all of the responding law schools conduct a program on an introduction or overview of clerkships, with most of them sponsored by the career services office. However, notably absent are specialized informational/support programs in this area for women and students of color—only about a quarter of the responding schools provide such programs. Also missing were programs on preparing for a clerkship, which are not offered by 64% of the law schools.

· **The vast majority of law schools offer a formal internship or externship program with local judges.** The schools with an externship or internship program generally believe that this has positively affected the number of clerkship applications, and the majority also perceive a positive effect on clerkship offers.

- **As a group, law schools allocate considerable resources to the judicial clerkship process.** Postings of letters from judges seeking clerks proved to be the most highly valued resource. Also highly valued by the schools are the clerkship handbooks published by their career services offices; however, 23% of schools, mostly the smaller schools, do not publish a clerkship handbook. Among the other resources most valued are the *NALP Federal and State Judicial Clerkship Directory*, the *Almanac of the Federal Judiciary*, and the WESTLAW® and LEXIS® resources.

- **Equally notable are the resources that the majority of schools do not have.** More than 71% reported that they do not have a judicial clerkship section on their Web site; of those that did have this resource, most found it to be useful. Largely missing as well were collections of written comments from faculty, and more than half of the schools did not have written feedback from alumni law clerks even though those who have such resources regarded them as valuable. Another significant resource, the *Directory of Minority Judges of the United States*, was not present at 49% of law schools, and the percent appeared even higher among certain school types; for example, 68% of the smallest school size and 52% of the public schools did not have this publication.

- **Universally, the law schools cited a need for more comprehensive resources regarding clerkship hiring procedures.** In the absence of a uniform comprehensive source on the timing of applications, hiring, contents of application packages, terms of clerkships, biographical and general information on judges, most schools maintain their own database of judges to which they allocate considerable time and resources.

- **Law schools in every category type and size of school indicated that the lack of uniform guidelines hinders the clerkship application process.** In their qualitative comments, this issue overshadowed all others, as the respondents addressed the problem this creates in their efforts to provide effective support for their students in the clerkship application process without draining the resources of their offices. Many schools commented that the clerkship applicant pool for the judges has been negatively impacted as well. Roughly half of the reporting schools noted that their schools are making programmatic changes in response to this issue, by moving up clerkship programming for second year students to earlier in the fall semester and by including first year students in their clerkship programming.

- **About half of the schools have a faculty clerkship committee.** Faculty generally are supportive of students applying for clerkships in terms of providing recommendations, but one-quarter of the schools experienced difficulty in getting the faculty to send letters of recommendation in a timely fashion.

- **Career services offices generally provide counseling or advising in connection with judicial clerkship applications but fewer offer clerical support.** A little more than half of the career services offices provide some kind of clerical support for students in connection with the processing of the clerkship applications, ranging from supplying students with a list of judges on a disk to mail merge to collecting and mailing the application package. These services, when provided by a career services office, are generally available to all students who would like to apply for judicial clerkships, although some schools select the students to which they will provide other kinds of support.

- **Financial assistance in connection with the clerkship application and interview process is limited at best.** Moreover, no school offers any other financial assistance for the judicial clerkship term except for a few schools that include clerkships within their loan forgiveness programs.

- **In their perceptions of student success, the career services professionals followed traditional expectations.** They named as the top criteria for success high class ranks, the law review/law journal credential, support of top faculty, and a summer or academic year judicial internship or externship. In the experience of career service professionals, a special connection to a judge does not emerge as a primary factor in acquiring federal and state clerkships.

- **Schools that offer more resources to students tend to have a higher percentage of graduates in clerkships.** Law schools that provide academic programs designed to support or encourage judicial clerkships had a higher percentage of their graduates obtaining clerkships than their counterparts without these programs and those schools that maintain a judicial database showed a similar tendency. In addition, the law schools with a faculty clerkship committee tended to have more of their graduates entering clerkships than those that did not have this committee; however, this positive correlation did not exist where the committee included a screening function. On a cautionary note, a causative link has not been established between these factors from the law schools and the clerkship rates of their students, nor can this be ascertained from the present data.

FINDINGS FROM THE LAW STUDENT SURVEY

- **Clearly students recognize the value of the clerkship relative to one's legal career.** For those who did apply for a clerkship, the factors that most influenced their decision to apply were the desire to gain the work experience of a clerkship; the impact of a clerkship on their future career; the prestige of clerkships; and discussions with others, primarily lawyers in practice.

- **The desire to clerk in the geographic locale or court of their future practice was the factor that most influenced the decision to apply to particular courts.** More than one-half of the students looked to the level of the court (trial/appellate), while almost as many focused on the type of court (federal/state/local). The reputation of the judge was also ranked by students as extremely significant in their decision where to apply. Other significant factors included the length of the clerkship term (one year versus two year); the atmosphere in chambers/ working conditions; and that the judge previously hired clerks from their law school. Considerably de-emphasized by the students were factors such as personal connection to the judge and the race/ethnicity, gender, sexual orientation or disability status of the judge.

· **A substantial number of students cited the financial differ-ential of a clerkship salary as a component of their decision not to apply for a clerkship at all.** While the financial burdens of applying for a judicial clerkship did not appear to play as large a role as expected for those students who chose to apply for a clerkship, the expense of the application and interview process did surface as a concern among some students.

· **The data do not support a finding that students chose not to apply for clerkships due to a perception of bias toward their gender, race or ethnicity.** Respondents who did not apply for a clerkship cited most often as a reason for not apply-ing that they preferred a different post-graduation option. A substantial percent of the students indicated that they did not think their applications would be competitive. More than one-third of the non-applying students stated as a reason that they lacked the finances to apply or interview for a clerkship and emphasized as a deterrent the financial differential of the clerkship salary given their considerable educational debt. Almost one-third of these students stated that they felt dis-couraged by some aspect of the application process; of these, most pointed to the timing or the arduousness of the process. Most of those students who did not apply for a clerkship reported that they would have done so if one or more of these factors were different.

· **The racial and ethnic patterns of judicial clerks appear to be a reflection of these patterns in the student applicant population of our study, rather than a difference in the suc-cess of their applications.** The overall success rate of those applying for a clerkship was quite high at 69.5%, and two of these groups, Asian/Pacific Islander and Hispanic/Latino, had even higher success rates. In order to increase minority repre-sentation among law clerks, efforts should focus on the need to increase the number of minority students who apply in the first instance, particularly among certain groups, such as Hispanics and African-Americans.

- **A gender differential in success rates emerged.** Sixty-six percent of the women who applied received a clerkship offer, in contrast to 74% of the male students in our study. The gender patterns in judicial clerks and applicants, while favorable when viewed in the context of the overall law school class, tend to vary with the type of court (federal versus state and local) and may also reflect a differential in the success rate of their applications.

- **A much lower percentage of students in the upper age category (36 and older) received an offer.** Moreover, more than any other demographic group, students in this category perceived their age to be a disadvantage leading to unsuccessful clerkship applications.

- **The results do not support the hypothesis of connections to judge as a significant component in obtaining a clerkship.** This fact contrasts with the perceptions among many of the students who offered as a reason for not applying for a clerkship, or for not succeeding with their clerkship applications, that they did not have the right "connections" to acquire a clerkship.

- **Grades, law review, and the academic record all play the largest roles in both the perceptions of students and the reality of a successful clerkship application.** These perceptions largely coincide with those of the career services personnel of their law schools.

- **Roughly one in ten applications at the federal level resulted in an invitation to interview, and one in four applications at the state level did so.** However, these numbers may not accurately reflect the practice common in some courts of submitting one application to a pool for distribution to many judges in that court. About one in three of the interviews with a state or federal judge resulted in an offer, although for state appellate courts the yield rate appeared somewhat higher at 43%.

- **The time given by judges to respond to a clerkship offer may not be as limited as has been widely believed and previously reported, but it is still a problem.** The response time most often described—identified by approximately one-third of the students—was "two days to one week." Still, a substantial proportion of students reported the prevalence of "on the spot" responses. Many students expressed frustration with the time pressure they experienced both in scheduling their interviews and responding to an offer.

- **One of the most problematic aspects of the application process for students was the obtaining and control of references.** Most strikingly, over one-third of the students indicated that they experienced difficulties in finding people to provide these references and an even greater percentage (36%) reported problems with the content of the letters. A large number of students expressed the concern that their professors did not know them well enough to write meaningful recommendations, due in part to the part to the earlier timing of the application process. In addition, almost one-third of the students experienced problems with the timely submission of these letters.

- **Students were generally satisfied with the assistance provided by their law schools.** In describing the level of assistance provided by their law schools overall, most of the students felt that they received adequate or very useful assistance in obtaining information or advice about their cover letter, resume, writing sample or letters of recommendation, and received adequate assistance in the area of interviewing. However, almost one-half of the students would have liked additional assistance from their law schools in collecting information or advice about the judges.

- **The lack of timing guidelines and standard application procedures makes the process chaotic and encumbered their experiences.** The absence of these uniform procedures, along with a lack of information about individual judges' application procedures and requirements, emerged repeatedly as significant factors in students' dissatisfaction with the clerkship application process.

· **The respondents to the alumni law clerk survey represented clerkships from a wide variety of types and levels of courts and judges nationwide.** In their demographic composition, the racial/ethnic and gender distributions were closely similar to the demographics observed for the student respondents who applied for a judicial clerkship, as well as the general law clerk population.

· **The qualifications of the clerks mirrored the perceptions of students as to the qualifications of successful candidates.** A significant percent of these law clerks reported that they had top grades/high class rank, had been a teaching or research assistant, were on the law review/ law journal, and/or had significant professional work experience prior to law school. Nearly one-third had a summer or academic year judicial intern/externship.

· **Only a relatively small percentage of the alumni law clerks reported having a special connection to a judge while in law school.** This fact provides further support for the findings of the student survey that, contrary to the perceptions among many of the students who did not apply for or receive a clerkship, very few of the students who applied and received an offer actually had a special connection to a judge.

· **The majority of law clerks responded that costs did not affect their choices during the application process.** A relatively small percentage applied to fewer judges as a consequence of the cost. Once again, the financial factor does not appear most significant for the choices made by applicants during the clerkship application process. However, some alumni did complain of the expense and, as noted above, some students pointed to financial considerations (i.e., the salary differential) as a reason for their decision not to apply for a judicial clerkship in the first instance.

- **The views of the law clerks did not entirely coincide with those of the students and career services professionals with regard to the important factors in judges' selections of law clerks.** Based on their past application experience and their observations as a law clerk, these alumni identified most often as "extremely important" to the judge the evaluation of the interview—even more highly than the academic record, which had received the strongest weight from their student counterparts. (Of course, it must be recognized that grades are an important component in obtaining this crucial interview.) According to the law clerks, second in importance were personal character traits. Not very important in the clerks' view were demographic characteristics and personal connection to the judge.

- **Almost one-third of the law clerks indicated that in retrospect they would have done something differently in the application process.** Many of them would have applied to more judges or more widely across the courts, applied sooner or started the application process earlier, built stronger recommendations from the faculty, pursued the clerkship more aggressively through phone calls to chambers, and/or researched additional information about the judicial ideology and the atmosphere of different judges' chambers, particularly by talking to former clerks.

- **Overall, the law clerks reported that their clerkship helped them acquire and improve a wide variety of legal and professional skills.** The substantial majority felt that the skills gained in their clerkships met or exceeded their initial expectations. Generally, clerks in trial courts (whether federal or state) ranked their skill development somewhat higher than those in appellate courts. The same pattern holds true with regard to the clerks' perception of the development of the relationship with their judges; most agreed that the relationship met or exceeded their expectations but trial court clerks ranked this slightly higher than appellate clerks.

- **When asked to characterize the degree to which their clerkship affected the ease of success in handling their post-clerkship duties, the former law clerks answered positively.** Significant variation appeared by court type, with the most positive response from law clerks in state trial and local trial courts, followed by federal trial courts, and a moderately positive response in federal appellate and state appellate courts.

- **Many respondents commented that their clerkship made them rethink their long-term goals and gave them a greater awareness of opportunities within the field.** They also cited an emphasis on quality of life issues, as well as consideration of personal happiness and the value of job satisfaction. In addition, many addressed their need for increased financial compensation and a pressure to enter private practice at the outset. Several indicated that the exposure to a variety of attorneys and law firms helped them decide which firm to join. As a result of their clerkship, some reported a heightened interest in government service or academia.

- **Almost half of the law clerks responded that their clerkship helped a great deal in obtaining their first post-clerkship position.** Almost one-quarter stated that it helped somewhat and over one-quarter believed that the clerkship did not substantially affect this factor. In essence, no one reported that the clerkship negatively affected the post-clerkship employment search.

- **In rating their clerkships, the law clerks resoundingly gave their overall experience high marks.** When asked whether they would clerk again, a remarkable 97% responded in the affirmative. In addition, their narrative comments reflect the strong positive feelings these alumni carry with them from their judicial clerkship experiences, as well as the valuable impact this professional experience has had on their future careers.

ACTION PLAN

Key Concerns

- **The lack of clerkship timing guidelines and uniform application procedures severely hampers law schools in their programming, information gathering and counseling efforts.** As a result, the clerkship applicant pool is negatively impacted, as some qualified students decide not to apply for a judicial clerkship at all. In addition, those students that do enter the process find their application experience—for most of them, their first contact with the judiciary—embroiled in chaos and turmoil.

- **A related problem is the lack of information on individual judges and their application requirements, procedures, and application and interview dates.** As repeatedly requested by law schools and students, there is a critical need for a centralized resource of information on judges and their hiring procedures. One student respondent suggested, "We need one comprehensive resource that contains accurate and complete information for all ... judges seeking clerks that year.... Anything that can be done to better synchronize the time frames on which judges operate would be an improvement—right now it's a free-for-all!"

- **In order to increase minority representation among law clerks, efforts should focus on the need to increase the number of minority students who apply in the first instance.** The data indicate that the representation of Hispanic and Black/African-American law clerks has been significantly lower than the representation of these groups in the general law school population, with some variation observed by court types. The racial and ethnic patterns characterizing judicial clerks appear to be a reflection of these patterns in the student applicant population, rather than a difference in the success of their applications.

- **Gender and age patterns vary among courts.** This study determined that the gender patterns in judicial clerks and applicants, while favorable when viewed in the context of the overall law school class, tend to vary with the type of court and may also reflect a differential in the success rate of their applications. In addition, students in the upper age category (36 and older), more than any other demographic group, believe their age to be a disadvantage leading to unsuccessful clerkship applications.

- **The expense of the clerkship application and interview process did surface as a concern among the comments by many students and alumni law clerks.** In addition, more than one-third of the students who did not apply for a clerkship cited the lack of the finances to consider a clerkship, emphasizing as a deterrent the financial differential of the clerkship salary given their considerable educational debt.

- **Obtaining valid and timely recommendations was problematic.** A large number of students expressed concern that their professors did not know them well enough to write meaningful recommendations, due in part to the early application deadlines. In addition, almost one-third of the students experienced problems with the timely submission of these letters, a fact that was supported by the reports of law school administrators.

ACTION PLAN TO ADDRESS THESE CONCERNS:

I. The Judiciary

- **There is a critical need for a resolution of the clerkship application deadlines.** It is hoped that this study will encourage federal judges to initiate viable timing guidelines and in the process set the application and interview dates further back in the student's career. If this process occurred later in the second year—or even in the third year—of law school, students would have more of an opportunity to develop a more complete academic record, important law school activities, professional work experience and meaningful faculty recommendations.

- **Universally, the law schools, students and alumni cited a need for more accurate and complete resources regarding the timing of applications, hiring, contents of application packages, the terms of the clerkships, biographical and general information on judges.** While there are a number of resources about judges now available, few deal specifically with hiring procedures. (Two resources that currently address this problem are NALP's *Judicial Clerkship Directory* and the new on-line database on federal clerkships offered by the Administrative Office of the Courts.) Such centralized, comprehensive sources would provide potential applicants with more information as to the judges' individual application preferences, requirements, and deadlines and would also benefit judges by reducing or even eliminating multiple inquiries from schools and others asking for similar information. The universality of the world wide web offers innovative avenues to accomplish this goal.

This request for informational resources applies to state and local courts as well as to federal courts. A law school respondent commented that biographical and evaluative information on state court and local judges is lacking in most materials. Another school suggested bar associations might develop directories for each state listing federal and state judges and addresses. These informational resources could be state-based or centralized with input provided by the state and local courts. Such an arrangement would be most logical in view of the fact that the students and law clerks named geographical considerations as the most important factor in their decision to apply to particular courts, with many desiring to clerk in the locale or court of their future practice.

- **Judges are strongly encouraged to provide applicants sufficient time to respond to a clerkship offer.** While the students most often described a response time of "two days to one week," they frequently reported that judges asked for "on the spot" responses to offers. Many students expressed frustration with the time pressure they experienced in scheduling their interviews and responding to an offer. More flexibility regarding responses could significantly improve the process for these students and allow judges access to a broader applicant pool.

· **Courts might adopt a regional or circuit interview process or a matching model of selection.** As one student commented, "Something needs to be done about the costs. Many judges could cooperate in their interviewing and do regional interview weekends so students wouldn't have to make so many trips." Similarly, innovative uses of videoconference technology for clerkship interviews might provide another way of controlling interview expenses.

As an alternative, some students offered the medical school model for consideration: "The process could be like the medical school system—we go through all of the interviews and are matched up' at the end. It would take the stress off the students and allow us to not worry so much about timing issues." Another suggested a centralized application process: "The judges could agree on a date at which they will begin accepting applications and set up a clearinghouse where applicants only send one application to a central location."

· **The judiciary is encouraged to join many other organizations who have embraced the goal of diversity in background, experience, race, ethnicity, gender, sexual orientation, and age for the legal profession by setting a similar goal for their clerkship ranks.**

II. Law Schools

· **The law schools should endeavor to gather and disseminate more information about the judges.** Overall, most of the students and alumni felt that they received adequate or very useful assistance from their law schools in obtaining information or advice about their cover letter, resume, writing sample or letters of recommendation, and received adequate assistance in the area of interviewing. However, almost one-half of the students would have liked additional assistance from their law schools in collecting information or advice about the judges. To address the need for a complete and current source of contact information, contents of application materials, and deadlines for judges, law schools should play a more active role in encouraging judicial participation in existing or newly developed directories.

- **Clerkship handbooks are valuable resources.** The study found that, although the clerkship handbooks published by their career services offices are highly valued by those schools, 23% of law schools, mostly the smaller schools, do not publish a clerkship handbook. More schools might find this type of resource helpful.

- **Web resources are underutilized.** More than 71% of law schools reported that they do not have a section on their Web site for clerkship information; of those that did have this resource, most found it to be useful. Schools that do not wish to develop their own site can still benefit from a number of existing sites on the web. These web sites are continually growing and changing, but all schools should encourage among their students an exploration of the wide range of web resources available to them.

- **Comments by clerks are an important resource.** In expanding their library of resources, schools should not overlook the value to their students of collecting written feedback from alumni law clerks. More than half of the schools reported that they did not have this resource, but those that did regarded this information as valuable. Moreover, student and alumni respondents emphasized their need for particularized information from former law clerks as to the atmosphere in chambers, judicial style and their individual clerkship experiences.

- **More outreach efforts to the students are needed to increase their awareness and attendance of clerkship programs and counseling.** Although many of the law schools do provide a variety of clerkship programs, the student surveys indicate that many students either did not attend these types of programs or did not realize they were available. These data suggest that schools that offer these programs need to increase the promotion of such programs. Two types of programs that were highly rated by many student respondents were those covering introduction/overview of clerkships and mechanics of the application process. More such programs would be welcome.

- **Intern/extern programs play an important role.** The schools should strive for the development of more judicial internship/externship programs, which are regarded as beneficial to this process by those schools that have them. Internship or externship programs with local judges often provide an entre into the world of judicial clerkships, as well as a valuable experience and enhancement to the law school education. The vast majority of law schools report having a formal internship/externship program, which most believe has positively affected the number of clerkship applications and, to a lesser extent, offers from the judges. Moreover, almost one-third of the law clerks and students who successfully applied for a clerkship had a summer or academic year judicial intern/externship.

- **The applicant pool must become more diverse.** Law schools should adopt as a priority encouraging more minority students to apply for judicial clerkships by offering more programs, resources, and counseling for these students.

- **Some form of financial assistance or loan deferment from law schools is imperative.** Such assistance might facilitate applications for those who could not apply due to the financial factor (salary differential and educational debt burden), thereby increasing the diversity of the applicant pool and law clerks and expanding the availability of clerkships to all who are otherwise qualified. There is no readily ascertainable reason why judicial clerkships, which are a form of public service, cannot be treated like other public interest jobs, evoking eligibility for financial assistance, loan forgiveness or deferral programs.

- **Law schools should encourage more faculty involvement.** Methods should be found to facilitate ways in which professors can interact more with students and increase their awareness of student writing. Faculty letters of recommendation are critical to the process and must be submitted to the judges on time. Schools should implement measures to facilitate the mechanics of the application process for their students, particularly in instituting follow-up efforts to improve the timeliness of the letters of recommendation from their faculty.

III. Students

- **Students are encouraged to find out more information about the judges.** Using the growing availability of resources (see appendix), students should research the atmosphere and relationships in chambers, particularly through information from former law clerks. Since web sites are continually growing and changing, students should explore the many on-line resources that are available.

- **Students should apply widely.** They should remain open minded and flexible as to the types of courts and judges. There are many opportunities available for a valuable judicial clerkship. Students should not be discouraged by their lack of connections to a judge in applying for a clerkship, since the data demonstrate that only a small percentage of students and law clerks have such connections.

- **Students should take advantage of all the resources offered by their law schools.** They should work on developing their relationships with faculty though writing, class participation, and serving as research assistants so that they can enhance their law school experiences and obtain more meaningful faculty recommendations. Students should take advantage of the programs on judicial clerkships provided by their law schools (and ask for more, if needed).

- **Almost one-third of the law clerks indicated that in retrospect they would have done something differently in the application process.** As general advice to students from the alumni respondents, their substantive narratives revealed that many of them would have applied to more judges or more widely across the courts, applied sooner or started the application process earlier, built stronger recommendations from the faculty, pursued the clerkship more aggressively through phone calls to chambers, and/or researched more to try to obtain additional information about the judicial ideology and the atmosphere of different judges' chambers, particularly by talking to former clerks.

SELECTED RESOURCES AS OF SEPTEMBER 2000

On-Line Resources

· **www.courts.net**

  This site was developed to provide access to web sites maintained by courts nationwide and offers links to both state and federal court sites.

· **www.uscourts.gov**

  The official site of the Administrative Office of the Courts, this site offers links to other federal sites and will be the home of a database that will contain information supplied by federal judges regarding their law clerk hiring schedules and application criteria, along with possible other features accessible by the law schools and judges.

· **www.judicialclerkships.com**

  This site, now under construction, will provide a central source of information and advice for law schools and students on judicial clerkships, as well as a forum for law clerks.

· Many law school web sites on judicial clerkship resources are also available and may be found through a browser search for information on judicial clerkships.

Directories

- *The NALP Federal and State Judicial Clerkship Directory*, available in print and on-line through the LEXIS® services, offers detailed information on judges' hiring criteria and practices. Judges may list in the directory at no charge by contacting the NALP office (202–667–1666).

- *Directory of Minority Judges of the United States, Chicago*: American Bar Association, Judicial Division, Task Force on Minorities in the Judiciary.

- *Almanac of the Federal Judiciary*, Englewood Cliffs, N.J.: Aspen Law and Business. Available on line through WESTLAW® .

- *BNA's Directory of State and Federal Courts, Judges, and Clerks*. Washington, DC: The Bureau of National Affairs.

- *Federal-State Court Directory*. Washington, DC: WANT Publishing Co. Available on line through www.courts.com.

- *Guide to State Judicial Clerkship Procedures*. Vermont Law School.

Data on Minorities, Women, and Clerkships from the National Judicial Clerkship Study[1]

Table 2. **Racial/Ethnicity Distribution of Judicial Clerkships by Level of Clerkship: 1994–1998**

Type of Clerkship	Race or Ethnicity	1994		1995		1996		1997		1998	
		NUMBER	PERCENT	NUMBER	PERCENT	NUMBER	PERCENT	NUMBER	PERCENT	NUMBER	PERCENT
All Clerks	American Indian	4	0.1%	15	0.5%	10	0.3%	8	0.2%	19	0.6%
	Asian/P. Islander	130	4.3%	166	5.3%	146	4.5%	161	5.0%	191	5.6%
	African American	171	5.7%	180	5.8%	190	5.9%	181	5.6%	204	6.0%
	White	2,622	87.1%	2,667	85.6%	2,783	86.3%	2,787	85.9%	2,918	85.1%
	Hispanic	83	2.8%	87	2.8%	95	2.9%	108	3.3%	95	2.8%
	TOTAL	3,010	100.0%	3,115	100.0%	3,224	100.0%	3,245	100.0%	3,427	100.0%
Federal clerks	American Indian	3	0.2%	4	0.3%	5	0.4%	2	0.2%	5	0.4%
	Asian/P. Islander	62	5.0%	81	6.4%	61	4.9%	74	5.9%	90	6.9%
	African American	61	4.9%	70	5.5%	66	5.3%	61	4.9%	63	4.9%
	White	1,089	87.3%	1,065	84.3%	1,073	86.1%	1,067	85.4%	1,106	85.3%

		NUMBER	PERCENT	NUMBER	PERCENT	NUMBER	PERCENT	NUMBER	PERCENT	NUMBER	PERCENT
	Hispanic	33	2.6%	43	3.4%	41	3.3%	46	3.7%	32	2.5%
	TOTAL	1,248	100.0%	1,263	100.0%	1,246	100.0%	1,250	100.0%	1,296	100.0%
Local clerks	American Indian	—	—	2	1.2%	1	0.4%	—	—	—	—
	Asian/P. Islander	8	4.1%	10	5.8%	5	2.0%	13	4.7%	10	4.0%
	African American	17	8.8%	17	9.8%	22	8.6%	26	9.4%	17	6.8%
	White	162	83.9%	136	78.6%	221	86.3%	232	83.5%	216	86.1%
	Hispanic	6	3.1%	8	4.6%	7	2.7%	7	2.5%	8	3.2%
	TOTAL	193	100.0%	173	100.0%	256	100.0%	278	100.0%	251	100.0%
State clerks	American Indian	1	0.1%	8	0.5%	4	0.2%	6	0.4%	12	0.6%
	Asian/P. Islander	60	3.9%	74	4.5%	80	4.7%	72	4.2%	90	4.8%
	African American	87	5.6%	90	5.4%	101	5.9%	94	5.5%	124	6.7%
	White	1,353	87.6%	1,448	87.5%	1,478	86.5%	1,475	86.7%	1,579	85.0%
	Hispanic	44	2.8%	35	2.1%	46	2.7%	55	3.2%	53	2.9%
	TOTAL	1,545	100.0%	1,655	100.0%	1,709	100.0%	1,702	100.0%	1,858	100.0%

Note: Excludes graduates for whom race or ethnicity was not reported.

Source: National Association for Law Placement, employment data for the Classes of 1994–98.

Table 3. **Racial/Ethnic Distribution of Federal Clerks by Circuit: 1994–1998**

Circuit	Race or Ethnicity	1994		1995		1996		1997		1998	
		NUMBER	PERCENT	NUMBER	PERCENT	NUMBER	PERCENT	NUMBER	PERCENT	NUMBER	PERCENT
First	Asian/P. Islander	2	4.3%	1	2.2%	5	9.1%	4	5.9%	2	3.9%
	African American	1	2.1%	2	4.4%	2	3.6%	2	2.9%	2	3.9%
	White	42	89.4%	41	91.1%	47	85.5%	57	83.8%	47	92.2%
	Hispanic	2	4.3%	1	2.2%	1	1.8%	5	7.4%	—	—
	TOTAL	47	100.0%	45	100.0%	55	100.0%	68	100.0%	51	100.0%
Second	American Indian	1	0.7%	—	—	—	—	—	—	—	—
	Asian/P. Islander	6	4.3%	11	7.8%	10	8.1%	6	4.6%	12	7.4%
	African American	4	2.9%	7	5.0%	8	6.5%	6	4.6%	10	6.1%
	White	128	92.1%	121	85.8%	101	81.5%	114	87.7%	134	82.2%
	Hispanic	—	—	2	1.4%	5	4.0%	4	3.1%	7	4.3%
	TOTAL	139	100.0%	141	100.0%	124	100.0%	130	100.0%	163	100.0%
Third	Asian/P. Islander	6	5.7%	7	6.0%	4	3.9%	3	3.1%	4	4.1%
	African American	5	4.8%	5	4.3%	6	5.8%	10	10.3%	10	10.2%
	White	88	83.8%	97	83.6%	92	89.3%	81	83.5%	83	84.7%
	Hispanic	6	5.7%	7	6.0%	1	1.0%	3	3.1%	1	1.0%
	TOTAL	105	100.0%	116	100.0%	103	100.0%	97	100.0%	98	100.0%
Fourth	American Indian	—	—	1	0.8%	—	—	—	—	—	—
	Asian/P. Islander	4	2.9%	4	3.2%	2	1.6%	2	1.9%	8	6.8%
	African American	6	4.4%	8	6.5%	11	8.7%	5	4.8%	5	4.2%
	White	127	92.7%	109	87.9%	113	89.0%	96	91.4%	103	87.3%
	Hispanic	—	—	2	1.6%	1	0.8%	2	1.9%	2	1.7%
	TOTAL	137	100.0%	124	100.0%	127	100.0%	105	100.0%	118	100.0%

Fifth	American Indian	—	—	3	2.3%	2	1.4%	—	—	—	—
	Asian/P. Islander	5	4.1%	7	5.3%	3	2.2%	5	3.9%	7	5.3%
	African American	4	3.3%	4	3.1%	5	3.6%	8	6.3%	3	2.3%
	White	105	86.1%	109	83.2%	120	86.3%	105	82.7%	116	87.2%
	Hispanic	8	6.6%	8	6.1%	9	6.5%	9	7.1%	7	5.3%
	TOTAL	122	100.0%	131	100.0%	139	100.0%	127	100.0%	133	100.0%
Sixth	American Indian	—	—	—	—	1	1.1%	—	—	—	—
	Asian/P. Islander	3	3.7%	4	4.3%	3	3.4%	2	2.1%	2	1.8%
	African American	8	9.9%	11	12.0%	5	5.6%	14	14.7%	9	8.2%
	White	69	85.2%	75	81.5%	78	87.6%	77	81.1%	99	90.0%
	Hispanic	1	1.2%	2	2.2%	2	2.2%	2	2.1%	—	—
	TOTAL	81	100.0%	92	100.0%	89	100.0%	95	100.0%	110	100.0%
Seventh	Asian/P. Islander	3	4.2%	—	—	2	2.9%	3	3.9%	7	10.1%
	African American	2	2.8%	1	1.3%	5	7.4%	1	1.3%	4	5.8%
	White	65	91.5%	69	92.0%	59	86.8%	69	90.8%	56	81.2%
	Hispanic	1	1.4%	5	6.7%	2	2.9%	3	3.9%	2	2.9%
	TOTAL	71	100.0%	75	100.0%	68	100.0%	76	100.0%	69	100.0%
Eighth	American Indian	—	—	—	—	1	1.3%	1	1.4%	—	—
	Asian/P. Islander	—	—	4	5.6%	2	2.6%	5	6.8%	6	7.7%
	African American	6	9.0%	4	5.6%	3	3.8%	2	2.7%	1	1.3%
	White	61	91.0%	63	87.5%	72	92.3%	66	89.2%	70	89.7%
	Hispanic	—	—	1	1.4%	—	—	—	—	1	1.3%
	TOTAL	67	100.0%	72	100.0%	78	100.0%	74	100.0%	78	100.0%
Ninth	American Indian	1	0.5%	—	—	1	0.5%	—	—	1	0.5%
	Asian/P. Islander	25	12.4%	28	13.3%	23	10.7%	30	14.0%	24	12.2%
	African American	7	3.5%	8	3.8%	11	5.1%	3	1.4%	6	3.0%
	White	160	79.2%	170	80.6%	166	77.2%	170	79.4%	159	80.7%
	Hispanic	9	4.5%	5	2.4%	14	6.5%	11	5.1%	7	3.6%
	TOTAL	202	100.0%	211	100.0%	215	100.0%	214	100.0%	197	100.0%
Tenth	American Indian	1	2.8%	—	—	—	—	—	—	2	4.2%
	Asian/P. Islander	—	—	3	7.7%	—	—	—	—	4	8.3%
	African American	2	5.6%	2	5.1%	—	—	2	4.9%	1	2.1%
	White	33	91.7%	32	82.1%	43	93.5%	37	90.2%	40	83.3%
	Hispanic	—	—	2	5.1%	3	6.5%	2	4.9%	1	2.1%
	TOTAL	36	100.0%	39	100.0%	46	100.0%	41	100.0%	48	100.0%
Eleventh	Asian/P. Islander	5	4.4%	1	1.1%	3	2.9%	6	5.1%	7	6.5%
	African American	8	7.1%	9	9.6%	8	7.8%	4	3.4%	2	1.9%
	White	97	85.8%	80	85.1%	90	87.4%	103	88.0%	97	89.8%
	Hispanic	3	2.7%	4	4.3%	2	1.9%	4	3.4%	2	1.9%
	TOTAL	113	100.0%	94	100.0%	103	100.0%	117	100.0%	108	100.0%
DC	American Indian	—	—	—	—	—	—	—	—	2	2.0%
	Asian/P. Islander	2	2.1%	6	6.5%	2	2.6%	7	7.4%	6	6.0%
	African American	5	5.3%	8	8.7%	2	2.6%	4	4.3%	9	9.0%
	White	85	90.4%	75	81.5%	73	93.6%	82	87.2%	83	83.0%
	Hispanic	2	2.1%	3	3.3%	1	1.3%	1	1.1%	—	—
	TOTAL	94	100.0%	92	100.0%	78	100.0%	94	100.0%	100	100.0%

Excludes graduates for whom race/ethnicity was not reported.

Source: National Association for Law Placement, employment data for the Classes of 1994–98.

The **First Circuit** includes Maine, Massachusetts, New Hampshire, Rhode Island, and Puerto Rico.

The **Second Circuit** includes Connecticut, New York, and Vermont.

The **Third Circuit** includes Delaware, New Jersey, Pennsylvania, and the Virgin Islands.

The **Fourth Circuit** includes Maryland, North Carolina, South Carolina, Virginia, and West Virginia.

The **Fifth Circuit** includes Louisiana, Mississippi, and Texas.

The **Sixth Circuit** includes Kentucky, Michigan, Ohio, and Tennessee.

The **Seventh Circuit** includes Illinois, Indiana, and Wisconsin.

The **Eighth Circuit** includes Arkansas, Iowa, Minnesota, Missouri, Nebraska, North Dakota, and South Dakota.

The **Ninth Circuit** includes Alaska, Arizona, California, Guam, Hawaii, Idaho, Montana, Nevada, Northern Mariana Islands, Oregon, and Washington.

The **Tenth Circuit** includes Colorado, Kansas, New Mexico, Oklahoma, Utah, and Wyoming.

The **Eleventh Circuit** includes Alabama, Florida, and Georgia.

The **D.C. Circuit** includes both the District of Columbia Circuit and the Federal Circuit.

Table 4. Gender Distribution of Judicial Clerkships by Level of Clerkship: 1994–1998

Type of Clerkship	Gender	1994		1995		1996		1997		1998	
		NUMBER	PERCENT	NUMBER	PERCENT	NUMBER	PERCENT	NUMBER	PERCENT	NUMBER	PERCENT
All Clerks	Women	1,549	49.3%	1,601	48.7%	1,685	50.3%	1,766	51.6%	1,840	51.2%
	Men	1,596	50.7%	1,687	51.3%	1,663	49.7%	1,657	48.4%	1,752	48.8%
	TOTAL	3,145	100.0%	3,288	100.0%	3,348	100.0%	3,423	100.0%	3,592	100.0%
Federal clerks	Women	589	46.0%	578	43.6%	605	46.3%	611	45.4%	650	47.3%
	Men	692	54.0%	748	56.4%	701	53.7%	734	54.6%	724	52.7%
	TOTAL	1,281	100.0%	1,326	100.0%	1,306	100.0%	1,345	100.0%	1,374	100.0%
Local clerks	Women	122	59.2%	104	57.1%	144	54.5%	158	54.1%	140	54.1%
	Men	84	40.8%	78	42.9%	120	45.5%	134	45.9%	119	45.9%
	TOTAL	206	100.0%	182	100.0%	264	100.0%	292	100.0%	259	100.0%
State clerks	Women	821	50.4%	908	51.7%	932	52.8%	987	55.8%	1,037	53.6%
	Men	809	49.6%	847	48.3%	833	47.2%	782	44.2%	896	46.4%
	TOTAL	1,630	100.0%	1,755	100.0%	1,765	100.0%	1,769	100.0%	1,933	100.0%

Note: Excludes graduates for whom gender was not reported.

Source: National Association for Law Placement, employment data for the Classes of 1994–98.

Table 5. **Initial Employer Types —
Men and Women: Class of 1998**

Men

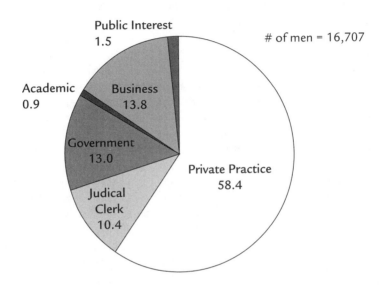

Public Interest
1.5

# of men = 16,707

Academic
0.9

Business
13.8

Government
13.0

Private Practice
58.4

Judical
Clerk
10.4

Women

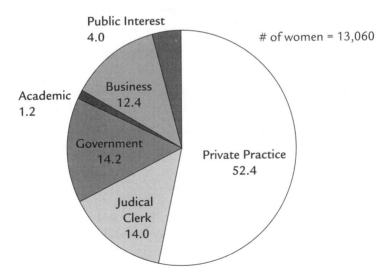

Public Interest
4.0

# of women = 13,060

Academic
1.2

Business
12.4

Government
14.2

Private Practice
52.4

Judical
Clerk
14.0

Note: Figures based on full-time jobs only. The unknown category is not shown on the chart.

Table 6. Gender Distribution of Federal Clerkships by Circuit: 1994–1998

Curcuit	Gender	1994		1995		1996		1997		1998	
		NUMBER	PERCENT	NUMBER	PERCENT	NUMBER	PERCENT	NUMBER	PERCENT	NUMBER	PERCENT
First	Women	23	47.9%	20	40.0%	30	50.8%	29	41.4%	29	52.7%
	Men	25	52.1%	30	60.0%	29	49.2%	41	58.6%	26	47.3%
	TOTAL	48	100.0%	50	100.0%	59	100.0%	70	100.0%	55	100.0%
Second	Women	60	42.3%	72	49.0%	61	47.7%	65	46.4%	81	48.2%
	Men	82	57.7%	75	51.0%	67	52.3%	75	53.6%	87	51.8%
	TOTAL	142	100.0%	147	100.0%	128	100.0%	140	100.0%	168	100.0%
Third	Women	42	37.8%	55	44.0%	61	51.7%	63	52.5%	49	45.8%
	Men	69	62.2%	70	56.0%	57	48.3%	57	47.5%	58	54.2%
	TOTAL	111	100.0%	125	100.0%	118	100.0%	120	100.0%	107	100.0%
Fourth	Women	69	49.3%	44	33.8%	60	46.5%	53	46.1%	50	41.0%
	Men	71	50.7%	86	66.2%	69	53.5%	62	53.9%	72	59.0%
	TOTAL	140	100.0%	130	100.0%	129	100.0%	115	100.0%	122	100.0%
Fifth	Women	50	41.0%	51	37.8%	61	42.4%	57	44.2%	56	40.3%
	Men	72	59.0%	84	62.2%	83	57.6%	72	55.8%	83	59.7%
	TOTAL	122	100.0%	135	100.0%	144	100.0%	129	100.0%	139	100.0%
Sixth	Women	49	59.8%	41	42.7%	45	48.4%	45	44.6%	55	48.7%
	Men	33	40.2%	55	57.3%	48	51.6%	56	55.4%	58	51.3%
	TOTAL	82	100.0%	96	100.0%	93	100.0%	101	100.0%	113	100.0%
Seventh	Women	30	41.1%	36	45.0%	28	40.6%	27	35.1%	41	58.6%
	Men	43	58.9%	44	55.0%	41	59.4%	50	64.9%	29	41.4%
	TOTAL	73	100.0%	80	100.0%	69	100.0%	77	100.0%	70	100.0%
Eighth	Women	30	43.5%	33	44.6%	37	47.4%	31	39.7%	41	50.0%
	Men	39	56.5%	41	55.4%	41	52.6%	47	60.3%	41	50.0%
	TOTAL	69	100.0%	74	100.0%	78	100.0%	78	100.0%	82	100.0%
Ninth	Women	99	47.1%	118	54.4%	104	45.8%	117	51.5%	113	52.8%
	Men	111	52.9%	99	45.6%	123	54.2%	110	48.5%	101	47.2%
	TOTAL	210	100.0%	217	100.0%	227	100.0%	227	100.0%	214	100.0%
Tenth	Women	21	52.5%	13	31.0%	23	47.9%	18	38.3%	24	45.3%
	Men	19	47.5%	29	69.0%	25	52.1%	29	61.7%	29	54.7%
	TOTAL	40	100.0%	42	100.0%	48	100.0%	47	100.0%	53	100.0%
Eleventh	Women	59	51.8%	42	42.0%	46	43.4%	56	43.8%	54	46.2%
	Men	55	48.2%	58	58.0%	60	56.6%	72	56.3%	63	53.8%
	TOTAL	114	100.0%	100	100.0%	106	100.0%	128	100.0%	117	100.0%
DC	Women	40	41.7%	38	39.2%	36	41.9%	44	44.4%	46	42.6%
	Men	56	58.3%	59	60.8%	50	58.1%	55	55.6%	62	57.4%
	TOTAL	96	100.0%	97	100.0%	86	100.0%	99	100.0%	108	100.0%

Excludes graduates for whom gender was not reported.

Source: National Association for Law Placement, employment data for the Classes of 1994–98.

Table 28. **Comparisons of Application and Offer Rates**

	Total #	% Applying	% Not Applying	Of Those Applying % Receiving Offer
Overall	1,651	48.2%	51.8%	69.5%
Gender				
Women	914	48.2	51.8	66.0
Men	736	48.1	51.9	73.7
Age				
20–25 years	679	50.1	49.9	72.6
26–30 years	693	49.2	50.8	69.8
31–35 years	163	39.9	60.1	67.7
36 and older	108	42.6	57.4	47.8
Sexual Orientation				
Heterosexual	1,536	47.5	52.5	69.5
Openly gay, lesbian, or bisexual	74	52.7	47.3	69.2
Other	13	46.2	53.8	66.7
Race/Ethnicity				
American Indian/Alaska Native	9	11.1	88.9	100.0
Asian/Pacific Islander	110	46.4	53.6	80.4
Black/African American	77	46.8	53.2	66.7
Caucasian	1,309	49.4	50.6	68.9
Hispanic/Latino	49	40.8	59.2	80.0
Other	—	34.8	65.2	62.5
Disability Status				
Not Disabled	1,536	48.5	51.5	69.9
Visually Impaired or Blind	5	60.0	40.0	66.7
Hard of Hearing or Deaf	3	66.7	33.3	100.0
Learning Disabled	10	10.0	90.0	100.0
Other	19	47.4	52.6	55.6

Notes

1. Reprinted from the NALP Report at 23–29, 46.

APPENDIX

F

Law Schools: The Ways
You Can Help Your Students

Law schools, this is for you! Having been there myself, developing a highly successful and comprehensive judicial clerkship program at Yale which led to a record number of students obtaining clerkships, and learning even more on the national level since, I cannot leave you this book without offering my suggestions and ways to help students in this process. Many of you have heard this from me before, in national conferences, speaking arrangements at your school and numerous articles, so I will keep it (relatively) brief with just a few key points as a guideline.

COUNSELING EARLY IN THE PROCESS

One of the best ways to help students is to connect with them through counseling early in the process, and offer information as to courts and judges, strategies, and help with individual issues. The earlier you reach them the better—aim for the spring of the first year of law school—because you can help them shape their law school careers in ways that will be beneficial in general but also specifically for the clerkship application process down the road. If you wait to initiate contact until the "clerkship season," when students are in the midst of the application process, you will find that the chaos can obstruct your message and words of advice. Also, many of the finely balanced elements of the application hinge upon what has taken place in that student's law school experience before that point, so your efforts now will largely be triage. For instance, many students will complain later that they do not know any professors well, or that they do not have anything to use as a writing sample. You will be able to assist them most effectively if you can offer them early guidance in building a successful law school experience—and in so doing, lay the groundwork for a successful clerkship application. So, here's the message for your students in a nutshell of 10 tips:

1. Make your grades and a strong academic record your priority.
2. Make an effort to get to know a few faculty members well by taking small seminar classes and/or serving as a research assistant.
3. In your course selection, keep in mind and be guided by the need for at least some of the useful subject matter (more black letter law content such as Evidence, Civil and Criminal Procedure, Business Organizations, First Amendment/Constitutional Law issues). Choose at least a couple of classes in which you will have the opportunity to write in class, rather than all exam courses. If possible, take at least one small class, as noted above.
4. Develop your legal research and writing skills early in your law school career (and over the summer), through writing class papers, briefs, memoranda and/or a journal note. Doing so will serve three purposes: getting to know a professor who will be familiar with your writing (*i.e.*, for letters of recommendation); developing a possible writing sample for clerkship applications; and fulfilling a graduation requirement early—plus, it's just plain good for you!

5. Try to work on a law journal. For prestige, the top journal of your school is the best, but if not "the" journal, then try any journal that interests you. The journal experience of writing and editing is valuable in and of itself, and may help you with a writing sample. Activities such as Moot Court, barristers union and trial advocacy are also beneficial for a clerkship and judges do look for them.

6. Pursue a judicial externship/internship, for exposure to the judiciary, to see what a judicial clerkship would be like, and to gain the potential support of a judge.

7. Be open-minded and flexible as to judges, types of courts and clerkships. Continue to expand your horizons—do not fall into the trap of limiting your options by thinking it has to be Judge X or the Xth Circuit.

8. Research early and continue to gather information through a variety of sources—printed, on-line, and people! This includes remaining aware of judges and courts, and on the alert for clerkship issues, during your summer job as well as throughout law school.

9. To this end, attend any lectures, events and functions that expose you to members of the judiciary. Nothing substitutes for the opportunity to mingle and exchange information directly with a judge!

10. Of course, encourage your students to attend the programs on judicial clerkships offered by your law school and to avail themselves of all those precious resources you have gathered in your office!

PRESENTING PROGRAMS

I am a big believer in programs, having conducted quite a few in my day. There can be a great variety of types of programs in the area of judicial clerkships, to address the issues from many different perspectives. One of the most interesting and valuable types of forum is the **judicial speaker**, whether in panels of judges or individually on clerkships or a broader substantive topic (*e.g.*, I have arranged panels on such themes as "gender and the bench," "state and federal court clerkships: views from the bench" and "jurisdictional issues and the interrelationship between the courts"). Another venue is the role of a guest lecturer representing his or her court. I find that students greatly appreciate seeing a real judge as a person, and remain transfixed on his or her words of wisdom. This event brings the judiciary to the students in a very meaningful way, additionally giving both student and judge the opportunity to exchange ideas and develop contacts. (As one judge later remarked to me, after speaking on the subject of clerking for his circuit—what cases you would be seeing if you were a law clerk during that term—"Not only did I have a great visit with the students, but I got a good clerk out of it!")

Another useful program is arranging **panels of former law clerks**, most easily done with graduates of your school. This is always exceedingly interesting for the students, who appreciate hearing about the clerkship experience and application process directly from someone with whom they can relate. To achieve the greatest breadth of information and experiences, the ideal panel includes former law clerks from a diversity of courts (federal/state, appellate/trial, geographic distribution), as well as a diversity of clerks in terms of their future practice after their clerkships (law firm, public sector, government, academia) so that students can envision the wide range of potential career paths. These can also be specialty panels, such as former U.S. Supreme Court law clerks speaking about applying and clerking for that Court.

A **student panel** of third year students who have been through the application process the prior year is particularly well received and heartening for first and second year students. Whether or not they receive a clerkship, it is good to know that you can get through the process and survive. Students always have some concrete tips to share with their peers.

Lastly, **faculty panels** on this subject can be very productive. Not only is it wise as a political matter to get the faculty involved in your programs, but they do tend to have more of a vested interest in this area. As a result, members of the faculty have valuable information to contribute to the students; they may have a great deal of their own knowledge about particular courts and judges that is important to have shared. Moreover, this is another opportunity to encourage further involvement of the faculty with the students. By facilitating the interaction of professors with students and increasing their amount of contact, you will be doing your part to improve this critical factor in the clerkship application process for your students.

Of course, my specialty is presenting **informational sessions and educational seminars**, on a wide variety of topics and issues, including: an overview of the federal and state courts; the judicial clerkship experiences and opportunities; the nuts and bolts of the clerkship application process; interviewing, cover letter, resume, and writing skills workshops; and preparing for your clerkship. But it is not my intention to be advertising my services here, so I will try not to jump up and down too much about this! If you have read through this book, you already know where and how to reach me if you would like further assistance with the judicial clerkship program at your school!

EXPANDING RESOURCES

As you can see, resources are of critical importance in this area. There is so little reliable and complete information out there (although glancing at my extensive resource chapter at first you may not comprehend this point) and it is, after all, a research project for students. For this reason, any information you have will be much appreciated by your students—and they invariably seek even more. Using my resource section as a guide to the value and limitation of each publication, you should be able to build quite a collection; then have your students use this book to guide them through the rest!

ENCOURAGING FEEDBACK

I believe that encouraging feedback via student surveys is an excellent way to obtain important information directly from the people who count the most. You will want to separate the myths and rumors from the reality of what actually happened in that year through surveys on the subject of their application process and ways to improve it in the future for others. In addition, solicit written feedback from graduates as to their judicial clerkship experiences; in sharing vital information about their clerkships, they can provide one of the best resources in assisting their fellow students. By the way, I have found the response rate of the students and alumni to be quite remarkable and they are very willing to spend considerable time and effort in writing substantial comments. Perhaps this is due to the cathartic effect for them— the healthy process of looking back and evaluating their experiences—especially if they think it will make a difference and their suggestions will be taken to heart.

Noteworthy Initiatives

Now, if you *really* want to take concrete measures to improve the process for your students in a significant way, add to the list these further initiatives arising from the National Judicial Clerkship Study:[1]

- In order to increase minority representation among law clerks, law schools should adopt as a priority encouraging more minority students to apply by offering specialized programs, resources and counseling for these students.

- With a goal of promoting diversity of the applicant pool, judicial clerkships—which are a form of public service—should be treated like other public interest jobs, evoking eligibility for financial assistance, loan forgiveness or deferral programs.

- Schools should also implement measures to facilitate the mechanics of the application process for their students, including procedures to improve the timeliness of the letters of recommendation from their faculty.

Well, these are just some suggestions for ways to improve the judicial clerkship application process for your students. Use them as you see fit, according to the goals, needs, and resources of your law school.

Notes

1. See "Action Plan" in *Courting the Clerkship: Perspectives on the Opportunities and Obstacles for Judicial Clerkships*, Report on the 2000 National Judicial Clerkship Study (National Association for Law Placement, October 2000), pp. 16–18 (reprinted in this Appendix); and my article, "Empowering the Participants: Initiatives from the National Judicial Clerkship Study," *NALP Bulletin,* Vol. 13, No. 12, December 2000.

Other Titles Available

What Law School Doesn't Teach You. . . But You Really Need To Know
Expert Advice for Making
Your Legal Career a HUGE Success

"Be yourself." "Avoid gossip." "There's no such thing as a stupid question." If you believe statements like these, you could jeopardize your job. Why? Because the new lawyers who stand out follow a much more subtle set of rules. Rules that you can use to transform your job, whether you work for a law firm, government entity, public interest organization, or any other legal employer!

In this book, you'll learn the trade secrets that make top lawyers say, "I wish I'd known that when I started out!" You'll discover hundreds of tips and strategies, including:

Author:
Kimm Alayne Walton, J.D.
ISBN: 0-15-900453-5
Price: $19.95

  · How to turn down work when you're swamped without saying the dreaded "no"
  · How to negotiate for more money
  · How to use gossip to your advantage
  · How to make an outstanding first impression
  · How to take criticism and make yourself shine

Author Kimm Alayne Walton talked to lawyers and law school administrators all over the country, asking them for their best advice for new lawyers. Whether you're going for a summer clerkship, your first permanent job, or you've already started your career you'll find a wealth of invaluable insider tips you can use right now. With *What Law School Doesn't Teach You . . . But You Really Need To Know*, you'll feel as though you have hundreds of top-notch mentors at your fingertips!

America's Greatest Places To Work With A Law Degree

And How To Make The Most Of Any Job, No Matter Where It Is!

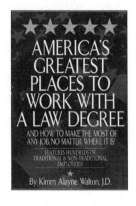

With *America's Greatest Places to Work With A Law Degree* you'll find out what it's really like to work at hundreds of terrific traditional and non-traditional employers—from fantastic law firms, to the Department of Justice, to great public interest employers, to corporate in-house counsel's offices, to dozens of others. You'll learn lots of sure-fire strategies for breaking into all kinds of desirable fields—like Sports, Entertainment, the Internet, and many, many more. You'll discover the non-traditional fields where new law school graduates pull down six figures—and love what they do! And you'll get hundreds of insider tips for making the most of your job, no matter WHERE you decide to work.

Author:
Kimm Alayne Walton, J.D.
ISBN: 0-15-900180-3
Price: $24.95
(776 Pages, 6" x 9")

The bottom line is, no matter what you like, there's a dream job just waiting for you. Discover it in *America's Greatest Places To Work With A Law Degree*.

Guerrilla Tactics For Getting The Legal Job Of Your Dreams

Regardless of Your Grades, Your School, or Your Work Experience!

Whether you're looking for a summer clerkship or your first permanent job after law school, this national best-seller is the key to getting the legal job of your dreams.

Guerrilla Tactics for Getting the Legal Job of Your Dreams leads you step-by-step through everything you need to do to nail down that perfect job! You'll learn hundreds of simple-to-use strategies that will get you exactly where you want to go.

Guerrilla Tactics features the best strategies from some of the country's most innovative career advisors. The strategies in *Guerrilla Tactics* are so powerful that it even comes with a guarantee: Follow the advice in the book, and within one year of graduation you'll have the job of your dreams . . . or your money back!

Author:
Kimm Alayne Walton, J.D.
ISBN: 0-15-900317-2
Price: $24.95
(572 Pages, 6" x 9")

Pick up a copy of *Guerrilla Tactics* today . . . and you'll be on your way to the job of your dreams!

The Best Of The Job Goddess
Phenomenal Job Search Advice From America's Most
Popular Job Search Columnist

"Should I wear my wedding ring to Interviews? How can I get
a job in another city? I was a Hooters girl before law school—
should I put it on my resume?" In her popular *Dear Job Goddess* column, legal job search expert Kimm Alayne Walton
provides answers to these, plus scores of other, job search
dilemmas facing law students and law school graduates. Her
columns are syndicated in more than 100 publications
nationwide.

The Best Of The Job Goddess is a collection of the Job Goddesses
favorite columns—wise and witty columns that solve every
kind of legal job search question! If you're contemplating
law school, you're a law student now, or you're a lawyer considering a career change—you'll enjoy turning to the Job
Goddess for divine guidance!

Author:
Kimm Alayne Walton, J.D.
ISBN: 0-15-900393-8
Price: $14.95
(208 Pages, 4¼" x 9")

Proceed With Caution
A Diary Of The First Year At
One Of America's Largest, Most Prestigious Law Firms

Prestige. Famous clients. High-profile cases. Not to mention
a starting salary exceeding six figures.

It's not hard to figure out why so many law students dream
of getting jobs at huge law firms. But when you strip away
the glamour, what is it like to live that "dream"?

In *Proceed With Caution*, the author takes you behind the
scenes, to show you what it's really like to be a junior associate at a huge law firm. After graduating from an Ivy League
law school, he took a job as an associate with one of New
York's blue-chip law firms.

He also did something not many people do. He kept a diary,
where he spelled out his day-to-day life at the firm in graphic
detail.

Proceed With Caution excerpts the diary, from his first day at
the firm to the day he quit.

Author: William F. Keates
ISBN: 0-15-900181-1
Price: $17.95
(166 Pages, 6" x 9",
hardcover)

The Official Guide To Legal Specialties
An Insider's Guide To Every Major Practice Area

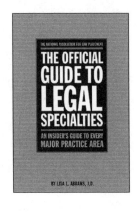

This fast-paced book presents an inside look at what it's like to practice law in major specialty areas, from entertainment to immigration, from tax to telecommunications. From day-to-day activities, to clients, to work environments in all types of settings—blue-chip firms to public interest organizations to government agencies—you'll find that lawyers in every specialty area have fascinating lives.

In this book, you'll find the insights and expertise of top practitioners—the issues they tackle every day, the people and clients they work with, and what they find rewarding about their work. You'll learn about the skills important in different practice specialties, the most helpful law school classes and extracurricular activities, and much more! Over 120 government, public interest, corporate, and private attorneys are featured, from solo practitioners to those in the country's largest firms.

Author: Lisa L. Abrams, J.D.
516 Pages, 6" x 9"
Price $19.95
ISBN 0-15-900391-1

Specialties included in this book:

Admiralty & Maritime Law	Intellectual Property Law
Antitrust Law	International Law
Appellate Practice	Labor & Employment Law
Banking & Commercial	Legislative Practice
Finance Practice	Military Judge Advocates /
Bankruptcy Law	JAG
Civil Litigation	Municipal Finance Practice
Corporate Practice	Public Interest Law
Criminal Law	Real Estate Law
Entertainment & Sports Law	Securities Law
Environmental Law	Solo, Small Firm, & General
Family Law	Practice
Government Contracts	Tax Law
Practice	Telecommunications Law
Government Practice	Tort Litigation: Personal
Health Care Law	Injury & Insurance
Immigration Law	Defense Litigation
Insurance Law	Trusts & Estates Law